W9-CHZ-352

TABLE OF CONTENTS

...joining any project or organisation prospective volunteers ...carefully read the Warning on page 3 and the Important ...pages 36–38.

World Volunteers

The World Guide to Humanitarian and Development Volunteering

Green Volunteers
Publications

World Volunteers
The World Guide to Humanitarian and Development Volunteering

Editors:	Fabio Ausenda, Erin McCloskey
Cover design:	Studio Cappellato e Laurent srl, Milano
Cover photo:	"Winnie and Kibibi", Makindu Children's Center, Kenya © The Register Guard/Nicole DeVito
Aknowledgements:	The Register Guard (Eugene, OR) and Winnie Barron of the Makindu Children's Center, Kenya, for the cover photo.

This Guide is not an annual publication: the useful websites section, the suggestions for contacting the organisations in the introductory pages and the updates page of our website (see bottom of next page) allow the reader to find continuous new opportunities and to keep the information in this Guide always up to date.

Copyright © 2005 Fabio Ausenda

Published by: Green Volunteers di Fabio Ausenda
Via Canonica 72
20154 Milano, Italy
www.greenvol.com
E-mail: network@greenvol

All Rights Reserved. Except as permitted under current legislation no part of this work may be photocopied, stored in retrieval system, published, performed in public, adapted, broadcast, transmitted, recorded or reproduced in any form or by any means, without the prior permission of the copyright owner.

US & Canada distribution: Universe Publishing
A division of Rizzoli International Publications, Inc.
300 Park Avenue South,
New York, NY 10010

UK distribution: Vacation Work Publications
9 Park End Street,
Oxford OX1 1HJ, England

Printed in January 2005 by: Consorzio Artigiano L.V.G. srl, Azzate (VA), Italy
ISBN: 88-89060-00-X
Library of Congress Control Number: 2004092034

This book is dedicated to Kibibi, the girl hugged by Winnie [in the] *photo, with the hope that all the Kibibis in the world may liv[e]* [a] *life, as they deserve. Kibibi passed away, at the age of 1...*

**The Editors highly recommend the following in...
are read. These pages explain what humanitarian...
volunteering involves and will increase the volu...
being accepted by an organisation.**

WARNING!

PLEASE NOTE THAT THE INFORMATION HER...
OBTAINED FROM THE RELEVANT ORGANISATI...
PUBLIC SOURCES. ALL PROJECTS LISTED IN T...
BE CHANGED OR CANCELLED WITHOUT NOTIC...
USERS SHOULD VERIFY CURRENT PROJEC...
PERIOD, COST, LOCATION, ACCOMMODATI...
PROGRAMME. ORGANISATIONS AND PROJEC...
CHANGE THEIR PROGRAMMES, OBJECTIV...
TELEPHONE, FAX AND E-MAIL ADDRESS, ...
OPERATING WITHOUT NOTICE AT ANY TIME...
PUBLISHER AND DISTRIBUTORS ACCEPT NO ...
FOR INACCURACY OF INFORMATION ...
PUBLICATION.

INDIVIDUALS WILL JOIN ANY OF THE ...
ORGANISATIONS LISTED IN THIS PUBLICATIO...
RISK. THE EDITOR, PUBLISHER AND DISTRIB...
BE LIABLE FOR ANY LOSS OR DAMAGE THAT...
ANYONE JOINING ANY OF THE PROJECTS OR ...
LISTED IN THIS PUBLICATION.

HOW TO RECEIVE ANNUAL UPDATES FROM T...

Regular annual updates of this guide will be avai...
reader. In order to obtain the updates from the Inte...
carefully read the following introductory pages...
section dedicated to useful websites and the **Imp**...
36–38. Free annual updates of this guide will b...
Publisher ceases operating for any reason.

INTR...

IMPO...

ORGA...

APPE...
A...
A...
A...

ORGA...

Before...
shoul...
Note o...

INTRODUCTION

The growing gap between North and South

In the past ten years, the division between North and South has deepened. The industrialised world—Europe, North America, and Japan—is running towards a consumerism that knows no limits. Seemingly limitless technological advancement is growing so fast that we had to coin a new phrase and "invent" a new branch of the economy: the *New Economy.* This economy is based on things virtual and potential—not only on technology but also on new forms of consumption, science, and biotechnology. However, the rest of the world is being left behind.

Up until the '80s, the East was undoubtedly tied to an image of totalitarian regimes without democracy. However, there was never an image of an economy in ruin, with hunger, poverty, and spreading diseases, or pro-capita income worst than many third-world countries. Increasingly we see frightening ethnic wars closer to our borders (such as in the Balkans) and poverty in many countries that previously were able to boast acceptable standards of living. Even countries not affected by war have been reduced to unimaginable poverty since the collapse of the Soviet block—think of the citizens of Moldova or Belarus, or of the street kids of Romania.

In the '90s, following the collapse of the Soviet Union, we came to realise that the South's boundary had moved closer and, tragically, the gap had become bigger. Today, many people are discovering this boundary, that was once at a comfortable distance, now only hundreds, at times only tens, of kilometres away. While in the past the western perspective of poverty and underdevelopment was perhaps only associated with the famines in Africa; today in many western European countries, it is not uncommon to see children, from countries such as Albania, begging for money from people stopped in their cars at traffic lights or taking the subway to work or to go shopping.

In Africa the situation has become even worse. Following the famine caused by climate conditions or conflicts triggered by the Cold War there are now also ferocious local conflicts with effects that are mostly ignored by the rest of the world. These conflicts, since they don't

5

have any external support, leave entire countries devastated and abandoned. Previously, at the end of a conflict, the prevailing superpower attempted to extend its political influence by helping the local economy and infrastructure. This is no longer the case: the wars are bloody and cruel and are caused by ethnic, tribal, religious, or economic reasons. This all happens often with complete indifference from the wealthy countries. Africa is ravaged by diseases such as Aids or Ebola. At the same time, western pharmaceutical companies care more about preserving profits and protecting patents than about the overwhelming number of deaths—a death toll that they have contributed to.

Finally, terrorism, such as the events of 11 September 2001, is a fanaticism, which can be the most dangerous by-product of poverty and underdevelopment and that increases the gap between the rich and the poor. Ultimately this justifies war by some countries and creates an isolationist attitude by others.

Thankfully, not everyone is insensitive to what is happening. The media are making the distances shorter and bringing to the attention of the western world the incredible gap in resource distribution and the consequential tragedies, such as natural disasters and wars, in the world.

Today, it costs much less to travel to far places and communication time and costs have decreased dramatically with the Internet and e-mail. All of these reasons have not only increased awareness, but also a willingness "to act". In addition, citizens in wealthy countries have more time and resources to allow them to travel or move abroad more easily. When a person does go abroad the ease of communication makes home feel less distant. Therefore, the increased awareness has caused a collective desire to act, with low transportation and communication costs making this desire more feasible.

Moreover, in the last few years, a "political" movement has emerged. In reality, it is a movement common to many ideologies: the political left, environmentalism, and various religious beliefs. This is the "anti-global" movement characterised (with some exceptions) by a strong, inspirational solidarity. It is not by chance that in the last few years, part of this desire to act has been directed towards developing countries. This Guide is a tool for those people (even without previous volunteer experience in poor countries) that no longer just want to be spectators but instead want to "act".

What can we do?

We have seen how the awareness of this gap between the North and South, and the growing number of catastrophes (more or less of human cause—even natural disasters can often be traced to human error, such as negative development, deforestation and other contributors to climate change, etc.) has awakened the desire to "do something" to help those who are less fortunate. Help can be given in many ways:

1)   **by donating money**
2)   **by donating material objects**
3)   **by donating time**

Donating money

It is an easy solution especially if you have limited time available. In effect, by donating money you delegate your willingness to act to others. The only difficulty is in deciding which organisation to choose. Many people are hesitant to donate because they are unsure of how their money will be spent. This topic is debatable: it would be like a dog biting its own tail. Small local organisations are able to use a higher percentage of donated money for projects as opposed to operating costs, however, because of their small size, the effectiveness for the cause is limited. The communities they help are quite small. Alternatively, large organisations with high administrative costs have a greater impact on the projects they support. Often these organisations are able to obtain additional funding from governmental or Inter-Governmental sources, ultimately supporting projects for many years. It is very rare that organisations divert funds from the original cause. The more common case is that of organisations spending a large portion of donated funds on excessive administrative costs. A good control method for someone who wants to regularly donate funds is to ask to see an organisation's certified financial statements. The larger organisations have balances that are certified by auditing firms. In almost all fiscal systems, donations to non-profit organisations are tax deductible, further facilitating the act of giving. Regardless, donating money to large or small organisations is always the right thing—without donations, many non-profit organisations would cease to exist.

Donating material objects

In the last few years there has been a decline in this action. We are in a time of abundance, globalization enables the production of items (such as clothing) in the far east at extremely competitive prices. Therefore, it is much cheaper and easier for aid organisations to purchase clothing—new, packaged, and sorted in the right sizes—directly from the producers, as opposed to selecting, washing, packing, sorting, and transporting used items from households. Up until a few years ago, used items had more value and donating objects was more common.

Other actions, such as donating food, have an impact if they are donated to organised programmes. Donating food items according to what an organisation requests, as opposed to casually giving extras from your kitchen cupboards, is much more efficient. Donated groceries are used to supply soup kitchens for the homeless in our own cities. When intervening in developing countries for emergency purposes and hunger relief, often times the food is donated by large producers and governments. It is much easier for large aid organisations, as with the clothing, to ship groceries well packaged and preserved, than to collect, select, and pack groceries donated by private individuals. Actions such as donating used toys, much like clothing, is often not a priority on a global scale, although there are exceptions. Systematically organised collections, such as the ones performed by many organisations, can be useful if they generate funds.

Donating time – Volunteering

Volunteering is the third donation possibility, which in the context of this Guide, is obviously the most important. Since it is not always true that volunteering is the best way to help those in need, with this book we try to give the potential volunteer the tools and advice that will make volunteering enriching for the participant, useful for the aid organisation, and essential for the cause.

Volunteering in developing countries, contrary to what most people think, is not always unpaid, but, in many cases, the volunteer, especially the professional volunteer, is paid for by the sending NGO. These funds are used for providing pocket money or a stipend. This stipend is sometimes equivalent to what would be earned in the volunteer's own country, or some times even higher.

Situations can vary from contract to contract and they also depend on the paying institution. Often salaries are in US dollars (a strong currency) and are tax free. Volunteers may receive a good salary or an additional indemnity because the paying NGO must compete for a qualified professional within the private sector. For those who may be concerned by the fact that volunteers will be paid a salary for staying a few months abroad, we can point out that these salaries are only for the most qualified people, working in development projects financed by large NGOs. The majority of volunteers in the long-term humanitarian projects receive a salary just enough to fulfil the basic needs. In this Guide we have included organisations that offer paid positions for qualified professionals because many still require unpaid volunteers. We will therefore provide information on finding a professional position, considering that a few months (or years) away from home, even if paid, is always a sacrifice—of family and friends, hobbies, sports, and comforts.

Time can be donated occasionally (e.g., for a fundraising event), regularly (for a few hours a week), or by going overseas (for a few weeks, months, or even years). This last case is the focus of this Guide, which aims to be a useful instrument for those who, for short or long term want to become volunteers. We give suggestions in order to have this experience fulfilled and also to help every prospective volunteer find the organisation nearest to his or her needs. We will talk about local volunteering in the following section, "how to start" (see page 11).

Volunteering organisations

Generally speaking, volunteering in developing countries is done with non-profit organisations that supervise and train the volunteers, allowing them to serve in a structured way and, most of all, guaranteeing continuity to the efforts of the organisation. If a volunteer wants to be more autonomous, we suggest joining a non-profit organisation directly that is working in a developing country. These organisations are greatly in need of help, both economically and in management because they are located in poor countries with limited resources. It may also be convenient to apply with an organisation from a developing country because if a volunteer is financially self-sufficient and can cover the travel and living expenses, they are often more easily and willingly accepted by the organisation.

The common classifications of international development organisations are: Government Organisations, Inter-Governmental Organisations (IGOs) and Non-Government Organisations (NGOs). The IGOs include all the national aid agencies. Almost all wealthy countries have their own development agency. In the US, for example it is USAID – the US Agency for International Development. Among the IGOs, the major donors are: the European Union, the World Bank, the Organisation of American States, and the numerous UN agencies acting independently or together with other NGOs such as UNDP (United Nations Development Programme), FAO (Food and Agriculture Organization), UNICEF (United Nations Children Fund), WFP (World Food Programme), and UNHCR (United Nations High Commission for Refugees).

This Guide does not consider Government or Inter-Governmental Organisations, either because they don't offer volunteering programs, or because they are managed in conjunction with private organisations. The United Nations have established one agency, UNV (United Nation volunteers) headquartered in Bonne, Germany, which recruits and sends volunteers to various UN agencies. UNV has been listed in this Guide. NGOs make the bulk of the organisations listed, although it is not a comprehensive list because the number of humanitarian NGOs is so large that surpasses the scope of this Guide. A thorough list of NGOs of a given country can be easily found on the web—the richest source of information (see "useful websites" page 18). In this Guide the reader can find a studied selection of organisations from all around the world (many of them from developing countries). There is a great variety of choices: from workcamps (for those with little or no experience) to professional contracts (for specialised doctors). Organisations listed have headquarters and projects in countries all around the globe. The type of organisations range from large religious organisations to small rural projects in a developing countries. There are many organisations from the developing countries that are in extreme need of help, such a hospital in Cameroon or an orphanage in Kenya. This Guide is a useful instrument for finding an organisation to volunteer for or for starting a search for other organisations on the Internet.

VOLUNTEERING OPTIONS

How to start: local volunteering

Whatever is the motivation to volunteer in a developing country it is important to keep in mind that one cannot improvise oneself into a volunteer. Motivation must be strong because the sacrifice is considerable and a good adaptability is recommended. Work is often done in difficult conditions, with little or no comfort, often by helping people in desperate situations and witnessing tragic realities. It is highly advisable to test this motivation before hand. The NGO itself must be aware of the volunteer's motivation, otherwise it would risk losing time and resources, and, worse of all, the unmotivated volunteer could negatively influence the project he or she is working on. However, the volunteer's motivation is generally perceivable from the volunteer's resume and interview.

If this is your first volunteering experience abroad, it is recommended to start local. This may turn out to be a practical activity such as visiting the elderly or the homeless or working in a food distribution centre for the poor in your own home town, or, if possible, you may choose to start working locally with the NGO you would later be interested in volunteering for on an overseas project. This can be a great occasion to get to know the work environment and to show your skills, initiative, and spirit of sacrifice. Activities can be of all kinds: from simple office work to fundraising or public awareness activities about the goals of the NGO. Every NGO, whether large or small, normally uses local volunteers and it always welcomes a person's intention to form a local small chapter or fundraising group, if an office of the organisation is not located nearby.

It is not absolutely necessary to volunteer locally with the NGO you will be joining overseas. Any social or humanitarian organisation is fine, the important thing is to be confident in your decision. If the local volunteer experience proves that your motivation is less than anticipated, you may reconsider the idea of a becoming volunteer overseas. Or you may discover that your sector of interest has changed. The "useful websites" section (see page 18) may be very useful in finding the organisation operating locally that is right for you.

Volunteering from home

With the increased use of computers, it is now possible to volunteer comfortably from home. Some organisations, such as NETAID (www.app.netaid.org) or Interconnection (www.interconnection.org), give you the opportunity to become a "vitualvolunteer" for an NGO in a developìing country with extreme need of tecnological help. A typical example of the work a virtual volunteer can provide is the construction of websites but there are many other tasks that can be performed with a computer communicating by e-mail. Some organisations from poor countries needing computer help are listed in this Guide. The section "useful websites" (see page 18) shows how to find other organisations on websites featuring international directories such as www.idealist.org.

Being a virtual volunteer allows you to become familiar with the NGO from a developing country with which a volunteering period is forseen. Volunteering directly for an NGO from a poor country is certainly a challenging choice as mentioned earlier. Such an organisation can have strong management difficulties and the working and living conditions may be very poor without having the help and the support of other expert volunteers. For this choice no particular prerequisites are needed. It is sufficient to have some professional qualification useful to a project and to be ready to bare all travel and living expenses. For these reasons this option must be strogley motivated and therefore a test period of virtual voluteering is advisable to start developing personal relations with the people you may laterbe working with.

The workcamp: an ideal experience for young people

A workcamp is the ideal setting for a volunteer with no previous experience who does not want to committ too much time. It is therefore particularly suitable for students and young people as a meaningful way to spend a summer vacation or visit a new country. It could be considered more of an alternative vacation than a true volunteering committment. Nevertheless workcamps are good introductory experience to volunteering, and they are an enriching life experience for the work accomplished and for meeting people from many different countriers and cultures who share the same interests and lifestyle.

The psychological commitment is minimal however, the risk of a workcamp is that it may not be taken very seriously by all the participants and the "holiday" aspect can takeover and shade the primary goal of the workcamp, which is to help those in need. This will depend on the motivation and dedication of organisers of the workcamp. If the organisation has a website, they may post feedback and often e-mail addresses from past volunteers. This is a good way to assess the philosophy or atmosphere of a particular workcamp. A balanced attitude towards "vacation" and the social or humanitarian commitment can be the best approach.

Often no previous experience is required for workcamps; the structure is organised to lodge and cater to a certain number of volunteers, the tasks to be accomplished are simple and the work is never in extreme situations. Often the only requirement is to know the language of the workcamp (most often English). For these reasons the workcamps are preferred by young people and students. Older volunteers may also be accepted, but they should first verify the kind of work to be done and the age group of other volunteers, in order not to feel too isolated from the rest of the group. More experienced volunteers can always apply for a coordinating position. In the Appendix Tables at the end of the Guide the organisations that offer workcamp opportunities are indicated.

Workcamps and unpaid volunteer positions obviously have less competition but they may not be able to take volunteers at the time you may apply. This may be owing to the available positions being already filled. They may also require specific qualifications to meet the needs of the association or project at that time. And even though volunteers may be financially self-supporting and willing to work, they still require considerable engagement on the part of the organisation. They require space, attention (in sometimes critical situations), coordination, assistance, transportation, and they must be provided with higher standards of hygiene and safety than what may be found in that country. A volunteer may become depressed, sick, or injured. An unneeded or, even worse, an unwanted volunteer can be of great hindrance. Make as large a search spectrum as possible to increase your chances of finding an organisation that is not only interested but ready to accept you to their project.

Short-term volunteering: for retired people or skilled workers

To volunteer in a developing country it is often not necessary to have extensive travelling experience, to speak a foreign language, or to have a university degree; tradesworkers such as mechanics, plumbers, electricians, brick layers, ironsmiths, carpenters, etc., who can teach their skills to others may be extremely desired by a project.

We recommend that only people with previous international experience apply directly to an NGO in a developing country. A considerable autonomy along with the ability to work independently in sometimes uncomfortable or unusual conditions may be necessary. For first-time volunteers with no previous travel or work experience in a developing country, it is advisable to apply with a larger, established sending organisation that coordinates projects with more provisions in place and larger groups of volunteers on site often with group leaders for support.

Religious missions are an ideal environment for skilled labourers or retired people to share their lifetime working experience. With these projects it is possible to work in a quiet environment and there is usually no necessity to speak a foreign language, since the resident missionaries act as interpreters and cultural mediators. Typically, volunteers accepted onto missionary projects are sent by a church or agency supporting the mission. There are countries with a strong Christian tradition, who have close ties with missions: Italy or Ireland are good examples. Volunteers on missions have typically already been involved with the church and its activities and events, such as fundraising, etc., to prove their skills, motivation, and faith. They become so acquainted with the group supporting the mission that going to work at the mission is a sort of spontaneous evolution.

Short-term volunteering: for skilled professionals

Many qualified professionals (medical doctors, engineers, architects, agronomists, etc.), during their professional life, may feel they want to help those in need through a professional experience working in a developing country. The response to this inclination can be

14

short-term professional volunteering, which can last as little as one month or a summer vacation period. Obviously the professional volunteer can be engaged for longer periods by taking a leave of absence from work.

The qualified professional is very often accepted because of possessing necessary qualifications and sometimes for having the ability to bear all the travel and living expenses. Under these circumstances the professional volunteer can be accepted in a project even without previous volunteering experience abroad. The higher the qualifications of the volunteer the higher the chance of being accepted to a project basis. For example, a dentist with several years of professional experience is the ideal candidate for spending a month in a dental clinic in Africa. It will be very difficult for a professional to be paid for short-term volunteering (less than one month). This can happen for longer term engagements - at least 2-3 months - or if a relationship between the candidate and the NGO is well established or the application is in response to an employment offer.

Many NGOs will ask to have preliminary meetings or to perform short training courses (during weekends, for example). These requests are absolutely legitimate and allow the organisation better to know the prospective volunteer and vice-versa.

Medium-term volunteering

Medium-term volunteering may involve both professional and unskilled volunteers. Normally it lasts from two to six months. In general, medium-term volunteers are either students or professionals who are familiar with the world of cooperation and have already served as volunteers in the past. The most experienced are often employed with contracts issued by financing institutions, such as the European Union. Highly specialised professionals, e.g., medical doctors, often receive placement for few months with a salary, even without previous volunteering experience. The Guide lists a few European and American organisations, mostly in the field of health, that tend to select only experienced professionals, paying them with sufficient, if not competitive, salaries. Keep in mind that there are rarely any expenses incurred by the volunteer: board and lodging are supplied and there are few amusements that require money.

Long-term volunteering

Long-term volunteering is a true choice in life. In general, the minimum period lasts at least two years and is renewable. The economic treatment is regulated by specific contracts and conditions issued by the organisations that co-finance the projects, such as the European Union. The approach to a career in cooperation must be made in a systematic way, as for any other field, starting from proper courses of instruction, of which many are run by the NGOs themselves. Humana (see listing) is a one such example.

Volunteering with organisations in developing countries

The following outlines the main characteristics of NGOs situated and working in developing countries:
- NGOs in developing countries need a considerable amount of help in view of the very scarce resources to which they have access, especially if they are not helped by partner organisations residing in the "rich countries".
- NGOs in developing countries are the least selective in accepting volunteers and often the length of the volunteering period is negotiable. Also, the requested qualifications are not very strict: even generic qualifications may be enough (e.g., teaching basic computer skills).
- The volunteer must pay for all of his or her expenses: certainly travel, often board, sometimes lodging, and at times also give a contribution.
- The volunteer may be without other volunteers to share experiences with or ask advice from. The project leaders may also have very high work expectations.
- The volunteer may find conditions of considerable lack of organisation, extreme scarcity of means, or with few comforts, in other words, the experience may be a difficult test on the volunteer's capabilities.

In spite of all the possible problems described, we continue to recommend this type of volunteering to those who have courage and initiative. These points are not meant to deter but to make sure a potential volunteer is not naive to the difficulties that may be involved. However, the rewards are even greater because they give the opportunity for the volunteer to be instrumental in contributing to changing the existing situations of extreme precariousness, allowing those organisations to better help their own people. We especially advise volunteers with language skills, who are endowed with considerable initiative and autonomy, to address themselves to these organisations.

In this Guide we have listed a good number of NGOs of developing countries, especially African ones. In the section "useful websites" (see page 18) and also on our website (see page 19) we have selected a list of sites with excellent links to many other NGOs not listed in the Guide.

Responsible tourism

Responsible tourism deserves a separate mention. Indeed, it is not volunteering, but as the term suggests, "tourism made on tiptoe".

The tourist tries to understand the local culture, to live with the locals, and to visit their villages, schools, farms, and cooperatives using the services offered by the local communities as much as possible so that they may increase their revenues. Responsible tourism is for those who want to travel, understand, and to be as little trouble to their host as possible. Several NGOs, in fact, are beginning to organise trips to the locations where their projects are carried out, so that the travellers may visit the volunteers and the communities being helped. Responsible tourism, in the context of this Guide, may be considered a gradual approach or introduction to volunteering.

Self-reflection before departure

Motivation is the best key to success in the volunteering experience, both for helping the project and oneself. Desire to leave should never be a flight or an escape from personal problems. Humanitarian volunteering means "to give oneself totally and sincerely" leaving behind, at least for a while, one's problems. A stressed and unhappy volunteer can cause many problems to a project where the objective is to help—not to be helped. For a meaningful and enjoyable experience and for the enhancement of the project, volunteers must pause for deep self-reflection before leaving to affirm their motivation and commitment and be ready to give their best effort.

USEFUL WEBSITES

The World Wide Web is the most comprehensive source of information on voluntary work worldwide. In this section we have highlighted the ones that we believe to be the most useful. However, if we were to list one book on voluntary work worldwide, *The International Directory of Voluntary Work* by Vacation Works Publications (Oxford UK), is the most comprehensive listing thousands of voluntary placements worldwide in different fields, many of them local, in the UK, the US, Europe, and other countries.

On the opposite page we have provided a links page from our website, to allow to reach easily the websites listed below. To obtain annual updates of this guide from the Internet please read carefully the "Important Note" on pages 36–38 of this guide. The links and the updates pages are not publicised to reserve them only for the readers of this Guide.

The Internet allows us to rapidly access information from almost anywhere in the world on practically every subject. The organisations involved in humanitarian volunteering are quite certainly a primary use of the Internet. Non-profit organisations in developing countries have little funding and considerable demand for communicating their calls for assistance, their needs, their public awareness campaigns, the collection of funds and, as concerns our field, their need for volunteers. After understanding which activity sector, the type of work, the country of destination, and the motivation behind volunteering, the Internet becomes a great tool in finding the most suitable volunteer opportunity. Search-engines, links to other sites, and, for constant information without having to navigate the Internet, select organisation newsletters are valuable tools for researching volunteer opportunities.

Practically every organisation, be it small or large, has a website. The volunteer positions are nearly always listed in the menu under the sign "Get involved!" or "How to help us". Most often, after a section dedicated to fundraising, there is a section concerning volunteering, both locally and at national headquarters. The national and international NGOs, which mostly run financed or co-financed cooperation projects, have a section dedicated to "Personnel search". In this case they are looking for qualified or specialised professionals to be hired on a contract basis (longer periods) in cooperation projects in developing countries. Therefore, answer these announcements as you would answer any employment offer: send a CV and wait for the answer (which may not arrive). As in all searches for employment it is advisable to send your CV to as many associations as possible. There are sites specialising exclusively in personnel searches for non-profit organisations.

The Internet is a fundamental tool for widening the search field and finding less competitive organisations.Naturally, the Internet is also quite useful in finding an association with which to perform local volunteering. Use a good search engine and look for "association + volunteering + the city name" to quickly find nearby associations. A good way to find workcamp organisations is to use a search engine and type in the key word "workcamp" and the country name.

Most of the websites of the organisations listed in this Guide are useful and often provide good links, however, we have chosen to make available to the reader a wide variety of useful websites which we have included in a link page of our website, accessible only to those who have purchased this Guide, which we will update periodically. The address of our links (for updates, please see pages 36-38) page is:

www.worldvolunteers.org/links.html

Below we have highlighted a few websites from organisations already listed in the Guide as well as selecting (as an example of what can be found in our website) a certain number of additional websites that may link you to hundreds of associations all over the world. The following websites should not be overlooked:
www.idealist.org
In our opinion, number one: the site with the largest data base of associations in the world, divided by sector of intervention and country; one can subscribe to a newsletter to receive the announcements of searches for volunteers, or even for professional persons on the part of associations listed in the data base.
www.avso.org
The site of the AVSO, Association of Voluntary Service Organisations, with links to all associated organisations.

www.alliance-network.org
The site of the Alliance of European Voluntary Service Organisations, a group of several European NGOs offering workcamps.

www.vfp.org
The site of Volunteers for Peace; it has a list of workcamps with opportunities in 80 countries.

www.oneworld.net
The international site of the Oneworld organisation; it lists volunteering opportunities offered by organisations all over the world, job opportunities, and links to all other Oneworld websites.

www.cnvs.org
The site of the Catholic Network of Volunteer Service; it has an excellent page of linked Catholic volunteering organisations both in the USA and elsewhere.

www.netaid.org
This site is already mentioned in "Volunteering from home" (page 12). Even for those not interested in doing volunteer work with their computer from home this is an excellent resource with several links.

www.interconnection.org
The site of an organisation of "virtual volunteers"; it has several links and information for volunteering opportunities all over the world.

www.volunteer.org.nz
A New Zealand-based site that offers volunteer programs through partner organisations; it includes information about post secondary education in development.

www.volunteermatch.org
A US-based database of volunteering opportunities for local non-profit and public organisations. Run a search by entering a zip code, then sort according to interest. Well organised, with icons to represent opportunities for different age groups. Excellent for local volunteering opportunities.

www.kabissa.org
A non-profit organisation that seeks to further democratic change and social justice in Africa by providing a space on the Internet for the African non-profit sector. Features include volunteering opportunities, NGO directory, newsletters, and more. It is an excellent directory of organisation for volunteering in Africa.

www.visionsinaction.org
This site has excellent suggestions for raising funds for voluntary work.

www.nonprofitcareer.com
Volunteering and job opportunities in the non-profit market, mainly in the US. Includes a job centre, directory of non-profit organisations, and information on workshops, conferences and job fairs, and a good list of volunteering organisations.

www.icva.ch
The website for the International Council of Voluntary agencies—a global network of human rights, humanitarian, and development NGOs, which focuses its information exchange and advocacy efforts primarily on humanitarian affairs and refugee issues. Great links to agencies worldwide, newsletters, and more. International Council of Voluntary Agencies. Good page of links worldwide.

www.ugandamission.org
The website of Mission to East Africa. The focus of this site is world missions, particularly in Uganda, East Africa, where they are based. There are over 1500 links to helpful Internet sites, including overseas missions, recent news articles, and extensive research topics.

www.bond.org.uk
BOND is a network of more than 250 UK-based voluntary organisations working in international development and development education. The site includes a current issues section, an extensive directory, a discussion room, and more. The website of a membership body for organisations engaged in international development work overseas or in the UK.

www.acfid.asn.au
An informational website for the Australian Council for International Development, that provides an overview of human rights activities in Australia It has an excellent directory, with links, to Australian Aid Organisations, as well as links by topic.

www.oneday.takingitglobal.org
A directory of 1514 international organisations. Browse by subject or by region and get a brief synopsis of the organisation or link to their website.

www.voluntario.org.br
Recife Voluntário - Centro de Voluntários do Recife   A well done website, with many links to partner organisation for volunteering all over Brazil.

www.youthactionnet.org
An excellent website with many volunteering and job opportunities for young people all over the world.

www.volunteerafrica.org
A simple and friendly website providing many links and advice for volunteering in Africa.

www.ngovoice.org
Voluntary Organisations in Cooperation in Emergencies within the Liaison Committee of NGOs to the European Union. VOICE is the largest European network of non-governmental organisations (NGOs) who are active in the field of humanitarian aid.

www.nvoad.org
National Voluntary Organizations Active in Disaster, Cooperation, Communication, Coordination, Collaboration in Disaster Response. A very useful infocentre, of many US organisations.

www.americorps.org
The official website for the domestic Peace Corps, excellent resource for getting involved in local community, cooperation for the National Service, and programmes for senior citizens, and more.

www.csv.org.uk
Community Service Volunteers (CSV) provides opportunities for all young people to volunteer full-time helping in communities throughout the UK.

www.charitypeople.com
A very large database in the UK for finding a job in the Non-profit world, ideal for people who return!

www.ihe.org.uk
The website and magazine "The Health Exchange" for Health Professionals Interested in Working in Developing Countries!

www.nursingabroad.net
Extremely useful website with medical and nursing positions worldwide.

www.servenet.org
Excellent for finding volunteering positions in the US with excellent links. SERVEnet.org is the premier website on service and volunteering. Through SERVEnet, users can enter their zip code, city, state, skills, interests, and availability and be matched with organizations needing help. SERVEnet is also a place to search for calendar events, job openings, service news, recommended books, and best practices.

www.miusa.org
As a US-based national non-profit organisation, the mission of Mobility International USA (MIUSA) is to empower people with disabilities around the world through international exchange, information, technical assistance and training, and to ensure the inclusion of people with disabilities in international exchange and development programs.

www.volunteerabroad.com
US website appropriate for Young people and students.

www.worldvolunteerweb.org
Extremely informative and updated UN Internet portal on worldwide volunteer resource established as a continuation of the International Year of the Volunteers (2001) web site. The site is maintained by UNV (see listing), the United Nations agency for Volunteering.

www.citizens4change.org/home.htm
A very informative website from a group of Canadian organisations, with excellent information on how to choose a project and for pre-departure preparation.

www.isp.msu.edu/NCSA/volteer.htm
A substantial list of Organisations (both African and not) offering volunteering opportunities in Africa, with contacts and description, compiled by the National Consortium for Study in Africa at the Michigan State University

www.aboutistc.org/iaewep/contact_members.html
List Student travel organisations in 26 countries, members of The International Association for Educational Work Exchange Programmes (IAEWEP). Good for contacting the organisation in the desired country directly.

www.reliefweb.int/w/rwb.nsf
The website of the United Nations Office for the Coordination of Humanitarian Affairs (OCHA). It features a vast Directory of Humanitarian Organizations and a very updated and resourceful list of professional vacancies.

www.developmentgateway.org/
The website of the Development Gateway Foundation. It has a very good directory of current development project in every country.

HOW TO READ THE GUIDE

World Volunteers is a directory. It lists organisations of different natures offering volunteering opportunities in developing countries. The Guide gives examples of the different kinds of opportunities but it can not be considered comprehensive. If an organisation of interest can not be found among the organisations listed, the section dedicated to resources on the Internet gives the reader the possibility of finding hundreds or thousands of additional organisations. Organisations are listed in alphabetical order. Should an organisation have an acronym, as many do, the organisation is listed in alphabetical order by the acronym. For example, MSF (Médecins san Frontières), UNV (United Nations Volunteers), and EVS (European Voluntary Service) are listed alphabetically by their acronym.

At the end of the Guide, there is an Appendix with two analytical tables. The first table lists the geographical area of the projects of each organisation in the Guide. It also indicates whether the organisations run workcamps or offer non-professional or short-term opportunites (up to 3 months). The second table lists the sectors of activity for each organisation.

Meaning of recurrent acronyms:

NGO: Non-governmental Organisation

EU: European Union.

Meaning of abbreviations

For each organisation the Guide lists:
The **address** and the **telephone** and **fax** numbers with the international codes. Remember to change the local area code according to the country's telephone system. For example, to call the UK (listed as ++44 (20) XXXX-XXXX), people calling from the UK should not dial ++44 (the international code), but should add 0 (zero) before 20 (the local area code). Calling from Europe add 00 before 44 to call the UK, whereas from the US only dial 011, then 44, the international access codes from the US to the UK. **E-mail** and World Wide Web (**www**) addresses are listed where available. Some organisations in developing countries do not have a website: it can be useful to ask via e-mail if they have implemented one since the printing of this Guide. If not, a prospective volunteer with good computer skills can help this organisation to make one: it is a good way to begin volunteering and an excellent introduction to the organisation. Organisations who do not have a website, therefore do not have their e-mail address linked to a domain name and tend to change their e-mail address quite often. If, after a reasonable number of solicitations an organisation does not answer to the e-mail messages, or a message bounces back, a search with the most common Internet search engines (such as google, altavista, or yahoo) or a quick phone call or fax will indicate whether a new e-mail address exists. It is also possible to send an e-mail message to an organisation from the same country or of the same sector, which probably knows the organisation in question. If an organisation exists and still operates, it is always possible to trace it through the Internet, and with a bit of investigation it is always possible to find the new coordinates. The reader should also realise that projects are dynamic and details such as sectors, costs and benefits, project duration, start and finish dates, or countries in which the organisations operate may vary from year to year. New projects arise and old projects may end. Periodic verification of the websites of interest is highly recommended.

Desc.: This section is the description of the activities and main objectives of an organisation, along with some general information on their history, partnerships, or other information relevant to prospective volunteers. Information on specific projects run by the organisation may be elaborated.

Sector: This section helps show the scope of the organisations' actions by describing the sectors in which the organisations operate. At the end of the Guide there is an Appendix with an analytical index, formatted as a table, to allow the readers to easily select organisations operating within their sectors of interest. The difficulty of this categorisation has been the grouping of various definitions in order to standardise the categories. Therefore when, in our opinion, it has not been possible to include an area of action of a given NGO in one of the specific categories chosen, we have introduced the category: various. Unfortunately, it may be that an organisations listed may have specific sectors not outlined in the Guide. It is also easy to see how many sectors overlap: for example, a project that works with the rights of women can be considered to be working in the sectors of women's issues, education, human rights, child welfare, skills training, and even agriculture. Therefore, the reader should not consider this classification rigid or absolute, and should contact or consult the website of the organisations of interest to confirm the full scope of the project and whether it works in a sector that has not been classified here.

Agriculture: Farming projects, irrigation, livestock breeding, treatment and processing of products and crops, and shipping to markets of the final products or commodities. Relevant professions vary from agronomists to veterinarians to hydrologists.

Child welfare: The defence of children rights for shelter, education, nutrition; protection against abuse or violence, prevention of child labour and exploitation; assistance with orphanages; providing attention to street children; or prevention of child prostitution.

Community Development: The development of all products and services that foster a sound and peaceful coexistence of a community. The promotion of grassroots organisations, small entrepreneur unions, sport groups, basic democracy, public administration, economic organisation, etc.

Construction: The constructions of public or private buildings, schools, hospitals, etc., urban planning and servicing a community, such as the planning and construction of water and sanitation systems.

Culture: Ranges from intercultural exchange and awareness to archeological preservation.

Education: Basic literacy and language courses, hygiene and health education, social skills, technology, and computers.

Emergency: Short term immediate actions, disaster relief such as after an earthquake or other natural disasters, or initial response to refugees from a conflict.

Environment: Natural resources, pollution treatment and cleanups, solid and organic waste management, forestry, wildlife management, protected areas management, aquaculture, etc.

Health: Basic healthcare; specialist medicine; health education and HIV/AIDS awareness; nutrition and hygiene; or first aid.

Housing: Homelessness, building homes, etc.

Human rights: This is a broadest sector and includes the defence and monitoring of human rights. These rights are legal as well as emotional and encompass prisoners' rights, torture prevention, labour and workers rights, as well as the rights of the elderly or disabled.

Hunger relief: Distribution of food in famine situations.

IT: Information Technology and communications, which also includes media.

Peacekeeping: Peace monitoring actions.

Refugee aid: Logistic assistance, providing food and shelter, health and administrative assistance, repatriation, and reconstruction of living conditions for refugees of political, conflicts, natural disasters, etc.

Religious: Religious worship, assistance, or practice; it usually pertains to the missions although it also may be a Christian organisation with a spiritual element that is not evangelical or a working component of the project.

Sanitation: Sewage treatment, potable water, etc.

Skills Training: May or may not be exclusively related to working to earn a salary. Skills taught may be personal financing or economics, craftsmanship, trades, computers, etc.

Small-enterprise development: The development of basic entrepreneurial efforts, including small shops or retail activities, community services, small craftsmanship activities, farm products manufacturing or processing, or small lodging, restaurants, and guiding services within a sustainable tourism context. Included within the small-enterprise development is micro-credit development, which is a fundamental tool for enterprise development.

Women's issues: Work towards raising the role of women in their societies, women's rights in submissive conditions, family planning, creation of women's organisations, protection from physical violence, etc.

Various: Anything that does not fall in the previous classifications, such as tourism, and specific trades or professions that would be listed under qualifications.

Country: Countries are grouped by continent. For cultural and geographical activity Mexico is included with Latin America instead of North America and the Caribbean is a separate group. The Middle East is kept distinct from the rest of Asia. Projects in Oceania, due to the small number of countries, are few, whereas those in Europe take place mostly in Eastern Europe. Organisations finish and start new projects continuously, and therefore the list of countries is extremely dynamic. It is recommended to verify with the organisation directly or with their website that the country of interest has a project currently taking volunteers.

Qualif.: The qualifications and skills required of a volunteer who wants to join a project. As a general rule for the workcamps no special qualifications are needed, other than a strong motivation and enthusiasm. Adaptation to harsh work, basic accommodation and little comfort is almost always required. For professional volunteering (whether short, medium, or long term) volunteers are chosen according to their qualifications. Therefore, the major qualifications required by an organisation are specified. These requirements however, must be considered dynamic, particularly for larger organisations. Active organisation have many projects at different phases, and start new ones continuously, therefore new professional skills are always needed. Smaller organisations tend to specialise in a specific field, and therefore tend to select mostly specific professional figures. For organisations hiring young graduates, if they do not have a technical preparation, it is difficult to identify them with a professional qualification, which will be acquired with years of experience. In this case someone's motivation, maturity, ability to work autonomously are taken into consideration, because of the great dedication needed to live and work for a few years in a very different country from what a recent graduate is used to. Often candidates for long-term volunteering are exposed to specific training courses by the sending NGO. These courses focus on the local culture, language, and specific aspects of the organisation and the projects the volunteers will be involved with. Often also qualified professionals are required to attend these training courses particularly if they don' have previous experience in working in developing countries.

Nonpro: This abbreviation stands for 'non-professional'. It indicates whether or not non-professional or unskilled volunteers are accepted by organisation. All organisations providing workcamp opportunities by definition accept non-professional volunteers. Many NGOs accept recent graduate students for long-term positions or internships in order to introduce them to a career in international development with training opportunities. Other organisations, particularly those in developing countries, may accept short-term volunteers with experience or skills in activities and industries such as fundraising, managerial, or computer.

Age: Some projects impose a minimum and maximum age on the volunteer profile. Typically the minimum age is 18 for workcamps or generic volunteer positions. Minors may be accepted for certain programs or with a guardian. Seniors are almost always accepted unless the physical demands of the project are considered too high. Where a specific professional is needed the age becomes irrelevant and experience the more appropriate criteria for acceptance.

Duration: The duration of the volunteering period can span from weeks to months or years. Typically, workcamps last two weeks to one month at the most, short-term volunteering up to three months, middle-term volunteering is six to twelve months, and long-term volunteering can last well beyond one year.

Lang.:   This important section states the languages that are required for a volunteer to work on a project. The importance of communicating with the project staff or with other local or international volunteers should not be overlooked. Often another international language (such as Spanish, Portuguese, or French) is used. It is very important to be able to speak at least a few words of the local language, especially when volunteering in the health sector. Prospective volunteers should never underestimate the importance of this aspect and never overestimate their ability to understand a foreign language in a working environment. It is often expected that long-term volunteers learn the local language in order to be more integrated in the project. Even a professional and experienced volunteer may not be accepted to a project if the foreign language needed is not spoken. In general, for unskilled volunteers, such as those participating in workcamps, English is sufficient.

Benefits: Volunteers working overseas receive many of the benefits provided in the private sector, but obviously with much lower standards. The benefits can vary greatly between the workcamp, short-term (professional or unskilled), and middle- or long-term volunteering situations. Middle or long-term volunteers often receive a salary, which will depend on the experience. It may seem to be a contradiction in terms to be a "paid" volunteer, but it is a necessity: Very few people can afford to leave home for months or years and return without any money, especially if the volunteers are young (and have little savings) or older with a family to support. NGOs therefore must offer a salary , even low, otherwise it would be very difficult to recruit the personnel to run the projects. Many NGOs, when possible, hire mostly local staff, but it is difficult when the necessary skills are not locally available. In many other cases, NGOs have projects funded by large Inter-Governmental organisations or National aid agencies, such as the EU (European Union) or USAID (US Agency for International Development), which bear most or part of the costs, including salaries. The European Union, or better the European Commission (which is the Government of the Union) has a DG (General Directorate, the Ministries of the Commission) devoted to development cooperation: the DG VIII. In general salaries for long-term volunteers are not very high except the ones for skilled professionals when the projects are co-financed. Volunteers are helped by the fact that they have little or no expenses, that international travel is often reimbursed, and room and board are part of the benefits, or, if room and/or board are not supplied, the cost of living in general in developing countries is very low. Therefore the salary, for a long-term volunteer, is in large part saved and it can be a small sum available for when a volunteer returns home. Other benefits can be, as already mentioned: international travel, room and board, travel allowances for family members or more. Co-financing institutions usually have set contracts that clearly spell out all the benefits for the volunteers; NGOs working in co-financed projects must follow these contracts for their personnel hired within these projects. The conditions for short-term volunteers are different, particularly if they are hired with individual agreements: the benefits depend exclusively on what is stipulated. International and/or local travel, room, board, and a small stipend (or "pocket money") may be paid. The organisations do appreciate volunteers who can afford to forego any of the benefits or personally fund any of the project costs. Skilled professionals who can afford the time and expenses should not hesitate to contact the organisation they would like to volunteer for, if they think that their skills can be used. NGOs in developing countries (the Guide lists a few dozen) may only provide room and board.

Costs: The costs that a volunteer incurs are what are obviously not covered in the benefits. Long-term professional volunteers with a co-financed contract will usually only pay their personal expenses; short-term volunteers and volunteers for local NGOs, with or without individual contracts, will usually bear all the costs (travel, room, and board) that the NGO can not pay, and may have to provide a donation, whereas participants to workcamps, have usually to pay for travel and a participation fee, which usually covers the costs of room and board, and often can also be a contribution to the project itself.

Applic.: This section briefly describes the application procedures required by the organisation. Applications may or may not require a CV (curriculum vitae or resume), letters of recommendation, or whether the prospective volunteer must fill out an on-line or printed application form, etc. When communicating with organisations in developing countries it is advisable to use e-mail, if they have it, because of the low cost and the velocity. However, some projects in Africa may have problems receiving e-mails, so it is recommended to telephone these organisations if the e-mail receives no response.

Notes: This section gives relevant additional information. For example if the organisation requires participation to pre-selection meetings or training courses, if they have local groups or international branches, or if a prospective volunteer must become member of the organisation before applying, etc.

TIPS FOR CONTACTING AN ORGANISATION

Having a copy of *World Volunteers* has been the first step. Below are some suggestions to help you find the organisation most suited to your interests and be accepted on their project.

1) **Have clear in mind what you want to do, the sector you prefer, the geographical location, the duration of your volunteering period, and the costs you can afford.** This will help you select and reduce the number of organisations you need to apply to. If you have a limited amount of time, leave out from your selection the organisations that only take long-term volunteers; vice-versa, if you want to work long-term, omit the organisations that don't offer this possibility. If you are professionally qualified in a specific field, and you think that your skills may be useful, look specifically for organisations in your sector where you would best be able to use your qualifications. Conversely, do not consider organisations that do not need your skills. A good approach can be to select a list of organisations and divide them into your first and second priorities. The first priority should include the organisations that are of primary interest to you, the second should include the organisations you would volunteer for only under certain circumstances; then start contacting both groups systematically.

2) **Use the fastest possible method to contact an organisation**. Remember that interesting projects or organisations also have many applicants, and they usually fill their available positions on a first come, first serve basis. Therefore, you want to be as fast as possible in letting them know that you are interested in taking a position with them. Do not lose time by sending a letter by regular mail, unless you are required to do so, but immediately start sending e-mails, even if only as preliminary enquiries. E-mail is usually a good way to make a first contact with an organisation and get to know who they are without being too committed. It is also a good idea to verify before applying whether or not you have a good chance to be accepted. If not, do not waste time, go on to the next organisation on your list. Should you not receive a reply within 3–5 days,

be prepared to send reminders or telephone them to confirm their e-mail address or verify whether or not it is worth continuing your application process with them, particularly if it requires filling out lengthy forms.

3) Inform the organisation you would like to work for about yourself as much as possible. With your request for information, send a description of your skills and interests and possibly a CV—which you always have ready so it would not be a waste of time to attach it. Always enclose a cover letter and ask if in addition to the CV other information about yourself is required.

4) If an organisation is in a developing country, make it easy for them to respond to you. Remember that organisations in poorer countries often are short of funds. Therefore, help them by enclosing self-addressed stamped envelopes should you exchange regular mail (for example you may need an original letter in their stationary paper to obtain the Visa). Always enclose one or more international postal reply coupon(s) as a form of courtesy, even if you are not required to do so. You may also offer an organisation to fax you collect (give them an appointment, because in order to receive a fax collect you should first be able to answer vocally, accept the call, then switch on the fax mode). Better still, since a fax goes both ways regardless of who calls, you can offer to call the organisation on their fax line and have them fax back the information. Remember that you should arrange this over the phone. If you interact with a large organisation, well equipped for recruiting volunteers, they will have all the means to contact you.

5) Do exactly what is required by an organisation for being accepted. If they require you to complete their application form, whether it is sent to you or whether you download it from their website, do fill it out, even if you have already submitted your detailed CV. Compile in a proper and clean manner both the CV and a cover letter, which you should always enclose. Should you be required to send material by regular mail, never hand write, not even the cover letter, unless you are required to do so. If you apply with an organisation where the official language is not

English but another major international language that you will be expected to use if accepted by them, send at least the cover letter in this language and be prepared to translate your CV if necessary. Many organisations with workcamp programmes, often require an advanced deposit or membership to their organisation. If accepted, do not miss an opportunity by not paying a deposit on time. Inquire about the fastest method to transfer funds: by international telegraph money order, credit card, money wire from bank to bank, etc. Finally, many organisations require preliminary meetings or training courses if you are accepted. You should obviously attend regularly.

6) **Contact many organisations.** Select an organisation, or a specific project, well in advance. Properly planning your vacation or time in advance will allow you to find the best airfares and select the best period suitable to you. Get detailed information on what to expect: the type of work, accommodation, food, climate, clothing, equipment necessary, etc. Owing to a lack of space this information can not be included in the organisations' description in the *World Volunteers* Guide. The Guide aims to give a general overview of a given organisation and give you tools to find many others. Never show up at a project location without having first applied and having been accepted and confirmed. Most projects have limited positions, lodging and personnel. Very rarely are they equipped to take on an unexpected volunteer. If you want to do so, because you were already travelling in a certain area, do not be disappointed if you are rejected.

Good luck with your "world volunteering"!

IMPORTANT NOTE

The Editors and the Publisher of *World Volunteers* do not endorse nor support any of the organisations listed in the guide; our intention is simply to present the reader with the widest possible choice to meet his or her interests and skills. Further and more detailed information about the organisations listed should be obtained directly by the reader from the organisations they wish to join. The Editors and Publisher of *World Volunteers* have also decided, both in order to offer prospective volunteers the widest possible choice and to help these extremely needy organisations, to cite, whenever possible, small organisations, particularly in developing countries, for the following reason:

1) **To allow extremely poor organisations to receive the help from volunteers** from developed countries and thereby use their valuable skills. We think that we should help this local grassroots potential as best we can, particularly if it comes directly from local organisations without an input from large organisations in the developed world.

However, prospective volunteers should consider that:

2) **Small organisations in developing countries often allow volunteers to come without excessive screening, and this may result in a negative experience for both the volunteer and the organisation.** We therefore recommend prospective volunteers to evaluate their own personal level of experience, both in travelling and in working abroad, and their capacity to live in extremely poor, remote, disorganised, and sometimes also unsafe conditions.

3) **A volunteer joining an organisation in a developing country directly, may find an excessive level of disorganisation, if judged by Western standards, that may not be perceived by the organisation's leaders. This may result in the volunteer being unable to conduct the task for which he or she has joined the organisation.** In such

cases, particularly if the volunteer judges that his or her help can not be useful to improve the situation, we highly recommend the volunteer to leave the organisation, without incurring in further costs or frustrations. In addition, we always recommend that the prospective volunteer carefully verifies the working conditions by reading the following instructions.

BEFORE JOINING PROJECTS AND ORGANISATIONS, PROSPECTIVE VOLUNTEERS SHOULD CAREFULLY READ THE FOLLOWING CONSIDERATIONS AND WARNINGS:

1) **Because of obvious cost reasons**, which would then reflect on the sale price of this book, **the Editors and the Publisher cannot personally visit every project or organisation** listed in this guide but have to trust what projects and organisations (or their websites, previous volunteers, or references cited by the organisations) declare.

2) **Small projects and organisations**, particularly in developing countries, mainly owing to a shortage of funding or qualified personnel or because of conflicts and emergency situations, **often change their programs or even interrupt their activities without informing the Editors and Publishers of this guide.**

3) **Before joining an organisation volunteers should carefully verify the validity of the information declared** in the project website (if one exists) or reported in this guide or its updates. To obtain annual updates of this guide from the Internet, readers must type the address of our webpage (see page 19), by replacing the words links.html with /updates/

4) **Prospective volunteers, before joining an organisation, should exchange frequent e-mails, or even fax or phone calls, with the organisation leaders** and ensure that communication is always prompt and clear. They should also confirm the project details, such as the living, working, and

safety conditions, prior to departure.

5)   **Prospective volunteers (before joining small projects or organisations directly, particularly in developing countries) should ask for names and addresses of previous volunteers and for international references to subsequently correspond with** to further verify the working and safety conditions.

6)   **Volunteers should never join an organisation by going directly to the location** without previous correspondence and verification of existing conditions.

7)   **Prospective volunteers should carefully read the WARNING on page 3 of this book.**

ORGANISATION LIST

Aang Serian 'House of Peace'

PO Box 13732 Arusha Tanzania
Tel.: ++255 (744) 318-548 or 673-368
or in the UK ++44 (2380) 402-575
E-mail: aang_serian@hotmail.com
www.aangserian.org.uk

Desc.: Volunteers work at the Aang Serian Community School in the Maasai village of Monduli, the Aang Serian office and recording studio in Arusha town, and occasionally other projects in the region. A variety of skills are needed to help build the Community School, and teaching, sports coaching, fundraising and secretarial skills are much in demand. Volunteer posts can start at various times of the year and can be of flexible duration. They are mainly community based and provide a unique opportunity for visitors to participate in the local culture and to better understand the values of the people. A 'Teach and Learn' program is also offered: volunteers study Swahili, indigenous knowledge, traditional dance and drumming.

Sector: Community development, construction, education, environment, small-enterprise development.

Country: Africa (Tanzania).

Qualif.: No particular skills required for short -term placements, initiative and adaptability are important requisites. Teaching qualification preferred for longer placements.

Nonpro: Yes, with relevant skills to the project.

Age: Minimum 18.

Duration: 2 months to 1 year, depending on project.

Lang.: English.

Benefits: Accommodation and food.

Costs: Program fee: GB£185(US$340) plus GB£60(US$110)/ week.

Applic.: References are required once applicatiopn is accepted.

Notes: E-mail contact in the UK: enolengila@yahoo.co.uk, bob@webzell.co.uk. There should be ample opportunity for personal travel in the country.

Abha Light Foundation

PO Box 236-00515, Nairobi, Kenya
Tel.: ++254 (20) 787310 – Cell.: ++254 733895466
Fax: ++254 (20) 787310
E-mail: abhalight@eudoramail.com
http://home.pacific.net.sg/~rucira/alf

Desc.: Abha Light Foundation is concerned with improving and maintaining the health of the people primarily using homeopathy, complementary and alternative medicines and health practices through health training programs and homeopathic and natural medicine mobile and permanent health clinics to further the well being and health of Africans in an economical and safe way. Homeopathic medicine can be very cheap and easily distributed by a qualified homeopath. The immediate goal is to provide medicine for the poor through mobile clinics. The long-term goal is to introduce homeopathy and other complementary medicines into Africa as part of the health-care solution for the people.

Sector: Health.

Country: Africa (Kenya).

Qualif.: Homeopaths (3rd–5th year students are possible if they can hold their own in case-taking and prescribing), acupuncturists, naturopaths, and other complimentary therapists.

Nonpro: No.

Age: Over 20. Qualifications is more required.

Duration: 4 – 6 weeks is minimum. Long-term (3 – 6 months) would be most beneficial for both the project and the volunteer.

Lang.: English. Translators will be available for patients speaking only Swahili or other tribal languages.

Benefits: Accommodation. Unusual clinical experience.

Costs: US$300. Volunteers are responsible for their food, local transportation, e-mail, etc. However, life in Kenya is cheap and $150–250 per month is a reasonable budget.

Applic.: On-line form.

ACDI/VOCA

50 F Street, NW, Suite 1075, Washington, DC 20001 USA
Tel.: ++1 (202) 383-4961 (or toll free in N. Am. 1-800-929-8622)
Fax: ++1 (202) 783-7204
E-mail: AV-CA@acdivoca.org or AV-OH@acdivoca.org or
volunteer@acdivoca.org
www.acdivoca.org or volunteeroverseas.com

Desc.: ACDI/VOCA identifies and opens economic opportunities for farmers and other entrepreneurs worldwide by promoting democratic principles and market liberalisation, building international cooperative partnerships, and encouraging the sound management of natural resources. Every year ACDI/VOCA carries out over 600 volunteer consultative assignments around the world. Recruiters manage a roster of some 4,000 volunteer experts, the largest agricultural volunteer network in the USA. They match client needs, who initiate and determine their own technical assistance requirements, with volunteers possessing the relevant background.

Sector: Agriculture, education, environment, small-enterprise development.

Country: A variety of countries in Africa, Asia, Eastern Europe and the Middle East. See website for updated list.

Qualif.: 10–40 years of experience in respective field. Volunteers and paid specialists in: banking and finance, commodity marketing, small- and medium-enterprise development, cooperative and association development, international agribusiness partnerships, and food monetisation are desired.

Nonpro: No.

Age: Dependent upon experience.

Duration: Inquire with the organisation.

Lang.: English.

Benefits: Employment opportunities updated on website.

Costs: Inquire with the organisation.

Applic.: On-line form.

Notes: ACDI/VOCA opportunities for non-US citizens are limited.

Action Against Hunger UK

Unit 7B, Larnaca Works, Grange Walk, London SE1 3EW   UK
Tel.: ++44 (20) 7394 6300
Fax: ++44 (20) 7237 9960
E-mail: info@aahuk.org or jobs@aahuk.org
www.aahuk.org

Desc.: Action Against Hunger UK is part of the Action Against Hunger International network, one of the leading international organisations in the fight against hunger and malnutrition.

Sector: Agriculture, health, hunger relief, sanitation.

Country: A varietey of countries in Africa, Asia, Eastern Europe and Latin America .See website for updated list.

Qualif.: Nutritionists, nurses,water engineers, agronomists, food security officers.

Nonpro: N/A

Age: N/A

Duration: Depending on project (from 3 months to 2 years or more). One year contracts.

Lang.: Working knowledge of English with French or Spanish.

Benefits: Salary depending on experience, all in-field expenses paid, as well as transportation, room and board, living expenses, per diem and full insurance package, including war risk, emergency evacuation, and medical.

Costs: No cost to the volunteers.

Applic.: Send on-line form and a CV to the appropriate office. Action Against Hunger New York: job@aah-usa.org or info@aah-usa.org; Action Contre la Faim France: info@acf.imaginet.fr; Accion Contra el Hambre Spain: sbernhardt@achesp.org (for administrators, logisticians, managers) or mmanzaneque@achesp.org (for nurses, nutritionists, hydros) (www.accionco ntraelhambre.org).

Adarsh Community Development Trust

Door No. 6-4-504 Maruthi Nagar
Anantapur 515 001 Andhra Pradesh, India
Tel.: ++91 (8554) 274-492 or 240-122
E-mail: Adarsh_3894@yahoo.co.in

Desc.: This Charitable Social Organisation was formed in 1982 by a group of enthusiastic and dedicated men and women who shared a deep concern and desire to serve the less fortunate and vulnerable people in and around of Anantapur District. The organisation headquarters are located in Anantapur and the District headquarters in the Rayalaseema region of Andhra Pradesh. The organisation has been working for the welfare of disadvantaged peoples for over 2 decades. Since late 1983 the organisation has been working with the assistance of the Christian Children's Fund (CCF) with 3,500 families throughout several in the Anantapur District.

Sector: Child welfare, community development, environment, sanitation, small-enterprise development, women's issues.

Country: Asia (India).

Qualif.: Water management/irrigation professionals and small enterprise and alternative livelihood experts desired.

Nonpro.: Yes.

Age: 18–40.

Duration: Minimum 2 weeks.

Lang.: English.

Benefits: Accommodation, internal transportation.

Costs: Travel, insurance and living expenses.

Applic.: Contact the organisation.

Notes: Once accepted the applicant will be put in contact with former volunteers who have been selected as Representatives in various countries. Please see "Important Note" on page 36.

AFS International
71 West 23rd Street, 17th Floor
New York, New York 10010 USA
Tel.: ++1 (212) 807-8686
Fax: ++1 (212) 807-1001
E-mail: info@afs.org
www.afs.org

Desc.: AFS is an international, voluntary, non-governmental, non-profit organisation that provides intercultural learning opportunities to help people develop the knowledge, skills, and understanding needed to create a more just and peaceful world. The worldwide network is run mostly by volunteers who connect to their community to place exchange students, community service students and teachers in host families.

AFS Community Service Program Participants volunteer with local organisations that address community needs such as environmental education and improvement, early child development or developing Human Rights programs. During the program, participants are exposed to new customs and values that challenge them to reflect on their own cultural norms. This intercultural learning process develops in participants not only a deeper understanding of another culture but, perhaps most profoundly, a richer awareness of their own background. AFS Educator Programs provide opportunities for teachers to live and work in countries around the world. Short programs allow teachers and administrators to travel abroad during their school holidays, to meet and work with other educators. Semester and year-long programs give teachers and administrators the opportunity to have in-depth cultural and pedagogical experiences. AFS Educator Programs include cultural lessons and events, family home stays, observation of local educational practices and teaching in schools in the host country.

Sector: Child welfare, community development, culture, education, environment, health, housing.

Country: AFS has offices in more than 50 countries with programs in more than 80.

Qualif.: All volunteers welcome. For participating in programs, see website for qualifications specific to program and country.

Nonpro: Yes.

Age: All ages of volunteers welcome. For participation in school-based programs students must be age 12—18. Community Service programs accept students 18 and over. Teacher programs vary according to country and certification.

Duration: 1–4 months to 1 year.

Lang.: According to country.

Benefits: Round-trip airfare, orientation, language training, health insurance. Check with nearest AFS representative for the fees for your preferred destination. —

Costs: The sending country sets costs that vary with the length of program and the destination. Australia (approx. AUS$7,600–10,000, or US$5,700-7,600, for 1 year; AUS$8,000, or US$6,000 for 6 months; AUS$1,100–5,200, US$830-3,950 for 1 month) UK (approx. GB£2,950 or US$ 5,500, for 6 month). Merit or need-based scholarships are available in some countries. A number of corporations offer scholarships to the children of their employees. Approximately 20% of AFS students worldwide receive partial financial assistance for their experience.

Applic.: Contact local AFS office (see website).

Notes: Volunteers must be sent through the AFS organisation in their country of citizenship.

AFSAI – Association for Training and Inter-Cultural Activities and Exchange

Viale dei Colli Portuensi 345, B2, 00151 Rome Italy
Tel.: ++39(06)537-0332
Fax: ++39(06)5820-1442
E-mail:info@afsai.it
www.afsai.it

Desc.: AFSAI started over 40 years ago when a group of young people decided to start an organisation with the goal of fostering intercultural exchange between young people from different countries. AFSAI is one of the Italian partners of EVS (see listing) and regularly organises workcamps.

Sectors: Community development, culture, education, environment, human rights, skills training, various.

Country: Various countries in Africa, Asia, Europe (European Union and Eastern Europe), Latin America, the Middle East.

Qualif.: No qualifications are necessary.

Nonpro: Yes. Volunteers must show flexibility, maturity and be willing to be fully engaged in a project with strong cultural, environmental, health, and/or social implications.

Age: 18–30 for Overseas Voluntary Service and EVS; minimum 18 for the workcamps.

Duration: 6–12 months for EVS. Shorter programs (3 weeks to 6 months) possible; 3–4 weeks for workcamps.

Lang.: Basic knowledge of English for the workcamps. For long-term programs volunteers receive language and cultural training upon arrival.

Benefits: Food, accommodation, travel costs and pocket money depending on the program.

Costs: None for EVS; travel plus a participation fee for Overseas Voluntary Service and for workcamps (EUR100–300).

Applic.: Form can be found on-line or requested to AFSAI.

Notes: Membership to AFSAI (approx. EUR 30 per year) necessary.

AFSC – American Friends Service Committee
Youth for Peace and Sustainable Community
1501 Cherry Street, Philadelphia, Pennsylvania 19102 USA
Tel.: ++1 (215) 241-7295
Fax: ++1 (215) 241-7026
E-mail: mexsummer@afsc.org
www.afsc.org/mexicosummer

Desc.: The Mexico Summer Project: Semilleros de Futuros (Sowing Futures) is a summer project in Mexico coordinated with AFSC's partner organisation, Service, Development and Peace, A.C. (SEDEPAC). The aim is for youth from different countries of the Americas, Europe, and the indigenous communities of Xilitla to work together on community projects, share from their diverse cultures and experiences, and learn ways to address political, ecological, and economic challenges. SEDEPAC has developed a long-term program to assist the people of Xilitla, San Luis Potosí, working in partnership with 2 principal organisations, the Sociedad Cooperativa Agropecuaria la Igualdad de Xilitla (SCAIX) and the Unión de Mujeres Campesinas de Xilitla (UMCX).

Sector: Community development, culture, various.

Country: Latin America (Mexico).

Qualif.: N/A.

Nonpro: Yes. Experience in service and advocacy and interest in political, social, and cultural issues in Latin America.

Age: 18–26.

Duration: Exact dates vary yearly, but runs between June and August.

Lang.: Fluent Spanish.

Benefits: Fees waived for co-facilitators. Some scholarship are available.

Costs: The project fee is on a sliding scale according to need but is normally US$1,250. US$150 (non-refundable) is due upon acceptance and the remainder 6 weeks prior to project start date. Participants are responsible for travel and personal expenses.

Applic.: By March 1 with notice given by April 1. Waiting list until April 15.

Notes: Remote living conditions. A physical exam is required.

AJED Youth Association for Education and Development

Cité Jardiparc X Cambérenne, Villa No. 3
PO Box, Dakar, Colobane, 12035 Senegal
Tel.: ++(221) 835-0320
Fax: ++(221) 855-2821
E-mail: ajed@sentoo.sn
www.go.to/ajed

Desc.: AJED was founded by a group of young people who wanted to contribute at the development of their country. Founded in 1979, the association was immediately recognised by the Senegalese government. The most important values of AJED are the solidarity, cultural exchanges, voluntary work, and the engagement in the development of the country. Since its foundation AJED organises different activities for young people like workcamps, a stay with guest family, and education programs. The youth programs have different goals: the economic and social promotion from the Senegalese youth, in an international solidarity perspective. The workcamps are organised to protect the environment (reforestation and the fertility of the soil) and to promote cultural exchanges.

Sector: Child welfare, community development, construction, culture, education, environment, health, small-enterprise development.

Country: Africa (Senegal).

Qualif.: No specific skills required.

Nonpro: Yes.

Age: Minimum 18.

Duration: 3 weeks to 1 month.

Lang.: English, French, Arabic.

Benefits: Room, board and pick-up from the airport.

Costs: Approx. US$800 plus mandatory insurance.

Applic.: Correspond via e-mail.

Notes: Please see note on page 36.

AJUDE – Youth Association for the Development of Voluntary Service in Mozambique

Rua da Mesquita 222, Flat 11, 1st floor, Maputo, Mozambique
Tel./Fax: ++258 (1) 312-854
E-mail: ajude@ajude.org
www.ajude.org

Desc.: AJUDE was born during the post-civil-war period in Mozambique, when the region faced deep transformations. The need of strengthening awareness, solidarity, and exchange between populations were the main motivations for the creation of the organisation. In Mozambique, the economic and social reconstruction and the reconciliation between Mozambicans constituted an important challenge, that's why young Mozambican students were the pioneers in this area, and through their actions AJUDE was created in 1995.

Sector: Child welfare, community development, construction, education, emergency, environment, health, human rights, women's issues.

Country: Africa (Mozambique).

Qualif.: No particular qualifications needed.

Nonpro: Yes.

Age: Minimum 18.

Duration: 2-week to 1-month workcamps.

Lang.: English, Portuguese preferred.

Benefits: Room and board, return transport from Maputo to the workcamp site.

Costs: Approx. US$220 for food and accommodation. The transport to and from the camp and the international airfare are not included

Applic.: On-line form.

Notes: For more information contact persons are available in the UK, Germany and France. Please see note on page 36.

AJVPE-TOGO Association des Jeunes Volontaires pour la Protection de l'Environnement

812 rue des Brueyeres, Nyekonakpoè (Togbato)
BP 4568 Lomé Togo
Tel.: ++(228) 901-2506 or 917-5313
E-mail: enquiries@ajvpe-togo.org or ajvpetogo@yahoo.fr or
sajvpetogo@yahoo.fr   www.ajvpe-togo.org

Desc.: AJVPE-TOGO, which stands for Young Volunteers Association for Environmental Protection, is a group of young people with a great desire to help in the field of environmental protection. To achieve these goals, the organization informs and raises awareness on the environment, supports local initiatives that promote community development (schools), creates public infrastructure (gardens, markets, public toilets, wells for water), develops voluntary programs with the public. The volunteers are able to work on various projects. They can help build a school, plant trees to prevent deforestation, or tutor young students. An artistic workcamp is also organised every year to teach participants music, dance, and the technique of Batik.

Sector: Community development, culture, education, environment.
Country: Africa (Togo).
Qualif.: No particular skills required; initiative and adaptability are important requisites. English, German, French, and math teachers desired.
Nonpro.: Yes.
Age:_ Minimum 18.
Duration: 3 weeks to 1 year dependent upon project.
Lang: English and French.
Benefits: Accommodation and food.
Costs: Volunteer contribution based on the duration of the program; 3–4 weeks costs approximately EUR150.
Applic.: E-mail a detailed CV.
Notes: Once accepted the applicant will be put in contact with former volunteers who have been selected as representatives in various countries. Please see note on page 36.

51

AJWS – American Jewish World Service

Jewish Volunteer Corps
45 West 36th Street, 10th Floor
New York, New York 10018 USA
Tel.: ++1 (212) 736-2597 (toll free in N. Am. 1-800-889-7146)
E-mail: jvcvol@jws.org
www.ajws.org

Desc.: This independent nonprofit organization was founded in 1985 to help alleviate poverty, hunger and disease among the people of the world regardless of race, religion or nationality. It provides humanitarian aid through financial and technical support, emergency relief, and skilled volunteers to grassroots groups that are implementing small-scale, self-sustaining development. The Jewish Volunteer Corps (JVC) places volunteers on short-term consulting projects with local, grassroots non-governmental organizations throughout Africa, Asia, Latin America and Russia and Ukraine. Volunteers come with a variety of skills and provide humanitarian aid in the form of technical assistance and training. Other opportunities for college students and recent graduates are with the International Jewish College Corps (IJCC). This is a seven-week immersion experience to explore international development, study social justice within a Jewish context, and serve on hands-on volunteer projects in the developing world and Ukraine. Following the summer, participants continue in the IJCC domestic program that includes educational seminars, retreats, public speaking engagements, article writing and volunteer service. AJWS also organizes an Alternative Spring Break in Central America for students and organizes delegations with synagogues, Jewish community centers and other groups wishing to learn more about international development issues.

Sector: Agriculture, education, health, small-enterprise development, various.

Country: Africa (Ghana, Kenya, Senegal, Uganda, South Africa, Zimbabwe), Asia (India, Thailand, Philippines), Europe (Russia, Ukraine), Latin America, (Belize, El Salvador, Honduras, Peru, Mexico, Nicaragua).

Qualif.: JVC volunteers must posses professional skills and expertise in a particular area such as: computer programming/systems, marketing, botany/agriculture, fundraising, strategic planning, journalism, staff training, micro-enterprise, public health and HIV/AIDS, midwifery, etc.

Nonpro: Interest, not expertise, is needed for college programs.

Age: JVC: Minimum 21.College programs: 18 to 25.

Duration:JVC: 1 month to 1 year, with the average volunteer serving 2 to 3 months.

Lang.: English, French, Spanish.

Benefits:Transportation and insurance is provided for JVC volunteers.

Costs: Modest, subsidized fees for college programs.

Applic.: On-line form or request application directly from AJWS. There is no application fee. After the JVC receives and reviews a completed application, an in-person or telephone interview will be arranged. Three written references will be required. Applicants will be notified in a timely fashion if a position is available.

Notes: AJWS receives applications exclusively from the U.S., Canada and Israel.

Alliance Abroad Group

1221 South Mopac Exwy, Suite 250 Austin, Texas 78746
Tel.: ++1 (512) 457-8062 (toll free in N. Am. 1-866-6ABROAD)
Fax: ++1 (512) 457-8132
E-mail: outbound@allianceabroad.com
www.allianceabroad.com

Desc.: The Alliance Abroad Group has been providing educational experiential travel programs for over 10 years. The Group offers a wide range of programs in countries all over the world, and can customize each program to fit the needs or the participants. Our programs offer you the opportunity to gain valuable experience in another country, learn about different cultures, gain work and interpersonal skills, and in some cases, earn money to support your stay. Volunteer projects vary, but all are committed to the conservation of the environment, fair trade and the improvement of the living standards of its members and their communities.

Sector: Agriculture, child welfare, community development, culture, education, environment, health, small-enterprise development.

Country: Africa (South Africa), Latin America (Costa Rica, Ecuador, Peru, Mexico), North America (Hawaii).

Qualif.: Willingness to contribute and help communities.

Nonpro: No.

Age: Minimum 18.

Duration: 1 week – 1 year. Programs run throughout the year, and allow to start at any time.

Lang.: English.

Benefits: Accommodation, food, in-country transportation, staff support, International ID card.

Costs: Varies by program and length of stay.

Applic.: Applications can be found on-line. Application should be submitted at least 2 months before the desired departure date.

Amaudo UK

Regent House, 291 Kirkdale, Sydenham
London SE26 4QD UK
Tel.: ++44 (20) 8776-7363
Fax: ++44 (20) 8776-7364
E-mail: amaudouk@btconnect.com

Desc.: Amaudo UK aims to support Amaudo Nigeria in achieving its goal of eradicating homelessness amongst mentally ill people by implementing systems of sustainable mental healthcare in Nigeria. Amaudo UK also supports Amaudo Nigeria in their work to care for and rehabilitate those who have become homeless through mental illness. Amaudo UK achieves this through awareness raising, assisting volunteers and visitors to the project, providing resources such as medical supplies, information and technology, co-managing projects, co-ordinating supporters and donors in the UK.

Sector: Health, human rights.

Country: Africa (Nigeria).

Qualif.: Various depending on post.

Nonpro: Possible without formal qualifications but with appropriate experience.

Age: No age restriction. Families with children may be accommodated.

Duration: Minimum 2 months.

Lang.: English, spoken and written.

Benefits: Flight, insurance, board and lodgings provided. No stipend.

Costs: Personal expenses.

Applic.: Request application form available from Amaudo UK.

Amazon-Africa Aid Organization

PO Box 7776 Ann Arbor, Michigan 48107 USA
Tel.: ++1 (734) 769-5778
Fax: ++1 (734) 769-5779
E-mail: info@amazonafrica.org
www.amazonafrica.org

Desc.: The mission of this organisation is to create a world of healthy, educated, and happy children who have clean water to drink and fresh air to breath. It started with the dream of affecting change in existing conditions and in people's attitudes. It provides financial, technical, and volunteer support to health, education, and welfare organisations along the Brazilian Amazon and in Portuguese speaking Africa and relies heavily on volunteer and donor support.

Sector: Child welfare, education, environment, health.

Country: Latin America (Brazil). Currently re-examining the Africa program and looking for new collaborating partner organisations in Mozambique, Guinea Bissau, and Angola.

Qualif.: The health clinic depends on volunteer dentists and physicians to provide care for the needy people of the Amazon. Some professions including osteopathic physicians, podiatry, optometry, and chiropractic are not legalised in Brazil, and therefore we are unable to accept volunteers in these professions. Volunteers interested in teaching English as a second language, must have a university degree with teaching experience.

Nonpro: See Amizade.

Age: 26 or older.

Duration: 2 weeks to 2 months. Physicians, dentists, teachers stay a minimum of 4 weeks. Surgeons and ophthalmologists stay a minimum of 10 days. Clinical and dental volunteers stay a minimum of 2 weeks – preferably 1 month.

Lang.: No requirements.

Benefits: Food, lodging, laundry, and airport transfers in Santarém. If a Rotary volunteer, room and board, and travel may be covered by Rotary International. Contact the office for details.

Costs: Volunteers will need to make their own arrangements for transportation to and from Santarém and pay for their own Visa (contact the organisation for details).

Applic.: Send as early as possible: a brief CV, copies of professional licenses, copies of professional diplomas, and a copy of the passport.

Notes: Visa processing is different for different countries; contact home country embassy and AmazonAfrica for details including information on vaccinations and medical insurance. Non-volunteer spouses are discouraged from coming, as there isn't much to do here without a translator. The cost is US$25/day for room and board for non-volunteers.

AMIGOS – Amigos de las Américas

5618 Star Lane, Houston, Texas 77057 USA
Tel.: ++1 (713) 782-5290
(toll free in N. Am. 1-800-231-7796)
Fax: ++1 (713) 782-9267
E-mail: info@amigoslink.org
www.amigoslink.org

Desc.: AMIGOS creates opportunities for young people to excel in leadership roles promoting public health, education, and community development. Founded in 1965, AMIGOS is a non-profit organisation that provides exceptional leadership training and volunteer service opportunities in the US and Latin America.

Sector: Child welfare, construction, culture, education, environment, health.

Country: Latin America (Brazil, Bolivia, Costa Rica, Dominican Republic, Panama, Paraguay, Mexico, Honduras, Nicaragua).

Qualif.: No specific qualification required.

Nonpro: Yes.

Age: Minimum 16. Aimed at youth (high school and college students).

Duration: 4–8 weeks.

Lang.: Minimum of 2 years of high school Spanish or Portuguese.

Benefits: The program fee includes International Insurance (with US$100,000 coverage), however all volunteers are required to carry their own health insurance.

Costs: The program fee is approximately $3,600. Transportation to regional workshops or the gateway city not included.

Applic.: March 15 Full Application Deadline and $250 deposit due if not previously submitted. Send the on-line registration form, CV, and US$40 application fee. Following a successful telephone interview, the International office will mail the volunteer training materials and workshop registration forms.

Notes: A 3-day workshop prior to departure is required. Regional workshops are conducted in the spring in some U.S. cities. Workshops may also be conducted in the gateway city (Houston or Miami) immediately prior to departure to Latin America.

Amizade, Ltd.

920 William Pitt Union
Pittsburgh, PA 15260
Tel.: ++1 (888) 973-4443
Fax: ++1 (412) 648-1492
E-mail: Volunteer@amizade.org
www.amizade.org

Desc.: Amizade programs offer a mix of community service and recreation that provide volunteers with the unique opportunity to participate first hand in the culture of the region where they are working. Volunteers do not need any specialised skills, just a willingness to help.

Sector: Construction, education, environment, various.

Country: Africa (Tanzania), Asia (Nepal), Europe (Northern Ireland), Latin America (Brazil, Bolivia), Oceania (Australia), North America (Arizona, Montana, Washington DC).

Qualif.: No qualifications needed.

Nonpro: Yes.

Age: Minimum 18; contact the organisation if younger.

Duration: 1 week-1year.

Lang.: English.

Benefits: Room and board, recreational, and educational activities, project materials, on-site director, on-site transportation.

Costs: Average fee is US$400–900 per week, but varies with project.

Applic.: On-line form plus a deposit of US$250 for international and domestic programs.

Notes: Amizade also has programs with Elderhostel (an organisation offering short-term educational adventures for people 55 and over). For more information call Elderhoste 1(617)426-8056. Amizade also organises: Customized Group Programs (for groups ranging from college, to church or corporate), Alternative College Breaks (a college program during the semester allocated vacations) and Alternative Family Vacations (family packages will including community service and recreation). See website for details.

Amnesty International

International Secretariat
1 Easton Street, London WC1X ODJ   UK
Tel.: ++44 (20) 7413-5500
Fax: ++44 (20) 7956-1157
E-mail: info@amnesty.org.uk
www.amnesty.org

Desc.: Amnesty International is a worldwide campaigning movement promoting all the human rights enshrined in the Universal Declaration of Human Rights and other international standards. It campaigns to free all prisoners of conscience; ensure fair and prompt trials for political prisoners; abolish the death penalty, torture, and other cruel treatment of prisoners; end political killings and "disappearances"; and oppose human rights abuses by opposition groups. Activities encompass public demonstrations, letter-writing, human rights education, fundraising, individual and global appeals.

Sector: Human rights.

Country: Worldwide. Consult website for country of interest. The International Secretariat's program is only in the London office.

Qualif.: The Health Professional Network comprises individuals, groups, and networks of doctors, nurses, mental health specialists, and other health professionals. Other professional job placements are posted on the website regularly but are mostly with the International Secretariat based in the UK.

Nonpro: Consult website for volunteer opportunities in country of interest.

Age: Restrictions may apply.

Duration: Minimum 8 weeks full time or 3 months part time in London. Other work and volunteer opportunities may vary in duration.

Lang.: English and/or local language of placement.

Benefits: Consult the organisation directly. In the US, The Patrick Stewart Human Rights Scholarship is for students interested human rights work for summer internships or short-term projects.

Costs: Expenses vary with each country and volunteer opportunity.

Applic.: Directions provided from the national office offering the work.

AMURT Global Network

6810 Tilden Lane, Rockville, MD 20852 USA
Tel.: ++1 (301) 984-0217
Fax: ++1 (301) 984-0218
E-Mail: amurtglobal@amurt.net
www.amurt.net

Desc.: AMURT (Ananda Marga Universal Relief Team) is one of the few private voluntary organisations of Third World origin, being founded in India in 1965. Its original objective was to help meet the needs of victims of disasters that regularly hit the Indian subcontinent. Over the years AMURT has established teams in 80 countries, to create a network that can meet development and disaster needs almost anywhere in the world. AMURT works in communities providing individuals with education and training to give them self-reliance and self-esteem. AMURTEL is a sister organization that strives to elevate the living standard of women and children .

Sector: Child welfare, community development, education, housing, hunger relief, women's issues.

Country: Africa (Burkina Faso, Congo, Ghana, Kenya, Mozambique, Rwanda, South Africa), Asia (India, Mongolia, Philippines, Thailand), Europe (Albania, Romania).

Qualif.: Teachers welcome, homeopaths needed for certain projects.

Nonpro: Young graduates may be accepted.

Age: Enquire with organisation.

Duration: Negotiable, enquire with organisation.

Lang.: English, other languages depend on destination.

Benefits: None.

Costs: US$200 for short-term (2—3 months) and US$350 for long-term. Volunteers are responsible for all expenses—food, travel, medical, etc., during their stay.

Applic.: E-mail CV and enquiry about volunteer opportunities.

Notes: See website for contacts in other countries.

The Apostolic Hospital Banga Bakundu

PO Box 93, Muyuka, SWP, Cameroon
Tel.: ++(237) 35-41-31
Fax: ++(237) 35-41-31
E-mail: tahbb@yahoo.com

Desc.: Network of Medical institutions. The project mission is to provide patient healthcare management, rehabilitation, and staff training. To provide affordable medication to the rural population and promote a healthy rural environment. Nurses should be able to work effectively in the wards (medical, surgical, and paediatric wards, etc.) theatre, teach, and train young nurses in the nursing school. Familiarity with tropical diseases would be an added benefit. Surgeons (orthopaedic consultant/surgeon able to perform corrective surgeries for children, manage close and open fractures, teach and train young general practitioners for continuity) are often desired.

Sector: Education, health.

Country: Africa (Cameroon).

Qualif.: Medical doctors, pharmacists, nurses, laboratory technicians, other hospital workers, computer specialists/programmers, teachers.

Nonpro: Young graduates may be accepted.

Age: N/A.

Duration: Minimum 2 weeks.

Lang.: English, French.

Benefits: Accommodation and food can be arranged.

Costs: US$50 per month for lodging; US$100 per month for food.

Applic.: Apply through e-mail, fax, or regular mail.

Notes: See Note on page 36.

ARC – American Refugee Committee

430 Oak Grove Street, Suite 204
Minneapolis, Minnesota 55403 USA
Tel.: ++1 (612) 872-7060
Fax: ++1 (612) 607-6499
E-mail: archq@archq.org
www.archq.org

Desc.: ARC works for the survival, health, and well being of refugees, displaced persons, and those at risk, and seeks to enable them to rebuild productive lives of dignity and purpose, striving always to respect the values of those served. ARC has provided multi-sector humanitarian assistance and training to millions of international beneficiaries for 25 years.

Sector: Child welfare, construction, education, emergency, environment, health, refugee aid, sanitation, small-enterprise development, women's issues, various.

Country: Africa (Guinea, Liberia, Rwanda, Sierra Leone, Sudan), Asia (Pakistan, Thailand), Europe (Bosnia, Kosovo, Macedonia, Montenegro, Serbia), Middle East (Iraq).

Qualif.: Minimum 3 years professional experience in development work.

Nonpro: No. Unpaid internships in Minneapolis Headquarters and short-term overseas positions may be available.

Age: Dependent upon experience.

Duration: Most positions require a 1-year commitment with the option to extend based upon mutual agreement.

Lang.: English.

Benefits: Stipend, round-trip transportation, housing (group), medical insurance, and Visa procurement when necessary.

Costs: Personal expenses.

Applic.: Send CV and cover letter, specifying dates of availability. Apply at the above address or e-mail: recruitment@archq.org.

Notes: Recruitment is very competitive. Applicants should update their status and availability regularly. ARC has representatives in Chicago and Washington. See website for details.

Australian Volunteers International

PO Box 350
71 Argyle Street, Fitzroy Victoria 3065 Australia
Tel.: ++61 (3) 9279-1788 (toll free in Australia 1-800-331-292)
Fax: ++61 (3) 9419-4280
E-mail: info@australianvolunteers.org
www.australianvolunteers.org

Desc.: Australian volunteers live, work, and learn in partnership with other cultures. This development agency aims to contribute to a peaceful and just world by fostering cross-cultural relationships and international understanding between people through social and economic development of communities.

Sector: Agriculture, community development, culture, education, environment, health, human rights, IT, skills training, small-enterprise development, various.

Country: Africa (Botswana, Eritrea, Kenya, Malawi, Mozambique, Namibia, South Africa, Zambia, Zimbabwe), Asia (Afghanistan, Bangladesh, Cambodia, China, India, Indonesia, Laos, Maldives, Mongolia, Nepal, Pakistan, Philippines, Sri Lanka, Thailand, Vietnam), Middle East (Palestine), Oceania (Australia, Cook Islands, Micronesia, Fiji Islands, Kiribati, Marshall Islands, Niue, Palau, Papua New Guinea, Samoa, Solomon Islands, Tonga, Tuvalu, Vanuatu), Latin America (El Salvador, Guatemala, Mexico, Nicaragua).

Qualif.: Profession, trade, or commercial qualification with experience.

Nonpro: Yes. Youth projects with Youth Challenge Australia (YCA).

Age: Minimum 20.

Duration: 2 years (1 year or less sometimes possible).

Lang.: Training provided in language needed.

Benefits: Airfare, pre-departure briefings, and medical insurance. Professional volunteers are paid; salaries and conditions vary.

Costs: Personal expenses.

Applic.: On-line request for information package to be mailed to prospective volunteer. Consult website for other offices.

Notes: Australian citizens and permanent residents only.

AVSO – Association of Voluntary Service Organisations

174 Rue Joseph II
B-1000 Bruxelles Belgium
Tel.:++32 (2) 230-6813
Fax:++32 (2) 231-1413
E-mail: avso@bigfoot.com
www.avso.org

Desc.: AVSO forms a European platform for national and international non-profit organisations active in the field of longer term voluntary service. They lobby for the legal status of volunteers and enhanced mobility within Europe and aim to broaden participation in voluntary service among new organisations in non-profit sector and among individuals who may traditionally not have access to volunteer opportunities (disabled, socially/economically disadvantaged, and ethnic minorities).

Sector: Community development, culture, education, environment, human rights, various.

Country: Avso members have projects worldwide.

Age: 18–25.

Duration: 6–18 months, depending on the organisation.

Lang.: Language and intercultural training provided.

Benefits: Accommodation, food, small stipend, appropriate insurance against illness and accidents, other benefits in accordance with the status of a volunteer.

Applic.: Contact project organisation.

Notes: Residents of the European Union or an applicant country only. Applicant countries to the EU include: Estonia, Latvia, Lithuania, Poland, Czech Republic, Slovakia, Hungary, Slovenia, Bulgaria, Romania, Malta and Cyprus). AVSO does not itself organise volunteer exchange programs.

AYAD – Australian Youth Ambassadors for Development

Level 2, 81 Flinders Street
Adelaide, SA 5000 Australia
Tel.: ++61 (8) 8232-3050 (toll free in Australia 1-800-225-592)
Fax: ++61 (8) 8223-4703
E-mail: AYAD@austraining.com.au
www.ausaid.gov.au/youtham

Desc.: This Australian Government initiative is funded and managed through the Australian Agency for International Development (AusAID). The Program identifies and places skilled young Australians on development assignments throughout the Asia Pacific region. The Program aims to strengthen mutual understanding between Australia and the countries of the Asia Pacific and make a positive contribution to development.

Sector: Agriculture, community development, construction, education, environment, health, sanitation.

Country: Asia (Bangladesh, Cambodia, China, Laos, Mongolia, Nepal, Philippines, Sri Lanka, Thailand, Vietnam), Oceania (Papua New Guinea, Fiji, Samoa, Tonga, Vanuatu).

Qualif.: Professions relevant to the above mentioned sectors.

Nonpro: Yes, with skills beneficial to the project.

Age: 18—30.

Duration: 3—12 months (departing March or August).

Lang.: Volunteers should learn the local language but all assignments will be with English speaking counterparts and supervisors.

Benefits: AUS$600-1,000 settlement allowance; AUS$1,200-1,500/ month (depending on location) living/accommodation allowance; AUS$350 per 6 month assignment support allowance; AUS$600 resettlement allowance after service. Pre-departure training costs, return airfare to host country, medical preparation, and insurance, Debrief on return home.

Costs: AYADs Youth Ambassadors should incur no costs.

Applic.: CV, response to key criteria, 3 references, academic transcripts, photographs, and passport. See website for details.

Notes: Australian citizens only. Police and medical check required.

Balkan Sunflowers

Prishtina Office, Bregu i Dielliet 2, block 13 apt. 32
Prishtina, Kosovo/a
Tel.: ++381 (38) 222-087 or ++377 (44) 501-819
Fax: ++44 (870) 138-5528
E-mail: bsfkosovo@yahoo.com
www.balkansunflowers.org

Desc.: Balkan Sunflowers has set up various relief and community work projects in Albania, Macedonia, and Kosovo/a with an expanding scope of activities. They have implemented hundreds of projects of various nature, size, and duration, from day-long events and celebrations to long-term educational courses. They establish activity centres, implement park development and environment programmes, and organise major campaigns for social reconstruction and renewal. Their mandate is to promote understanding, further non-violent conflict transformation, and celebrate the diversity of the lives and cultures of the Balkan region.

Sector: Child welfare, community development, culture, education, environment, human rights, refugee aid, women's issues.

Country: Europe (Albania, Macedonia, Kosovo/a).

Qualif.: Specific skills are required for some project placements.

Nonpro: Yes.

Age: Minimum 18.

Duration: A few weeks or many months.

Lang.: English. Local language skills are assets.

Benefits: Accommodation, food, basic insurance, travel to the project sites, and office costs. Orientation and on-going training provided. Some SCI branches provide training sessions.

Costs: EUR150 contribution, plus travel expenses, Visas if necessary, EUR10 entry fee at point of entry, and personal expenses A EUR 80-100 weekly budget is advised.

Applic.: On-line form e-mailed directly to the project or via the relevant SCI branch.

Notes: Applications can be submitted via SCI branches (see listing).

BERDSCO – Benevolent Community Education and Rural Development Society

P.O.Box 368, Buea, South West Province, Cameroon
Tel.: ++ (237) 752-5206
Fax: ++ (237) 332-2106 or 237 332 25 14
E-mail: berdsco_65@yahoo.com

Desc.: Founded in 1990 as a non-governmental organisation (NGO), non-political, non-profit and non-religious society and recognised by the Government of Cameroon in Sept. 1993. Gained special consultative status with the economic and social council of the United Nations in July, 2001. BERDSCO was created to alleviate poverty and hunger among the rural poor, especially women. The aims are to improve living conditions, create awareness to help integrate women in development activities, carry out programs on environmental education and sustainable development, and sensitise the public on issues of health drug abuse, addiction, and misuse. The NGO is also active in diagnoses of community diseases, awareness programme on HIV/AIDS pandemic and setting up of community HIV/AIDS Control Committees.

Sector: Agriculture, community development, education, environment, health, small-enterprise development, women's issues.

Country: Africa (Cameroon).

Qualif.: Professionals with degree in business studies domain or accounting for micro-finance sector and related disciplines or marketing; computer accounting; poverty alleviation; sound knowledge and experience in project proposal writing and fundraising. People with medical disciplines or highly qualified nurse for the health unit, teaching at nursery and elementary level (3 to 12 years old, information and communication technology needed, those with engineering degrees with sound knowledge on community social projects (such as construction of health post, bridges, culverts, schools, community halls etc.

Nonpro: Yes, with skills in communication, computer repairs, computer literacy, accounting clerks and community mobilisation and group leadership, etc.

Age.: Minimum 18.

Duration: 6 – 24 months renewable if necessary.

Lang.: English.

Benefits: Volunteers gain new skills, learn new ways of life and culture of various people, acquire knowledge on development issues of third world countries for an eventual academic or professional advancement.

Costs: BERDSCO contribution's to host each volunteer will be free accommodations, household equipment, arrival training, socialisation into his or her job, and continuous coaching throughout employment. Volunteers are only responsible for their own food and utilities. Volunteers may come in with their own equipment such as computers, vehicles and other equipment. Volunteers are welcome all around the year. Groups of 5 – 10 are also accepted.

Applic.: CV and cover letter mailed by post to the Director and advanced information by e-mail. Photocopies of relevant certifications required after recruitment.

Notes: See Note on page 36.

BESO

164 Vauxhall Bridge Road, London SW1V 2RA (B) UK
Tel.: ++44 (20) 7630-0644
Fax.: ++44 (20) 7630-0624
E-mail: registrar@beso.org
www.beso.org

Desc.: BESO is a development agency whose volunteers share experience and professional expertise with organisations in less developed communities worldwide that cannot afford commercial consultants. BESO focuses on the poorest countries by responding to requests for assistance from private and public sector organisations unable to afford commercial consultants. Volunteers give advice to small businesses and local industries, and help governments and local authorities, media bodies, and education and health institutions.

Sector: Agriculture, community development, education, environment, skills training, small-enterprise development.

Country: Various countries in Africa, Asia, Caribbean, Europe, Latin America, Middle East, Oceania.

Qualif.: Technical or professional experience of at least 5 years in at least 1 relevant field.

Nonpro: Only with skills useful to the project.

Age: N/A; many volunteers are retired or close to retirement age.

Duration: A week to max. 4 months at a time.

Lang.: English.

Benefits: GB£30 per week stipend, accommodation, food, transport.

Costs: Volunteers do not receive any fees for their work and no fees are charged to the overseas client.

Applic.: Contact the organisation directly. Offices also in Moscow, and Scotland (see website). BESO only responds to requests for assistance from overseas organisations and cannot predict which volunteers will be needed.

Notes: UK residents only.

BMS World Mission

PO Box 49, 129 Broadway
Didcot, Oxfordshire OX11 8XA UK
Tel.: ++44 (1235) 517-700 or 751-7647
Fax: ++44 (1235) 517-601
E-mail: missionteams@bmsworldmission.org
www.bms.org.uk or www.bmsworldmission.org/shortterm

Desc.: BMS world mission currently has approximately 150 workers serving overseas. They include 129 full-time missionaries and candidates, professional and summer student volunteers, and Youth Action Team members. BMS teams combine high-energy people with the needs of the world.

Sector: Agriculture, child welfare, community development, education, health, religious.

Country: Africa (various), Asia (Bangladesh, India, Indonesia, Nepal, Thailand, Sri Lanka), Europe (Albania), Latin America (Brazil).

Qualif.: Medical professionals can contact BMS for details.

Nonpro: Yes. Students, professionals taking unpaid leave, retirees.

Age: Minimum 18. BMS Action Teams for ages 18-28.

Duration: 3 months to 2 years. Summer teams in July and August. Action teams from September to April.

Lang.: English.

Benefits: Program expenses, flights, food, accommodation, insurance, Visa, training, and debriefing are covered in project fee.

Costs: Individual volunteers are self-financing. Summer teams GB £800–1,500, action team GB£3,300. Vaccinations, travel to the airport and training centre, and spending money not included in costs. Individual volunteers must be self-financing.

Applic.: Request application form, and info video. Individual/specific skills placements e-mail volunteers@bmsworldmission.org or call (1235) 517-654. October to February for Action Teams (gap-year), October to March for Summer Teams, e-mail mission teams@bmsworldmission.org or call (1235) 517-647.

Notes: UK residents only. Committed Christians with local church recommendations. Criminal record disclosure required.

Brethren Volunteer Service

1451 Dundee Avenue, Elgin, Illinois 60120 USA
Tel.: ++1 (800) 323-8039 (toll free in N. Am.)
Fax: ++1 (847) 742-0278
E-mail: bvs_gb@brethren.org or dmcfadden_gb@brethren.org
www.brethrenvolunteerservice.org

Desc.: This program of the Church of the Brethren has been working for peace, advocating justice and serving basic human needs since 1948. Volunteers give their time and skills to help solve deep-rooted problems in the work for justice and peace.

Sector: Agriculture, child welfare, community development, education, environment, health, housing, hunger relief, refugee aid, religious.

Country: Africa (Nigeria), Asia (Japan), Europe (Belgium, Bosnia-Herzegovina, Croatia, Czech Republic, France, Germany, Ireland, Netherlands, Northern Ireland, Serbia, Slovakia, Switzerland, UK), Latin America (Dominican Republic, Guatemala, Honduras), North America (United States).

Qualif.: Generalists or persons willing to learn a new skill. If a volunteer wants to use their specific skill, the BVS office will try to help.

Nonpro: Yes, with college degree or similar life experience. BVS also provides special orientation units for adults over 50 years.

Age: Minimum 18, except for international placements where the minimum age is 21.

Duration: 1 year for US placements, 2 years for overseas projects; this includes a 10-day to 3-week (depending on project) orientation.

Lang.: English, other languages useful.

Benefits: Accommodation (group, individual, on-site, or home-stay), monthly stipend, orientation, health insurance.

Costs: US$500 fee for international projects. Volunteers provide their own transportation to the orientation site.

Applic.: Deadline 6 weeks before each orientation. CV, photo and transcripts sent with application. Consult website for details.

Notes: Overseas assignments for US and Canadian citizens only.

The Bridge Foundation

No. 8 Third Ringway, Ringway Estate
PO Box 13463
Accra, Ghana
Tel.:+233 (21) 229-933
E-mail: planet35@hotmail.com
www.africatrust.gi

Desc.: The Foundation works in promoting human resource development focusing on assisting disadvantaged children or youth in deprived rural and informal peri-urban settlements, individually and collectively, to assess their values and skills required in improving their natural talents, especially in the fields of sports, literacy, and Information Communication and Technology (ICT). The organisation is running a Youth Sports Development Resource Centre, comprising of a gymnasium, library, and ICT Training Unit. Also, engaged in environmental management and protection of a fishing village on the Atlantic Coast, west of Accra.

Sector: Education, environment, IT, various.

Country: Africa (Ghana).

Qualif.: English teachers, environmentalists, volunteers with strong computer skills, and experienced sport coaches desired.

Nonpro.: Yes, with relevant skills.

Age: 18–35.

Duration: 3–6 months.

Lang.: English

Benefits: Subsidised accommodation.

Costs: US$15 per day plus budget for food and personal items.

Applic.: CV and 2 references required.

Notes: Once accepted the applicant will be put in contact with former volunteers who have been selected as Representatives in various countries. Please see note on page 36.

BRIDGES

1203 Preservation Park, #300
Oakland, California 94103 USA
Tel.: ++1 (510) 271-8286
Fax: ++1 (510) 451-2996
E-mail: info@grassrootsbridges.org
www.grassrootsbridges.org

Desc.: BRIDGES supports young community organizers from low-income and ethnically diverse backgrounds to increase their capacity for direct, grassroots organizing with a vision centred on global justice. Through extensive training and mentorship, plus international travel and internship placements, BRIDGES builds responsible international dialogues for grassroots communities in the US and the Global South to exchange ideas on sustainable solutions to common issues.

Sector: Culture, education, environment, health, small-enterprise development.

Country: Africa, Asia, Latin America.

Qualif.: Young adults from San Francisco Bay Area, who participate in the work of community-based organizations, actions, campaigns and numerous volunteer services.

Nonpro: Yes, see notes below.

Age: Minimum 18.

Duration: 8 months with 2—3 months abroad.

Lang.: English.

Benefits: Travel grant, training.

Costs: Contact the organisation for details.

Applic.: On-line form. Applications are due each December for Fellowships that begin in March of the following year.

Notes: US citizens or residents only. BRIDGES is committed to making these experiences available to ethnic minorities and individuals demonstrating financial need, who have worked for positive change in their communities, have had limited opportunity to travel abroad, and have not had previous international volunteer experience.

Buea Youth Foundation

PO Box 88 Buea, SWP Cameroon
Tel.: ++(237) 753-192
Fax: ++(237) 322-769
E-mail: bushu9@yahoo.com

Desc.: Buea Youth Foundation is committed to development and realisation of the potential of youths. It aims to achieve this through capacity building, education, technical training and intercultural exchange. The Foundation believes that global problems will be solved when the youths, the future of tomorrow, are well equipped to face the challenges of life and mankind as a whole.

Sector: Child welfare, community development, education, IT, small-enterprise development.

Country: Africa (Cameroon).

Qualif.: Required for some positions.

Nonpro: Yes. Students also welcome.

Age: Minimum 18. Families with children accepted.

Duration: Minimum 3 months.

Lang.: English. French is useful.

Benefits: Room and board. Stipends not available for all positions.

Costs: Return airfare from country of origin, US$30 application fee, personal expenses.

Applic.: Application forms provided upon request. Some volunteer positions require a cover letter and CV. Applications may be sent via e-mail, fax, or regular mail.

Notes: See Note on page 36.

BUNAC

16 Bowling Green Lane
London, EC1R OQH   UK
Tel.: ++44 (207) 251 3472
Fax: ++44 (207) 251 0215
E-mail: enquiries@bunac.org.uk or volunteering@bunac.org.uk
www.bunac.org

Desc.: BUNAC is a non-profit member organisation which looks to promote cultural exchange through work and voluntary work overseas.

Sector: Agriculture, child welfare, community development, culture, education, environment, health, human rights, IT, small-enterprise development, women's issues, various.

Country: Africa (Ghana, South Africa), Latin America (Costa Rica, Peru).

Qualif.: No qualifications needed.

Nonpro: Yes.

Age: Minimum 18.

Duration: 9 weeks—12 months.

Lang.: English, Spanish language skills required for Peru and Costa Rica.

Benefits: Group departures, in-country orientation, full support both in country and in the UK free time to travel at the end of the programmes.

Costs: Participants must contribute towards travel, insurance and programme costs (fees range from GB£ 390 to GB£600).

Notes: Nationality requirements vary, however volunteers must be resident in the UK. See www.bunac.org for full details of eligibility. Bunac has also an office in the USA (see website for details) and a partner organisation in Australia and New Zealand (IEP International Exchange Programs PTY Ltd (see websites: www.iep-australia.com and www.iep.co.nz)

BWCA – Bangladesh Work Camps Association

289/2, Work Camp Road, North Shajahanpur
Dhaka-1217, Bangladesh
Tel.: ++88 (2) 935-8206 or 935-6814
Fax: ++88 (2) 956-5506 or 956-5483 (Attn: BWCA)
E-mail: bwca@bangla.net
www.mybwca.org

Desc.: BWCA organises national and international workcamps, inter-cultural youth exchange programs, study tours, and leadership training on issues proclaimed by the UN/UNESCO towards establishing world peace. Being a member organisation of CCIVS (see listing), BWCA aims to expand and popularise workcamps around Bangladesh in collaboration with local partner NGOs. Volunteers may join local partner NGOs in on-going projects like assisting in the office, motivational campaigns, and environmental/agricultural/construction activities.

Sector: Agriculture, construction, education, environment, health, IT.

Country: Asia (Bangladesh).

Qualif.: No qualification or experience. Specific project volunteers should have some practical and professional experience in physiotherapy, nursing, agriculture, teaching, computers, etc.

Nonpro: Yes.

Age: Minimum 18 - 35.

Duration: Short-term projects (workcamps) are 12–15 days; RTYP (Round the Year Program) projects are 3–12 months.

Lang.: English.

Benefits: Accommodation and internal transportation.

Costs: US$150 per camp and US$150 registration fee for the first 3 months. US$50 per month for any additional period. The food charge is US$ 2/- (Two dollars) per day.

Applic.: Apply through partner organisations in applicant's own country. Individual applications are accepted only where there is no overseas partner organisation of BWCA with a payment of US$25.

Notes: Drugs and alcohol are prohibited. Couples are not accepted.

Canada World Youth (Jeunesse Canada Monde)

2330 Notre-Dame Street West, 3rd floor
Montreal, Quebec H3J 1N4 Canada
Tel.: ++1 (514) 931-3526 (toll free in Canada 1-866-786-9243)
Fax: ++1 (514) 939-2621
E-mail: cwy-jcm@cwy-jcm.org
www.cwy-jcm.org

Desc.: Created in 1971, Canada World Youth provides young people from Canada and around the world with the opportunity to travel, live, and volunteer in different communities, learn about local and international development, and gain professional skills for the future. Participants are paired with overseas counterparts, and together they learn about global citizenship in dynamic, cross-cultural settings. They get involved in a host community through volunteer service and live with a host family.

Sector: Agriculture, community development, education, environment, health, IT.

Country: Various countries in Africa, Asia, Latin America, the Caribbean, and Eastern Europe. Also programmes in Canada are offered.

Qualif.: No professional qualifications needed.

Nonpro: Yes.

Age: 17–29 (Core Program ages 17–24).

Duration: 4–7 months.

Lang.: English, French.

Benefits: Accommodation, food, small stipend, insurance, transportation.

Costs: A participation fee (CAD$250) and costs of a medical exam, vaccinations, a passport and travel accessories (e.g., backpack, sleeping bag, etc.). Participants must raise CAD$1,000 to CAD $1,950 (depending on program), although training and support for fundraising are provided.

Applic.: On-line form. For more information contact: imready@cwy-jcm.org or call 1(866)786-9243). See also website.

Notes: Canadian citizens or landed immigrants only. Participants must be in good health and are expected to pass a medical exam.

Canadian Crossroads International

317 Adelaide Street West, Suite 500
Toronto, Ontario M5V 1P9 Canada
Tel.: ++1 (416) 967-1611
Fax: ++1 (416) 967-9078
E-mail: info@cciorg.ca
www.cciorg.ca

Desc.: Canadian Crossroads is a unique volunteer and staff-driven organisation with more than 300 volunteers worldwide and 25 staff members that provides volunteers with an invaluable opportunity to share skills, expand experience, meet new people and contribute to global citizenship. The aim is to build a constituency committed to voluntarism, international development, and social action by developing partnerships with other countries, organising volunteer placements and internships, and educating the public on development issues.

Sector: Agriculture, child welfare, community development, education, environment, health, skills training.

Country: Over 25 countries in Africa, Asia, Latin America and Oceania.

Qualif.: Specific skill criteria are outlined in each job description.

Nonpro: State skills on application to aid in placement.

Age: Minimum 19 (18 in Quebec).

Duration: April to September. Length of placements varies according to the projects, usually 4–6 months. Departure is in May, September, or December/January of the year of application.

Lang.: English or French.

Benefits: Accommodation with host families, return airfare, and modest living allowance based on cost of living.

Costs: CAD$1,800–2,250 (approx. US$1,200–1,500) depending on program. Fundraising support is provided by CCI.

Applic.: Contact nearest Canadian Regional Office (see website).

Notes: Canadian citizens or landed immigrants, or a citizen of a host or partner country (consult website) only. There is no guarantee placement for preferred regions or countries to volunteer in.

CARE Corps Volunteer Program

47 Potter Avenue, New Rochelle, New York 10801 USA
Tel.: ++1 (914) 632-7788 (toll free in N. Am. 1-877- 227-3865)
Fax: ++1 (914) 632-8494
E-mail: carecorps@care.org
www.care.org

Desc.: This cultural exchange program is for people interested in social and development issues in Peru. Volunteers interact with Peruvian communities in a variety of locally driven projects such as income-generation activities, skill or vocational and computer skills training, sports training, child care, or arts and crafts programs. Located in the Andes Mountains, the program offers hands-on work opportunities, cultural exchange activities and educational sessions about global issues.

Sector: Child welfare, community development, education, environment, health, skills training.

Country: Latin America (Guatemala, Peru).

Qualif.: Healthcare professionals to work in hospitals, health posts, and rural communities.

Nonpro: Yes, with applicable skills experience.

Age: N/A.

Duration: 3 weeks with a maximum of 15 volunteers assigned to each session. New programs begin every month.

Lang.: Spanish helpful but not necessary.

Benefits All Peru/Guatemala-based expenses: airport transfers, daily transportation, meals, lodging (group house in the center of Ayacucho), professional staff guidance and supervision, orientation, medical insurance.

Costs: US$2175 (2 weeks). International airfare, insurance, and Visa fees not included. A non-refundable deposit of US$275 is due upon registration and the balance of payment is due 60 days before the program start date.

Applic.: On-line form and information survey.

Notes: CARE Corps is a Cross-Cultural Solutions program (see listing).

Casa de los Amigos
Service and Education Project
Ignacio Mariscal 132, Col. Tabacalera
Mexico DF, 06030   Mexico
Tel.: ++52 (55) 5705-0521/5705-0646
Fax: ++52 (55) 5705-0771
E-mail: amigos@casadelosamigos.org   www.casadelosamigos.org

Desc.: The Casa de Los Amigos, a volunteer-operated Quaker guest house and service centre in Mexico City, places volunteer interns (the Convive Volunteers) for full-time work with Mexican social service organisations at varying times of the year.

Sectors: Child welfare, community development, environment.

Country: Latin America (Mexico).

Qualif.: Technical skills are helpful, but not necessary.

Nonpro: There are no restrictions. Only motivation is needed, ability to speak Spanish and to sustain all the expenses.

Age: Minimum 18.

Duration: Minimum commitment of 3 months or more.

Lang.: Proficient Spanish is a requirement for Convive Volunteers. Intermediate level is accepted for Casa Volunteers (see notes).

Benefits: Lodging in the Casa is extremely affordable and Convive Volunteers receive a further discount (see costs).

Costs: There is an initial US$50 fee plus US$25 per month to cover administrative costs. Interns should budget a minimum of an additional US$150-275 per month for room (the dorm bed in the Casa costs approx. $ 26 for the first week and $32 for the following weeks), board (a common kitchen is available) and personal expenses. Volunteers must pay also for travel costs.

Applic.: For more information contact Casa de los Amigos or send via e-mail the application form on the website.

Notes: The Casa offers a variety of housing options and helps coordinate the volunteers. They also offer suggestions and opportunities for leisure activities. It is possible also to volunteer in the Casa, with the programme Casa Volunteers.

Catholic Institute for International Relations

International Cooperation for Development
Unit 3 Canonbury Yard, 190a New North Road
London N1 7BJ UK
Tel.: ++44 (20) 7354-0883 Fax: ++44 (20) 7359-0017
E-mail ciir@ciir.org
www.ciir.org

Desc.: CIIR, also known as International Cooperation for Development (ICD), is an international development agency tackling poverty and exclusion and pursuing lasting change in policy and practice. It works with partner organisations and people of any or no faith. It offers a progressive Catholic perspective independent of church structures. Development workers might work with peasant farmers in the Caribbean to find markets for their products, set up HIV and AIDS counselling services in Africa, support primary healthcare in the Middles East, or work with a women's group in East Timor.

Sector: Agriculture, community development, education, environment, health, human rights, IT, skills training, small-enterprise development, women's rights, various.

Country: Africa (Namibia, Zimbabwe), Asia (East Timor), Caribbean (Dominican Republic), Latin America (Ecuador, El Salvador, Honduras, Nicaragua, Peru), Middle East (Yemen).

Qualif.: 2 years work experience in the above mentioned sectors, and preferably with a background in training—formal or informal.

Nonpro: No.

Age: N/A with the necessary experience.

Duration: Minimum 1–2 years.

Lang.: Training in local language of host country provided.

Benefits: Local stipend plus home country and a discretionary dependants allowance, accommodation, return airfare, pre-departure grant, insurance and national contributions.

Costs: Personal expenses.

Applic.: For each post there is a job description and selection criteria. See website for openings.

Catholic Medical Mission Board

10 West 17th Street, New York, New York 10011 USA
Tel.: ++1 (212) 242-7757 (toll free in N. Am. 1-800-678-5659)
Fax: ++1 (212) 242-0930
E-mail: RdeCostanzo@cmmb.org
www.cmmb.org

Desc.: The Catholic Medical Mission Board places healthcare professionals in clinical facilities in developing countries. Volunteers serve in hospitals and clinics in collaboration with the local healthcare staff.

Sector: Health.

Country: Africa (16 countries), Asia (7 countries), Eastern Europe (4 countries), Caribbean (5 countries), Latin America (12 countries)

Qualif.: All candidates should be currently licensed in the US or Canada and must present all educational and professional credentials for review.

Nonpro: Yes.

Age: Minimum 21, no maximum but in good health. Families accepted.

Duration: Short term: 2 weeks to several months; long term: 1 year.

Lang.: Varies with project. Spanish necessary in Latin America.

Benefits: Room and board provided free to all volunteers. All volunteers receive coverage for medivac, malpractice and life insurance and assistance with visas. Those volunteers going 1 or more years, also receive full health insurance coverage, all travel expenses and a modest monthly stipend.

Costs: Immunization and prophylactic medications. Short term also need to pay for airfare.

Applic.: Request application form and return the completed form along with notary copies of licenses and diplomas, a physical examination form, a CV or resume, a passport-size picture and 3 letters of recommendation by regular mail.

Notes: Candidates must be licensed in the US or Canada. No opportunities for non-medical or medical students.

CCIVS – Coordinating Committee
for International Volunteers

Unesco House 31, François Bonvin   75015 Paris France
Tel.: ++33 (1) 4568-4936
Fax: ++33 (1) 4273-0521
E-mail: ccivs@unesco.org
www.unesco.org/ccivs

Desc.: CCIVS is an international non-governmental organisation that plays a coordinating role in the sphere of voluntary service. CCIVS has 250 members and branches in 90 countries. The aims of the CCIVS are to fight against the dangers of war, social and racial discrimination, underdevelopment, illiteracy, and the consequences of neo-colonialism; to promote international understanding, friendship, and solidarity as preconditions to firm and lasting peace on earth; to enable social and national development; and to establish a just international economic and social order. Volunteers from different countries live and work together on a common project to benefit the local population.

Sector: Construction, culture, education, environment, health, peacekeeping.

Country: Members are in over 90 countries in the 5 continents.

Qualif.: CCVIS members require volunteers with a broad spectrum of qualifications.

Nonpro.: Yes; many CCVIS members organise workcamps and seminars in above domains.

Age: Generally from 18 for non-professional volunteers, older for skilled volunteers.

Duration: 3–4 weeks. Projects for 1–6 months or 1–3 years.

Lang.: Local languages of the member organisations. Common languages are English, Spanish, French, and Portuguese.

Benefits: Contact the member organisations.

Costs: Contact the member organisations.

Applic.: Apply with member organisations directly.

Notes: CCIVS produces several publications on volunteer service.

CECI – Canadian Centre for International Studies and Cooperation

Volunteer Cooperants Overseas (VC/OS)
3185 Rachel Street East, Montreal, Quebec H1W 1A3 Canada
Tel.: ++1 (514) 875-9911 Fax: ++1 (514) 875-6469
E-mail: info@ceci.ca
www.ceci.ca

Desc.: CECI is a non-profit organisation whose mission is to fight poverty and exclusion in the developing world and in other countries.

Sector: Agriculture, environment, human rights, small-enterprise development.

Country: Africa (Algeria, Burkina Faso, Burundi, Guinea, Ivory Coast, Mali, Senegal), Asia (Cambodia, Nepal, Vietnam), Latin America (Guatemala, Haiti).

Qualif.: A certified copy of diploma if application will be requested, but professional experience is the determining factor.

Nonpro: Minimum 2 years of professional experience and a diploma corresponding to qualifications are required. All candidates are strongly urged to take training courses in international cooperation. Young graduates with no experience can be eligible for the International Youth Internship Program (IYI) (see notes).

Age: Families are accepted and children may be covered by CECI if they are under 18 years of age. It is strongly recommended that dependants over 18 years of age (or who will reach this age during the assignment) are not brought.

Duration: 2 years, except for certain humanitarian aid or reconstruction programs where assignments may be shorter.

Lang.: English, with some French. Training in local languages may be provided.

Benefits: A stipend is provided and the amount depends on the cost of living in the host country and the number of dependants. The mean allowance is around US$1,000 per month for a volunteer who is single. A 40% supplement of this sum for a dependent. spouse and a 20% supplement for each dependent child who accompanies the volunteer is provided. Travel, accommodation, insurance, schooling for children under 18, and reinstatement grant upon completion provided.

Costs: Personal expenses.

Applic.: On-line form. The CECI Recruiting Department will arrange an interview when a position in the prospective volunteer's field of competence becomes available. Once an application is accepted, there are 2 weeks of pre-departure training. Allow for about 3 months between interview and departure.

Notes: Canadian citizens and landed immigrants only.

International Youth Internship Program

The International Youth Internship Program offers young Canadians the chance to participate in an international internship in their field of competency. The program includes a preparation session for an overseas stay, a 6-month internship in a cooperation project and, upon returning to Canada, activities to assist the transition to a first job. Interested applicants must be 19–30 years of age; be Canadian citizens or eligible to work in Canada; be on the verge of graduating from college or university or have graduated less than 2 years ago; be unemployed or underemployed. Complete the on-line application form. For more information e-mail: jeuness-jsi@ceci.ca.

CESVI – Cooperazione e sviluppo

Via Broseta 68/a
24128 Bergamo Italy
Tel.: ++39 (035) 205-8058
Fax: ++39 (035) 260-958
E-mail: cesvi@cesvi.org
www.cesvi.org

Desc.: CESVI established in 1985, it is an independent organisation, working for global solidarity. CESVI believes to transform the moral principles of human solidarity and social justice into humanitarian aid and development, reinforcing an affirmation of universal human rights. CESVI believes strongly that helping the underprivileged in developing countries, or those in difficulty due to war, natural calamities, and environmental disasters, does not only helps those who suffer, but contributes also to the wellbeing of all of us on the planet, our "common home" to be looked after for future generations.

Sector: Community development, construction, emergency, health.

Country: Africa (Angola, Egypt, Eritrea, Kenya, Morocco, Mozambique, Senegal, Somalia, South Africa, Sudan, Swaziland, Uganda, Zambia, Zimbabwe), Asia (Afghanistan, Burma, Cambodia, (East Timor), India, Laos, North Korea, Tajikistan, Vietnam), Europe (Albania, Bosnia-Herzegovina, Romania, Serbia), Latin America (Brazil, El Salvador, Peru, Uruguay, Venezuela), Middle East (Iraq, Jordan, Lebanon, Palestine).

Qualif.: Professional qualifications necessary, e.g., engineers, etc.

Nonpro: No, professionally qualified personnel only.

Age: N/A with necessary experience.

Duration: 1–3 years; shorter term may be possible with private partners.

Lang.: English, French, Spanish, or Portuguese; it is expected that long-term volunteers learn the local language.

Benefits: All costs covered plus salary based on experience.

Costs: Covered by contract except extraneous personal expenses.

Applic.: On-line form.

Notes: Training is provided for all prospective volunteers.

CFHI – Child Family Health International

953 Mission St. #220, San Francisco, California 94103 USA
Tel.: ++1 (415) 957-9000
Fax: ++1 (501) 840-0486
E-mail: tudents@cfhi.org
www.cfhi.org

Desc.: This non-profit organisation is promoting international healthcare, service-learning, Spanish literacy and cultural competency to medical students through clinical electives in developing countries. Ecuador, Mexico, Bolivia, South Africa and India have many qualified and experienced physicians, however, it is the uneven distribution of healthcare that allows many impoverished communities to go underserved. CFHI actively encourages students to develop a high level of community health awareness, and to examine the ways in which every healthcare system is socially and culturally constructed. In this manner students can better understand how to serve all segments of the population

Sector: Education, health.

Country: Africa (South Africa), Asia (India), Latin America (Ecuador, Mexico, Bolivia).

Qualif.: Pre-medical nursing, dental, psychology, PA, MPH and medical students.

Nonpro: Yes, with college education.

Age: Minimum 21.

Duration: 4–12 weeks.

Lang.: English, Spanish.

Benefits: In-country accommodation, food, orientation, training, travel insurance, alumni services, staff support, and medical supplies to carry with you as a donation. Academic credit is available. Scholarships are available.

Costs: US$850–1,950 on average.

Applic.: On-line form.

Chantiers Jeunesse

4545, Avenue Pierre-De Coubertin , PO Box 1000, Branch M
Montreal, Quebec H1V 3R2 Canada
Tel.: ++1 (514) 252-3015 (toll free in N. Am. 1-800-361-2055)
Fax : ++1 (514) 251-8719
E-mail : cj@cj.qc.ca
www.cj.qc.ca

Desc.: The goals of Chantiers Jeunesse (Mouvement Quebecois des Chantiers Jeunesse) are to support and strengthen the development of the autonomy (self-reliance) of young people, mainly by the realisation of workcamps, which encourage community involvement; to initiate social involvement and encourage the intercultural communication and understanding between people from different countries and cultures. Most exchanges are between Quebec and European volunteers.

Sector: Community development, construction, culture, environment.

Country: Europe (Lithuania, Estonia, Belarus, Ukraine, Russia, Turkey), Latin America (Mexico).

Age: 16–17; or 18–30 at the beginning of the project.

Duration: 3 weeks; occasionally projects for 2 months or longer.

Lang.: French, English.

Benefits: Food, accommodation, transportation from home to workcamp site, recreational activities, and a minibus to explore the region.

Costs: CAD$15 application fee, CAD$125 participation fee. Extra fees for Mexico (CAD$270), former Soviet Union (Lithuania, Estonia, Belarus, Ukraine, Russia) countries (CAD$125), and Turkey (CAD$80). Personal expenses including public transportation costs (CAD$500–1,400), expenses while not at the camp, medical insurance, passport and Visa costs.

Applic.: On-line form. International volunteers must contact a workcamp organisation in their country of residence. See members of Alliance of European Voluntary Service Organisations at www.alliance-network.org/members

Notes: Canadian citizens or permanent residents with permanent residence in Quebec.

The Chol-Chol Foundation For Human Development

Casilla 14, Nueva Imperial, IX Región, Chile
or, 4431 Garrison Street NW Washington, DC 20013 USA
Tel./Fax: ++56 (45) 614007 or 614008
E-mail: info@cholchol.org
www.cholchol.org

Desc.: The Chol-Chol Foundation is a non-profit human development organisation that works in indigenous communities in the ninth region of Chile. The Mapuche people had been extirpated from their ancestral homeland since the arrival of the Spaniards, and the communities had been isolated from the current of modernity; without sufficient food, without passable roads, lacking medical facilities and secondary schools, and immersed in poverty, marginalisation, and an overwhelming lack of opportunities. The Foundation has grown from the work of an American missionary who arrived in Chol-Chol in 1953. Today there are several programs including housing, women's education, agriculture, and textile production.

Sector: Agriculture, construction, culture, education, health, housing, skills training, small-enterprise development, women's issues.

Country: Latin America (Chile).

Qualif.: Agronomists, veterinaries, grant writers, and social workers are especially welcome.

Nonpro: Yes, with at least an undergraduate degree.

Age: Enquire with the organisation.

Duration: Minimum 3 months.

Lang.: Spanish fluency.

Benefits: A small stipend for accommodation in certain cases, lunch during work days. Medical professionals may be funded. Enquire with the organisation.

Costs: Some projects are sponsored by international development agencies who fund the volunteers. Enquire with the organisation.

Applic.: On-line form. Volunteers should send a CV.

Christian Peacemaker Corps

PO Box 6508
Chicago, Illinois 60680-6508
Tel.: ++1 (773) 277-0253
Fax: ++1 (773) 277-0291
E-mail: personnel@ cpt.org
www.cpt.org/corps.php

Desc.: Since 1993, Christian Peacemaker Teams has been recruiting and training individuals for the Christian Peacemaker Corps. Corps members, trained in peacemaking skills and non-violent direct action, are available on a full-time basis to enter emergency situations of conflict and areas of militarisation at the invitation of local peacemakers, and responding to confront injustice and violent situations. The objectives are to advance the cause of lasting peace by giving skilled, courageous support to peacemakers working locally in situations of conflict; to inspire people and governments to discard violence in favour of non-violent action as a means of settling differences; to provide home communities with first-hand information and resources for responding to worldwide situations of conflict and to urge their active involvement; to interpret a non-violent perspective to the media; and to accompany individuals or communities who are threatened.

Sector: Human rights, peacekeeping, religious, various.

Country: Latin America (Colombia), Middle East (Palestine, Iraq), native communities in North America (Grassy Narrows, Ontario, Oneida, New York).

Qualif.: Experience in non-violent direct action.

Nonpro: No particular professional skills are required just a strong motivation for peace and a willingness to communicate.

Age: Minimum 21.

Duration: 3 years. Members are available for short-term organising, speaking, training, or other peace work within their home communities when not on project site. The Reserve Corps commit to 2 to 12 weeks each year for 3 years.

Lang.: English, Spanish, Arabic

Benefits: Modest stipend for full-time corps members. All living expenses and travel on project sites (while not serving on a project site, corps members live in locations throughout North America where housing is provided by friends or families or within existing group housing).

Costs: Reserve corps members fund their own work. Enquire with organisation.

Applic.: On-line application or request form directly from office. The application process includes a phone interview, contact with references, and participation in a short-term CPT delegation (cost dependent on destination). The selection process continues through a period of training with final discernment about acceptance into the Corps occurring at the end of the training period.

Notes: Volunteers must be of Christian faith. The organisation has representatives in Chicago and in Toronto, Canada. See website for contacts.

CIEE – Council on International Educational Exchange

7 Custom House Street, 3rd floor, Portland, Maine 04101 USA

Tel.: ++1 (800) 40-STUDY (toll free in N. Am.)

Fax: ++1 (207) 553-7699

E-mail: volunteer@ciee.org

www.ciee.org

Desc.: Designed to promote international cooperation and understanding, CIIE International Volunteer Projects offer unique opportunities for US residents to participate on short-term, team-oriented projects overseas. Volunteers immerse themselves in a new community and culture. A group of 10–20 volunteers from different countries spend 2–4 weeks working and living together while helping a community.

Sector: Child welfare, community development, construction, culture, education, environment.

Country: Hundreds of projects in over 25 countries in Africa, Asia, Europe, Latin and North America.

Qualif.: No previous experience or particular skills required.

Nonpro: Yes.

Age: Minimum 18.

Duration: 2–4 weeks.

Lang.: English.

Benefits: Pre-departure and in-country support, group accommodation, meals, medical insurance.

Costs: US$325 for a 2–4-week project. Some projects have additional fees. Contact the organisation for details. International travel is paid by the volunteer.

Applic.: On-line form.

Notes: US residents with valid passport and Visa (if required) only. Non-US residents in Europe contact the Alliance of European Voluntary Service Organisations at www.alliance-network.org. Individuals or organisations in other countries contact the CCIVS (see listing) or UNESCO (www.unesco.org/ccivs).

The Clearwater Project

PO Box 130124, Carlsbad, California 92018-9002 USA
Tel.: ++1 (760) 736-2465
Fax: ++1 (760) 929-2955 or 602-9794
E-mail: support@clearwaterproject.org
www.clearwaterproject.org

Desc.: The Clearwater Project deploys simple, affordable, and reliable solutions for communities searching for an answer to their water problems and needs. By combining immediate relief efforts with a comprehensive approach, the Clearwater Project establishes sustainable solutions that communities can effectively manage and maintain. The primary goal of the Clearwater Project is to provide assistance and empowerment to people suffering from a lack of safe drinking water. Clearwater accomplishes this goal by taking a hands-on approach and working directly with people to give them the tools, knowledge, and resources they need to improve the quality of their lives.

Sector: Culture, education, environment, health, sanitation.

Country: Africa (Tanzania), Asia (India, Bangladesh, India, Philippines, Tibet-China), Latin America (Brazil, Chile, Ecuador, Guatemala, Honduras, Mexico).

Qualif.: Environmental scientists, water chemists, microbiologists, water and civil engineers, anthropologists, educators, writers, computer programmers, photographers, video editors, fundraisers.

Nonpro: Yes, contact the organisation for details.

Age: Minimum 18.

Duration: Depends on the projects.

Lang.: English, Spanish, Hindi, Chinese, Swahili, Bangladeshi, Bengali.

Benefits: To be determined on and individual basis.

Costs: Vary with each project.

Applic.: Write or e-mail CV with cover letter.

CNFA – Citizens Network for Foreign Affairs

Agribusiness Volunteer Program
1111 19th Street, NW, Suite 900
Washington, DC 20036 USA
Tel.: ++1 (202) 296-3920 (toll free in N. Am. 1-888-872-2632)
E-mail: twhite@cnfa.org
www.cnfa.org

Desc.: US farmers, agribusiness professionals, and other agriculturalists help build democracy and market economies by sharing their expertise with aspiring entrepreneurs across the globe. In order to achieve the greatest impact, CNFA sends multiple volunteers to long-term projects, with each volunteer assignment building upon previous ones. CNFA's long-term projects seek to develop private farmer associations, cooperatives, private agribusiness, women's and young farmer groups, and other organisations that can help people increase their incomes and wellbeing. Volunteers provide help to a wide variety of groups, including dairy processors and producers, beef cattle farmers, mushroom producers, honey producers, fruit growers, and greenhouse producers.

Sector: Agriculture, small-enterprise development.

Country: Europe (Ukraine, Moldova, Belarus).

Qualif.: Agribusiness professionals: farmers and ranchers, cooperative specialists, food processing professionals, agribusiness executives, extension agents, organisation leaders, etc.

Nonpro: No.

Age: N/A with necessary experience.

Duration: 3–4 weeks.

Lang.: English.

Benefits: Airfare, lodging, meals, local transportation, and other project-related costs.

Costs: Volunteers donate only their time and unique skills.

Applic.: On-line form or request form via phone or post.

Notes: US citizens only.

COMENGIP – Community Engineering Programme

PO Box 29027 Dakar Airport Highway, Senegal
Tel./Fax: ++1 (775) 845-9343 (US telephone number)
E-mail: comengip@hotmail.com

Desc: COMENGIP refers to the valuable engineering work known to indigenous communities and their basic daily concerns: therefore COMENGIP aims at diagnosing, documenting and sustaining the contributions of the Indigenous Knowledge to World Ecological Rebuilding Programme and promoting such issues through volunteering worldwide.

Sector: Agriculture, child welfare, community development, education, environment, health, housing, human rights, sanitation, small-enterprise development, women's rights, various.

Country: Africa (Gambia, Guinea Bissau, Mali, Mauritania, Senegal, Equatorial Guinea, Congo, Cabo Verde).

Qualif.: No professional skills required.

Nonpro: Yes, but must possess good writing and communication skills, good computer literacy, etc.

Age: Minimum 18. Families with children are accepted.

Duration: 1–4 months or more.

Lang.: English, French, Spanish (or Portuguese).

Benefits: Accommodation provided and board negotiated.

Costs: Variable.

Applic: Send a letter of interest and CV to speed application procedures via e-mail, fax, or regular mail. If additional details are requested, COMENGIP will communicate in due time.

Notes: There are always more requests than can be met; if application, expressly sent via e-mail, fax, or regular mail with contact addresses included, receives no feedback within 20 days, likely the request is not being considered, in terms of dates and preferences. Applicants should send reminders.

Concern America

PO Box 1790, Santa Ana, California 92702 USA
Tel.: ++1(714)953-8575
or 1 (800) 266-2376 (toll free in N.Am.)
Fax: ++1(714)953-1242
E-mail:concamerinc@earthlink.net
www.concernamerica.org

Desc.: Concern America is a small non-profit, non-sectarian, non-governmental development and refugee aid organisation. The organisation was created to partner with materially poor communities living in impoverished regions of developing countries and with materially poor communities living in refuge outside of their homeland, for the purpose of improving the life situations of those communities.

Sector: Agriculture, child welfare, community development, education, health, refugee aid, sanitation, small-enterprise development.

Country: Africa (Mozambique, Sierra Leone, Liberia), Latin America (Mexico and countries in Central and South America).

Qualif.: Medical doctors, public health specialists, educators, agriculturalists, engineers, and other experts. Degree or experience in public health, medicine, nutrition, nursing, agriculture, community development, education, or appropriate technology.

Nonpro: No.

Age: Minimum 21.

Duration: Minimum commitment of 1 year; 2 preferred. There are no short-term internships or assignments.

Lang.: Fluency in Spanish (Portuguese in Mozambique) or ability to learn the language at own expense.

Benefits: Accommodation, board, round-trip transportation, annual trip home, health insurance, small monthly stipend, support services from the home office, simple repatriation allowance.

Costs: Personal expenses.

Applic.: Additional information on the website.

Notes: Work experience abroad is desirable.

Concern Worldwide

52-55 Lower Camden Street, Dublin 2 Ireland
Tel.: ++353 (1) 475-4162
Fax: ++353 (1) 475-7362
E-mail: hrenquiries@concern.ie or info@concern.net
www.concern.net

Desc.: Concern was founded initially as a response to the disastrous famine in Biafra. The famine was largely precipitated by the conflict that followed Biafra's attempt to secede from Nigeria. However, what began as a once-off operation quickly grew into a fully-fledged emergency and development organisation. Today, Concern is Ireland's largest relief and development agency, with operations in 24 countries worldwide. The chief focus of the work is on people living in extreme or absolute poverty. To this end, the organisation is guided by 2 main priorities: emergency response to humanitarian crises; longer-term development projects targeted at the poorest in society.

Sector: Education, emergency, health, human rights, hunger relief, sanitation.

Country: Africa (Angola, Burundi, Congo, Eritrea, Ethiopia, Kenya, Liberia, Mozambique, Rwanda, Sierra Leone, Somalia, Sudan, Tanzania, Uganda), Asia (Afghanistan, Bangladesh, Cambodia, East Timor, India, N.Korea, Laos), Caribbean (Haiti), Europe (Kosovo, Turkey), Latin America (Honduras, Venezuela).

Qualif.: Professional job postings are listed on website.

Nonpro: No.

Age: N/A with necessary experience.

Duration: Varies with each project.

Lang.: English (Spanish, French, Portuguese helpful).

Benefits: Stipend varies with position and project.

Costs: Personal expenses.

Applic.: Vacancies are posted on the website. Apply on-line.

Notes: Concern has branches in Northern Ireland, England, Scotland, and the USA. Consult the website for further details.

Concordia

Heversham House, 20-22 Boundary Road, Hove BN3 4ET UK
Tel.: ++44 (1273) 422-218
Fax: ++44 (1273) 421-182
E-mail: info@concordia-iye.org.uk
www.concordia-iye.org.uk

Desc.: Concordia is committed to international youth exchange in the hope of promoting greater international understanding, cultural awareness, and peace. The charity runs 2 schemes promoting youth exchange, a Seasonal Agricultural Work Scheme for non-EU students coming to the UK and a more recent programme of International Volunteer Projects, which offers 16-30 year olds the opportunity to join international teams of volunteers working on short-term projects in over 50 countries world-wide. Projects are community-based initiatives that would not be possible without volunteer action, focusing as much on the aspect of intercultural exchange – both within the group and the local community - as on the work itself.

Sector: Child welfare, construction, culture, education, environment.

Country: Africa (Botswana, Ghana, Kenya, Malawi, Namibia, South Africa, Tanzania, Togo, Uganda, Zimbabwe), Asia (Bangladesh, Cambodia, Japan, South Korea, India, Mongolia, Nepal, Thailand), Latin America (Ecuador, Guatemala, Mexico) Europe, North America.

Qualif.: No particular skills required.

Nonpro: Yes, with some previous relevant experience.

Age: 16-30, minimum age of 20 for projects in Africa, Asia and Latin America.

Duration: 2–4 weeks.

Lang.: English

Benefits: Food and accommodation. Travel not included.

Costs: GB£80 - £125 (US$120-180) plus travel.

Notes: Volunteers must join the Supporters' Network.

COOPI – Cooperation International

Via De Lemene 50
20151 Milano Italy
Tel.: ++39 (02) 308-5057
Fax: ++39 (02) 3340-3570
E-mail: coopi@coopi.org
www.coopi.org

Desc.: COOPI is an NGO founded in 1965. Its mission is to foster international solidarity by developing multi-sector projects in order to respond to the various needs of the local communities and by working in close relationship with local partners. COOPI intervenes in emergency situations in areas affected by war or natural disaster. COOPI has 120 projects in 37 countries.

Sectors: Agriculture, community development, construction, education, emergency, environment, refugee aid, skills training, sanitation, small-enterprise development, various.

Country: Africa (Cameroon, Central Africa Rep., Chad, Congo, Ethiopia, Djibuti, Kenya, Guinea B., Eritrea, Malawi, Morocco, Mozambique, Rwanda, Senegal, S. Leone, Somalia, Tanzania, Tunisia, Uganda), Asia (Afghanistan, Bangladesh, China, Pakistan, Tajikistan), Europe (Albania, Kosovo, Romania, Serbia), Latin America (Bolivia, Colombia, Ecuador, El Salvador, Guatemala, Honduras, Paraguay, Peru), Middle East (Yemen, Lebanon, Palestine).

Qualif.: Agronomists, engineers, hydrologists, healthcare professionals, emergency relief, and social workers, etc.

Nonpro: Yes, for workcamps only. Professionals for mid-/long-term projects.

Age: Minimum 21, dependent upon experience.

Duration: 3 months to 3 years for professionals; 3–4 weeks for workcamps.

Lang.: English, Spanish, French, and Arabic.

Benefits: Long-term professionals are fully funded with the standards of the funding organisation, such as the EU and UN agencies.

Costs: Workcamp participants pay for travel, insurance, room, and board.

Applic.: Send application via fax or e-mail selezione@coopi.org. For the workcamps contact campiestivi@coopi.org.

Notes: Available positions are always announced on the website.

CORD – Christian Outreach Relief and Development

1 New Street, Leamington Spa, Warwickshire CV31 1HP UK
Tel.: ++44 (1926) 315-301
Fax: ++44 (1926) 885-786
E-mail: personnel@cord.org.uk or info@cord.org.uk
www.cord.org.uk

Desc.: CORD is a UK-based Christian relief and development agency, established in 1967 to help war-orphaned and abandoned children in Vietnam. CORD works with marginalised and vulnerable people, especially children and people displaced by conflict. CORD's overall objective is to enable communities and individuals to have greater control over situations that affect their lives, to encourage self-reliance and to provide sustainable solutions to problems. CORD emphasises an integrated approach and brings specialist expertise in areas such as health, education, water/sanitation, and agriculture.

Sector: Agriculture, education, health, sanitation.

Country: Africa (Tanzania, Liberia, Zambia), Asia (Afghanistan, Cambodia, India, Philippines, Thailand), Europe (Albania).

Qualif.: Health professionals, managers, accountants, administrators, agronomists, logisticians.

Nonpro: No.

Age: N/A with necessary experience.

Duration: Initial placement is 1 year, with 1-year extension desired.

Lang.: English. French, Spanish, and Portuguese useful.

Benefits: All expenses covered plus stipend. Group accommodation.

Costs: Remuneration package for overseas positions covers all costs.

Applic.: Send CV to Head of Personnel and outline Christian commitment. Apply only for specific vacancies on the website.

Notes: Only Christians with free right of entry into the UK. Strict medical check-up before departure.

Cotravaux

11 Rue de Clichy
75009 Paris
France
Tel.: ++33 (1) 4874-7920
Fax: ++33 (1) 4874-1401

Desc.: Cotravaux coordinates 12 French workcamps. Its role is to promote voluntary work and community projects concerning environmental protection, monument restoration, and social projects. The organisation offers many workcamps in different regions of France. Many of the organisations members of Cotravaux work with foreign partners.

Sector: Culture, environment, various.

Country: Europe (France).

Qualif.: No specific skills needed.

Nonpro: Yes.

Age.: Minimum 18.

Dur.: 2–3 weeks. Certain projects offer 4–12 month volunteering.

Lang.: A few projects require French.

Benefits: Room and board provided (some camps require a daily contribution).

Costs: Volunteers must pay for their own transportation to the camps.

Applic.: Contact Cotravaux by fax or mail to obtain the list of partner workcamps in France or other specific countries.

Council for Mayan Communication in Sololà

Barrio Jucanya
Panajachel, Sololá Guatemala
Tel.: ++ (502) 293-5756
E-mail: padma@mayacom.org
www.mayacom.org

Desc.: The Mayan Council for Communication in Sololá is a small group of citizens and community leaders living in the ´Department´ of Sololá who have a continual interest in supporting the advancement of equitable access to communications technologies in the region. The motivation of each member is to secure free access to communications technologies, most specifically the Internet, for all people, organisations, and agencies that show interest and need. The specific objective is to create a network of rural Telecenters that provide community access to regional and international information resources with satellite reception, the ability to connect 24 hours a day and support 10–40 computers on-line. The Sololá network could consist of from 10–20 independent and self-administrating Telecenters, strategically situated around the lake to provide the most practical use for the region.

Sector: Education, IT, skills training, small-enterprise development, women's issues, various.

Country: Latin America (Guatemala).

Qualif.: Each volunteer program is tailored to suit the particular interest and abilities of the volunteer.

Nonpro: Yes.

Age: Minimum 18.

Duration: Minimum 1 month. Short-term stays available by negotiation.

Lang.: Spanish, English. The population is mainly indigenous, representing 3 of the 24 official indigenous Guatemalan languages: Kaqchikel, Tsutujil, and K´iche. Spanish is a second language to the majority and basic knowledge is essential.

Benefits: The application fee covers volunteer placement, administration, marketing, program information, and arrangements with host communities. The program fee covers 3 meals a day plus lodging. The projects are rurally located, high up in the mountains or in small villages around the lake. Most places are accessible by a combination of 'chicken' bus, pick-up, and hiking. Accommodations will have a shower, a flush toilet, and a bed with a mattress. Alternatively, modern services are available in Panajachel, and a program can be created to include day visits to the project with transport by boat or bus to nearby villages.

Costs: Flights, travel/health insurance, and corresponding airport departure taxes, plus a weekly budget of up to US$20. US$275 application fee and US$350 per month participation fee (variable according to accommodation and meal requirements), both paid prior to arrival. Costs are lower for committed long-term volunteers. Additional costs for transport are US$100–10 for airport transfer, US$60–1 for local travel; accommodation ranges from US$100 per night, week, or month.

Applic.: On-line form. Volunteers select a participating organisation in the Mayacom Network.

Cross Cultural Solutions

2 Clinton Place, New Rochelle, New York 10801 USA
Tel.: ++1 (914) 632-0022 (toll free in N. Am. 1-800-380-4777)
Fax: ++1 (914) 632-8494
E-mail: info@crossculturalsolutions.org
www.crossculturalsolutions.org

Desc.: Cross-Cultural Solutions, a non-profit organisation founded in 1995, is headquartered in New Rochelle, New York, with an office in Brighton, United Kingdom. Cross-Cultural Solutions offer two types of Programs, Volunteer and Insight. Volunteer Programs, focus on cultural immersion through volunteering and cultural learning opportunities, are year-round, and normally range from 2-12 weeks. The Insight program, which also focuses on cultural immersion but without the volunteering component, is Insight Cuba.

Sector: Child welfare, community develoment, culture, education, health, small-enterprise development, women's issues.

Country: Africa (Ghana, Tanzania), Asia (China, India, Thailand), Europe (Russia, Kosovo, Macedonia), Latin America (Brazil, Costa Rica, Guatemala, Cuba, Peru).

Qualif.: Open to people of all nationalities and ages.

Nonpro: Yes.

Age: Minimum 18, without adult companionship.

Duration: 2–12 weeks; all programs begin on specified start date; end date will vary, depending on length of stay.

Lang.: English.

Benefits: All program-based expenses: airport transfers, daily transportation, meals, lodging, professional staff guidance and supervision, orientation, medical insurance.

Costs: US$2,175 (2 weeks). International airfare, insurance, and Visa fees not included. A registration deposit of US$275 is due.

Applic.: On-line form and information survey.

Notes: United Kingdom Office, see website for contacts.

CUSO

500-2255 Carling Avenue,
Ottawa, Ontario K2B 1A6 Canada
Tel.: ++1 (613) 829-7445 (toll free in N. Am. 1-888-434-2876)
Fax: ++1 (613) 829-7996
E-mail: cuso.secretariat@cuso.ca
www.cuso.org

Desc.: CUSO is a Canadian organisation that supports alliances for global social justice. They work with people striving for freedom, gender, and racial equality, self-determination, and cultural survival. They achieve their goals by sharing information, human and material resources, and by promoting policies for developing global sustainability. CUSO contributes to the sustainable development of developing countries by helping to reduce poverty, by promoting democratic governance and human rights, and by supporting sustainable and equitable natural resource management practices.

Country: Africa (Benin, Burkina Faso, Ghana, Kenya, Mozambique, Nigeria, South Africa, Tanzania, Togo), Asia (East Timor, Indonesia, Laos, Thailand), Caribbean (Jamaica), Latin America (Belize, Brazil, Bolivia, Cuba, Chile, Costa Rica, El Salvador, Guatemala, Mexico, Nicaragua, Peru) Oceania (Fiji, Papua New Guinea, Solomon Islands, Vanuatu).

Sector: Agriculture, child welfare, culture, environment, health, housing, human rights, IT, small-enterprise development, women's issues, various.

Qualif.: Skilled and experienced in professional fields with an interest in and personal commitment to social movements.

Nonpro: Enquire with organisation.

Age: Occasionally cooperant placements are with host government agencies where age considerations may apply.

Duration: 2 years. Durations may vary to accommodate in-field language training programs.

Lang.: English, Spanish Portuguese.

Benefits: CUSO provides a benefit package that enables cooperants to live modestly overseas. Benefits are not linked to the type, level, or value of the work cooperants do, but are intended to cover the basic living expense of providing services overseas. All cooperants are entitled to a minimum of 4 weeks vacation for every year of service. Cooperants will receive return economy air travel (with possible restrictions), settling-in support, a modest living allowance, long-term (more than 12 months) cooperants receive a supplementary allowance, modest housing, language training if required, pre-departure and arrival orientation sessions, cost of required Visas, work permits, etc., an end of contract payment, healthcare benefits for placements of more than 6 months (see the website for more detailed information on health benefits and requirements). Spouses may be accepted with long-term cooperants and certain benefits may be included.

Costs: The overseas living allowance does not provide for additional personal expenses nor specialty food and consumer goods not essential to basic needs while overseas.

Applic.: Consult the website for the listing of Current CUSO Co-operant Opportunities and complete application details. Complete the on-line application form. Refer to Geographic Specialization for information on the connections between Canadian Area Offices and overseas programs. Each placement summary includes contact information for the responsible office. Successful application usually takes 3–6 months from application to departure, but may take longer to accommodate medical preparations, family needs, or to fit with pre-planned in-country training programs

Notes: Canadian citizens or landed immigrants only.

Dakshinayan

c/o Siddharth Sanyal, D-1/10 First Floor,
South City 2, Sohna Road,
Gurgaon 122101, Haryana India
Mobile: ++91 (981) 0687960
E-mail: sid@linkindia.com or dakshinayan@vsnl.com
www.linkindia.com/dax or www.dakshinayan.org

Desc.: Dakshinayan was set up in 1991 by Siddharth Sanyal to take over a tribal development project in Bihar, which was being managed by an international voluntary service organisation. Local villagers and activists manage the Cheo Project, which now falls within the newly formed tribal state of Jharkhand. Cheo is the name of the village where the project started in 1979, but now it's an acronym for Children, Health, Education, and Organisation. The project aims to initiate small locally-managed grassroots development projects at village level with emphasis on self-reliance; gather and disseminate information regarding development efforts and issues; promote development education for a better understanding of the cause, reality, and myths of rural and urban poverty; and create linkages between small projects and possible support sources within India and abroad.

Sector: Community development, education, environment, health.

Country: Asia (India).

Qualif.: No particular skills required, just a strong motivation.

Nonpro: Yes.

Age: Minimum 18.

Duration: 30 days minimum. There are no maximum limits.

Lang.: English.

Benefits: Accommodation at the project and food (vegetarian).

Costs: US$300 for 1 month; US$450 for 2 months; US$200 for every additional month. Volunteers must cover all expenses incurred while travelling to and from the project.

Notes: Open to all nationalities. Volunteers must arrive in New Delhi for orientation and placement before the 5th of the month.

Desteens Volunteering Services

PO Box 68130
Nairobi Kenya
Tel.: ++254 (722) 255-311(mobile)
E-mail: des_teencenter@yahoo.com or epeco99@yahoo.com

Desc.: Desteens organise workcamps for volunteers to come and help the community by teaching, working with the poor, working with local NGOs and local projects, and raising cultural understanding.

Sector: Community development, construction, education, environment, IT, small-enterprise development.

Country: Africa (Kenya).

Qualif.: Volunteers with skills are placed in relevant institutions. Mechanics, electricians, special education teachers, doctors, nurses, orthopedists, IT experts desired.

Nonpro.: Yes.

Age: 17–75.

Duration: 2 weeks to 2 years. Short-term teachers should note that schools closes for holidays in the months of April, August, and December.

Lang.: English. Swahili is the local language.

Benefits: Accommodation and food.

Costs: U$60 administration fee plus US$17 per day for living expenses. Cash donations, books, educational magazines, clothing, computers, toys, or any other donations gratefully received.

Applic.: Request application form via e-mail.

Notes: Once accepted the applicant can request to be put in contact with former volunteers. See note on page 36.

EMERGENCY

Via Orefici 2 - 20123 Milano Italy
Tel.: ++39 (02) 863-161
Fax: ++39 (02) 863-16336
E-mail: info@emergency.it
www.emergency.it

Desc.: EMERGENCY provides emergency surgical assistance and rehabilitation for the civilian victims of war and landmines. Its humanitarian programs require the collaboration of medical and technical staff with specific work experience in war zones. An essential component of EMERGENCY's activities is to train the national personnel in the clinical management and rehabilitation of landmine and war injuries thereby ensuring the sustainability of the programs. The international community is moving towards a global ban of these inhuman, indiscriminate, and persistent weapons. However, more than 110 million unexploded landmines are scattered in at least 67 countries, and they will continue to maim and kill for the decades to come. EMERGENCY's role is to provide surgical care and rehabilitation for these victims.

Sector: Emergency, health.

Country: Africa (Sierra Leone, Algeria), Asia (Afghanistan, Cambodia), Middle East (Iraq, Palestine).

Qualif.: Medical professionals: general surgeons, orthopaedic and plastic surgeons, anaesthesiologists, paediatrician, gynaecologist, nurses, physiotherapists, prosthetics, administration assistants.

Nonpro: No.

Age: N/A with the necessary experience.

Duration: 6 months minimum.

Lang.: English. Knowledge of a local language an advantage.

Benefits: Salary, room and board, round-trip airfare from Europe.

Costs: Personal expenses.

Applic.: Send CV via fax or e-mail to curriculum@emergency.it.

EVS – European Voluntary Service

European Commission
Rue de la Loi 200, B - 1049 Bruxelles Belgium
SOS Volunteer Helpdesk
Tel: +32 (2) 233.02.99 / Fax: +32 (2) 233.01.50
E-mail: volunteers@socleoyouth.be
http://europa.eu.int/comm/youth/ or www.sosforevs.org

Desc.: The European Voluntary Service (EVS) is an Action of the YOUTH programme, implemented by the European Commission and YOUTH National Agencies. It allows young people to do a voluntary service in a local host organisation in a foreign country. The volunteer gains a variety of personal, professional and intercultural skills, and brings some added value and intercultural flavour to the host organisation and the local community. Within the Euro-Med Youth Programme support is available also for voluntary service activities with partners in Mediterranean countries. The SOS Volunteer Helpdesk offers support to volunteers and organisations as well as to young people interested in EVS. The helpdesk works in close collaboration with the European Commission and national representatives of the programme in more than 40 European and Mediterranean countries.

Sector: Community development, culture, education, environment, etc.

Country: Programme countries are the EU Member States, Norway, Iceland, Liechtenstein, the 12 accession countries and Turkey. A smaller number of projects take place with partners in South Eastern Europe, Eastern European countries, Mediterranean countries, and Latin America.

Qualif.: Participation in the European Voluntary Service does not require any professional qualification. On the contrary, it is open to young people with no professional background in the field.

Nonpro: Programs are open with no particular expertise required.

Age: Minimum 18 - maximum 25 years.

Duration: There are two types of EVS projects: most of the projects are long-term with a duration between 6 and 12 months; short-term projects have a duration of 3 weeks to 6 months, aiming at young people with fewer opportunities, for example who never had an opportunity to travel abroad, have individual difficulties or a disability, or are temporarily in difficult circumstances.

Lang.: EVS volunteers do not need extended language skills. Linguistic support is available in the project.

Benefits: The projects receive grants as a contribution for preparation, travel, accommodation, food, activity costs directly related to the project plus a monthly allowance for the volunteer (pocket money).

Costs: Volunteers cannot be charged for participating in EVS. Sending and host organisations are responsible for project expenses. EU grants are supposed to cover most of the costs.

Applic.: Each EVS project is built on a partnership triangle between sending organisation, host organisation and volunteer. The organisations can be any type of non-governmental organisation, an association, a local authority or any non-profit-making local initiative. National Agencies / National Coordinators in the country of the prospective volunteer can provide contacts with existing sending organisations. Sending organisations would establish an agreement with a host organisation. For volunteers going from one Programme country to another both organisations submit grant applications to the National Agencies in their country. In other projects it is the project partner in the Programme country or Mediterranean partner country submitting one grant application.

Notes: The programme is accessible to young people with legal residence in the EU and some nearby countries (see website for details). Prospective volunteers must contact the YOUTH National Agency in their country, the Euro-Med National Coordinators or the SOS Volunteer Helpdesk for more information.

Foundation for Sustainable Development
59 Driftwood Court
San Rafael, California 94901 USA
Fax: ++1 (415) 482-9366
E-mail: info@fsdinternational.org
www.fsdinternational.org

Desc.:	FSD provides year round community development internships in Latin America and Africa with local non-profits organizations. Each intern is placed in a separate host organization and family for immersion purposes. A support network is provided by a country director, host organization supervisor, and host family. The program provides an opportunity for complete language immersion, practical hands-on experience working in community development, and a cultural experience living with a host family. Programs are geared mainly for college and graduate students, or recent graduates interested in a career in development.
Sector:	Community development, various.
Country:	Latin America (Bolivia, Nicaragua, Ecuador, Peru) and Africa (Tanzania and Uganda).
Qualif.:	No particular skills required. Conversational level Spanish for the Latin American programs.
Nonpro:	College or graduate students, graduates, with a high GPA and a strong interest in development and/or Latin America or Africa.
Age:	Minimum 18.
Duration:	8–24 weeks.
Lang.:	English, 2 years of college Spanish, or 4 years of high school Spanish and 1 year of college Spanish (for Latin American).
Benefits:	In-country travel, accommodation (home-stays), food, stipend, tourist excursions, staff support. Academic credit is available.
Costs:	US$1,600–3,000 plus US$25 application fee.
Applic.:	In duplicate with CV (in Spanish if applying to the Latin American programs), unofficial transcripts, and passport, 1 letter of reference, due by March 1st for the summer program and at least 2 months before departure for individual program.

Fundación Aldeas De Paz – Peace Villages Foundation

Lomas de Piedra Canaima
Santa Elena de Uiarén, Municipio Gran Sabana, Estado Bolívar
Venezuela
Tel.: ++58 (414) 245-6307
E-mail: aldepaz@yahoo.es
http://mipagina.cantv.net/peacevillages/about.htm

Desc.: The Peace Villages Foundation (PVF) is an NGO dedicated to promoting volunteerism, providing community service, encouraging collaboration and improving cultural awareness. PVF is a community based organization in the small village of Santa Elena de Uiarén in the beautiful "La Gran Sabana" Region in the southeastern corner of Venezuela next to the Brazilian border. PVF offers volunteer programs that are a mix of community service, educational opportunities and recreational activities. We provide volunteers with the unique opportunity to experience first hand the culture of the region where they participate in volunteering projects that are both beneficial to the community and rewarding to the volunteers. PVFsupports and contributes to the psychological, emotional, physical, cultural and social development of local indigenous communities, specially woman and children

Sector: Agriculture, child welfare, education, environment, health, housing, small-enterprise development, women's issues.

Country: Latin America (Venezuela).

Qualif.: Carpenters, plumbers, psychologists, medical doctors, etc.

Nonpro: Yes.

Age: Minimum 20.

Duration: 1–3 months.

Lang.: English, Spanish.

Benefits: Room and board, weekend leisure excursions.

Costs: US$30–35 per day.

Applic.: Send CV and cover letter.

Notes: Leisure time, during week-ends, includes: discovering the Amazon's forest beauty through river trips, trekking, etc.

Geekcorps, Inc.
1121 MASS MoCA Way
North Adams, Massachusetts 01247 USA
Fax: ++1 (413) 664-0032
E-mail: volunteer@geekcorps.org
www.geekcorps.org

Desc.: Geekcorps is a US-based, NGO that places international technical volunteers in developing nations, often working with small businesses. Objectives are to cooperate on specific technical projects while transferring the high-level Information and Communication Technologies skills required for long-term sustainability. Volunteers are matched with projects based on the technical skills required, as determined by the detailed Scopes of Work received from partner businesses.

Sector: IT, small-enterprise development.

Country: Africa (Ghana, Rwanda, Senegal, Mali), Europe (Armenia, Romania, Bulgaria), Asia (Mongolia, Kyrgyzstan, Thailand) and Middle East (Lebanon).

Qualif.: Programmers, web designers, database and software developers, network administrators, graphic artists, and business and marketing professionals have all volunteered through Geekcorps.

Nonpro: IT professionals with at least five years of industry experience.

Duration: Six weeks to six months. The average Geekcorps assignment is three to four months.

Lang.: English.

Benefits: All costs are covered: airfare, vaccinations, insurance, a living stipend, accommodations, visas, etc.

Costs: Geekcorps covers all costs but asks volunteers and/or their employers to contribute if possible.

Applic.: On-line form at www.geekcorps.org

Notes: Geekcorps obtains Visas for US residents. Others must apply for a Visa at their country's Embassy. Write to info@geekcorps.org with any questions.

Global Citizens Network

130 N. Howell Street
St. Paul, Minnesota 55104 USA
Tel.: ++1 (651) 644-0960 (toll free in N. Am. 1-800-644-9292)
E-mail: info@globalcitizens.org
www.globalcitizens.org

Desc.: Team members have the opportunity to immerse themselves in the daily life of a developing community, while working closely with local residents on such projects as building a health clinic, teaching in a pre-school, planting trees, or renovating a youth centre. Local hosts provide volunteers with education in the local culture, language, social structure, environment, economy, and arts. Communities are visited that offer insight into specific issues or trends, such as environmental protection, women in development, and traditional medicine. Home visits, local farm and factory tours, and hikes in surrounding areas are common. Volunteers are often invited to watch or participate in local ceremonies and holiday festivities. Teams consist of 6–10 people, and are led by a trained team leader.

Sector: Agriculture, community development, construction, education, environment, women's issues.

Country: Africa (Kenya, Tanzania), Asia (Nepal), Caribbean, Latin America (Guatemala, Mexico), North America (USA).

Qualif.: No special skills are required to participate.

Nonpro: Yes. Families are welcome to join the teams.

Age: Minimum 18. Younger volunteers are welcome with families.

Duration: 1–3 weeks, typically 2.

Lang.: English.

Benefits: Travel, food, accommodation (group or home-stay), tourist excursions, staff support. Academic credit is available.

Costs: US$650–1,950 depending on the project plus airfare.

Applic.: Download application off the website or request via telephone or e-mail.

Global Corps

1201 Pennsylvania Avenue, NW, Suite 200
Washington, DC 20004 USA
Fax: ++1 (240) 465-0244
E-mail info@globalcorps.com
www.globalcorps.com

Desc.: GlobalCorps is dedicated to a mission of matching the most qualified professionals in the development, humanitarian, and disaster relief fields with organisations looking for these individuals. Members of this exclusive community have a strong desire to help others, and many positions GlobalCorps recruits for present challenges not found in any other career. The commitment does not end when the position is filled, GlobalCorps endeavours to maintain continuous contact with both the professionals recruited and the organisations involved. Furthermore, the GlobalCorps website is a valuable resource for organisations and professionals alike; a place to access information about organisations, projects, disaster relief efforts, field reports, latest research, and more.

Sector: Community development, emergency, human rights.

Country: Africa, Asia, Europe, Middle East, Latin and North America.

Qualif: See regular job postings on the website.

Nonpro: No.

Age: N/A with necessary experience.

Duration: Variable with each posting.

Lang.: Language of country of placement.

Benefits: A contribution against the actual cost of the annual health and life insurance costs; an allowance for temporary lodging, living quarters, post and supplemental post, and separate maintenance, education, and educational travel; post differential; payments during evacuation/authorized departure; danger pay; annual and sick leave, insurance.

Costs: Volunteers are responsible for their personal expenses.

Applic.: Contact the organisation directly and send CV.

117

Global Routes

1 Short Street
Northampton, Massachusetts 01060 USA
Tel.: ++1 (413) 585-8895
Fax: ++1 (413) 585-8810
E-mail: mail@globalroutes.org
www.globalroutes.org.

Desc.: Global Routes designs experiential community service projects and teaching internships that allow high school and college aged students to extend themselves by living and working with people in communities throughout the world. High school programs are 4, 5 and 6 weeks long and offered in the summer. A primary focus of the programs for high school aged students is to develop the individual student through the experience of working, travelling and living with a group of peers in new and compelling environments. Typical service projects include: constructing classrooms, laboratories and libraries for village schools, running educational workshops and day camps, and renovating community buildings. High school programs exist in Belize, China, Costa Rica, Ecuador, Dominican Republic, Ghana, Guadeloupe, New Zealand, St. Lucia, Thailand/ Vietnam and the United States. The college-level internship is 10 to 12 weeks long and is offered in the summer, fall and winter. A primary focus of this program is to develop the individual's sense of self and personal responsibility through the experience of living and volunteering in a remote community. The primary service project for our college interns is teaching, from the elementary to high school levels. College programs exist in Costa Rica, Ecuador, Ghana, Kenya, St. Lucia and Thailand.

Sector: Construction, education, environment, various.

Country: Africa (Ghana, Kenya), Asia (China, Thailand, Vietnam), Latin America (Belize, Costa Rica, Ecuador), Caribbean (Dominican Republic, Guadeloupe, St. Lucia), North America, Oceania (New Zealand).

Qualif.: Programs are open to those students who show great enthusiasm to contribute to a developing community and a genuine desire to further their own learning and growth.

Nonpro: Yes.

Age: 13 – 17 for high school programs; 17 and older for college programs.

Duration: 4 - 12 weeks depending on project.

Lang.: English. Minimum 2 years French or Spanish for some projects.

Benefits: Accommodations (home-stays), food, recreation, workshops and tourist excursions.

Costs: College Programs:US$4,300–4,600. High School Programs: US$3,750–5,350. Program fees do not include airfare.

Applic.: On-line application form.

Notes: Leadership Positions are available. Leading a high school program generally involves a 4–7-week commitment (late June through mid-August) as well as attending a 5-day orientation prior to departure in mid-to-late June. These are co-leadership positions: 2 leaders, 1 man and 1 woman, lead a group of up to 18 high school students. Qualifications for staff positions include: minimum age of 24 to lead high school programs and 26 to lead college programs; extensive experience working with North American high school and/or college students is necessary; travel experience in the desired region; Spanish language proficiency for Costa Rica, Dominican Republic, and Ecuador programs, French language proficiency for Guadeloupe program (local language proficiency highly desirable for programs in all other regions); certification in Standard First Aid and CPR (higher level certifications desirable); backgrounds in counselling, cross-cultural learning, wilderness and/or environmental education, and classroom teaching.

Global Service Corps

300 Broadway, Suite 28
San Francisco, California 94133
Tel.: ++1 (415)788-3666, ext. 128
Fax: ++1 (415)788-7324
E-mail: gsc@earthisland.org
www. www.globalservicecorps.org

Desc.: Global Service Corps provides cross-cultural learning and community service adventures for adults in Tanzania and Thailand. Volunteers live with local families In the Tanzania Sustainable Agriculture Program, volunteers work on small-scale organic agriculture projects in and around the Arusha region. In the HIV/AIDS Program, GSC participants assist in the fight against HIV/AIDS through education, by working with students, teachers, community members, and local organizations. In the Thai program, participants teach English, (also to Buddhist monks) work with teachers in media presentation, special education, HIV/AIDS and drug awareness projects, and classroom presentation skills.

Sector: Agriculture, education, health.

Country: Africa (Tanzania), Asia (Thailand).

Qualif.: No professional qualifications necessary.

Nonpro: Yes.

Age: Minimum 18. Volunteers with children accepted on Thai project.

Duration: 2 weeks to one year.

Lang.: English. Swahili lessons provided in Tanzania.

Benefits: None.

Costs: US$1,585 and up depending on length and program. 10 week programs approx.US$3,500. US$25/ day after 10 weeks.

Benefits: Room and board, mentorship by an in-country coordinator, local transportation, Swahili lessons, and a safari/excursion.

Applic.: On-line form (or from a brochure) to be completed, printed, each page signed, and returned via post with deposit.

Note: Volunteers live with local families in order to receive a full insider's prospective of the country.

Global Vision International

Amwell Farm House, Nomansland
Wheathampstead, St. Albans, Herts AL4 8EJ UK
Tel.: ++44 (870) 608-8898
Fax: ++44 (1582) 834 002
E-mail: info@gvi.co.uk
www.gvi.co.uk

Desc.: Global Vision International promotes sustainable solutions for a rapidly changing world by matching the general public with international environmentalists, researchers and pioneering educators. Through its alliance with aid-reliant organisations throughout the world, GVI provides opportunities to Volunteers to fill a critical void in the fields of environmental research, conservation, education and community development.

Sector: Community development, education, environment.

Country: Africa (South Africa, Swaziland, Madagascar), Asia (Nepal, Thailand, China, Indonesia), Latin America (Ecuador, Brazil, Mexico, Guatemala, Honduras, Panama).

Qualif: No particular skills necessary: Professionals are welcome.

Nonpro.: Yes.

Age: Minimum 18.

Duration: 2 weeks to 2 years.

Lang.: English.

Benefits: Accommodation, food, project equipment and training all included, as well as full pre-departure and in the field support. See www.gvi.co.uk for more information.

Costs: GB£250 to GB£3,000 depending on project and duration. Flights and insurance not included.

Applic.: Place in a project is secured with a non- returnable deposit of GB £250. This sum is deducted from the expedition cost. Full payment is due 2 month prior to the expedition start date.

Notes: Reasonable physical fitness and ability to swim over 200 metres is necessary. International volunteers welcome.

Global Volunteer Network

PO Box 2231, Wellington, New Zealand
Tel.: ++64 (4) 569-9080
(toll free in UK 0800-096-7864, in N. Am. 1-800-963-1198, in
Australia 1-800-005-342)   Fax: ++64 (4) 569-9081
E-mail: info@volunteer.org.nz
www.volunteer.org.nz

Desc. The Global Volunteer Network's vision is to support the work of local community organizations in developing countries through the placement of international volunteers. Local communities are in the best position to determine their needs, and GVN provides volunteers to help them achieve their goals. GVN's aim is to provide challenging and affordable volunteer opportunities around the globe, and the network continues to expand with new programs being researched and assessed. GVN places every year almost 1,000 international volunteers.

Sector: Culture, education, environment, health, sanitation.

Country: Africa (Ghana, Uganda), Asia (China, Nepal Vietnam), Europe (Romania, Russia), Latin America (El Salvador).

Qualif.: Varies from program to program, but most do not require specialised skills.

Nonpro: Yes.

Age: Minimum 18 unless otherwise noted.

Duration: 2 weeks to 1 year. Volunteers accepted year-round except June and July because of Monsoon and summer vacation.

Lang.: English.

Benefits: Training, accommodation, food, transportation, supervision.

Costs: Application fee of US$297. Program fees range from US$150 to US$ 3,600. Return air travel, Visa, vaccinations, and corresponding airport departure taxes.

Applic.: On-line form.

Notes: Volunteers may come from anywhere in the world. Prices and other details are subject to change. Consult website for updates.

Global Volunteers

375 East Little Canada Road
St. Paul, Minnesota 55117-1628 USA
Tel.: ++1 (651) 407-6100 (toll free in N. Am. 1-800-487-1074)
Fax: ++1 (651) 482-0915
E-mail: info@globalvolunteers.org
www.globalvolunteers.org.htm

Desc.: Global Volunteers, a private non-profit, non-sectarian development organisation, was founded in 1984 with the goal of helping to establish a foundation for peace through mutual international understanding. As a non-governmental organisation (NGO) in special consultative status with the United Nations, Global Volunteers is uniquely positioned to represent local leaders in a national and international arena, and to engage short-term volunteers in local development efforts with long-lasting results. At the request of local leaders and indigenous host organisations, Global Volunteers sends teams of volunteers to live and work with local people on human and economic development projects identified by the community as important to its long-term development. In this way, the volunteers' energy, creativity, and labour are put to use at the same time that they gain a genuine, first-hand understanding of how other people live day-to-day.

Sector: Community development, education, health.

Country: Africa (Ghana, Tanzania), Asia (China, India), Caribbean (Jamaica), Europe (Greece, Hungary, Ireland, Italy, Poland, Romania, Spain, Ukraine), Latin America (Costa Rica, Ecuador, Mexico), North America (USA-Hawaii), Oceania (Australia, Cook Islands).

Qualif.: No particular qualifications are necessary.

Nonpro: Yes.

Age: Global Volunteers welcomes individuals and groups of all ages and backgrounds.

Duration: 1, 2, or 3 weeks depending on the community and the site. Volunteers who wish to stay longer in the community may choose to sign up for additional Global Volunteers programs. Programs are often offered back-to-back, during consecutive weeks. See the program date page on the website for more specific information about the dates for each program.

Lang.: English.

Benefits: Accommodation, meals and the services of a team leader.

Costs: US$350 deposit is required with application. The service program fee for 1-, 2-, or 3-week international service programs, including non-continental US programs, ranges from US$1,295 to US$2,995, excluding airfare. The service program fee for 1-week continental US service programs is US$750 (or $650 with internet processing), excluding airfare. All expenses, including airfare, are tax-deductible for US taxpayers. See each program page for specific price information

Applic.: On-line form with credit card for deposit, or print the text form and mail or fax the application and deposit. Volunteers select the site and program dates during which they want to volunteer. More than 90% of all applicants are accepted. Make travel arrangements as soon as placement on the service program is confirmed. The balance is due 75 days before the team is scheduled to arrive in the community, or immediately if the application is received within 75 days of the team's arrival date.

Notes: Before applying carefully read the On-line Volunteer Booklet. For further questions, phone the organisation and ask to speak to a volunteer coordinator.

Global Works, Inc.

1113 South Allen St.
State College, Pennsylvania 16801 USA
Tel.: ++1 (814) 867-7000
Fax: ++1 (814) 867-2717
E-mail: info@globalworksinc.com
www.globalworksinc.com

Desc.: The programs are aimed to introduce students to new cultures and countries and positively affect the communities in which they visit. Students stay in a community and contribute their labour and in exchange begin to learn about other cultures, global issues, and often another language. Global Works summer programs are located in all types of climates and cultures around the world. Students live in places such as villages in the mountains of Fiji or castle ruins in Ireland. Students spend roughly sixty percent of the time doing community service projects and the remaining forty percent on travel and adventure activities.

Sector: Community development, construction, culture, environment.

Country: Europe (Ireland, France, Spain), Latin America (Puerto Rico, Yucatan, Mexico, Ecuador, Costa Rica, Bolivia, Peru), North America (Quebec), Oceania (Fiji, New Zealand).

Qualif.: N/A.

Nonpro: Yes, high school students.

Age: 14–18. High school students only.

Duration: Spring Break programs 8 days, and Summer programs, 21–30 days.

Lang.: Some English, other "Immersion" programs require 2 years of Spanish or French. Immersion programs include homestays and focus on conversational language learning.

Benefits: Food, accommodation, adventure activities.

Costs: US$2,950–3,950, depending on program. Airfare and insurance not included.

Applic.: On-line form. Health and medical insurance forms required.

Notes: Staff must be over the age of 23 to apply.

Good Shepherd Volunteers

337 East 17th Street
New York, New York 10003 USA
Tel.: ++1 (888) 668-6GSV
Fax: ++1 (212) 979-8604
E-mail: goodshpvol@aol.com
www.goodshepherdvolunteers.com

Desc.: The Good Shepherd Volunteers program provides opportunities for Christian men and women to utilize their strengths in challenging environments with those marginalised by poverty and violence. The Volunteers participate directly in agencies sponsored by the Sisters of the Good Shepherd and approach service with a focus on compassionate relationships. The program is inspired by the philosophy of the Sisters, and the life of Saint Mary Euphrasia, their foundress. Today the Good Shepherd Sisters are a truly global Catholic Congregation existing in over 67 countries worldwide. With non governmental status at the UN, and hundreds of active ministries throughout the world, they provide a needed service in the arena of human rights for women, children and families.

Sector: Child welfare, education, religious, women's issues.

Country: Latin America (Paraguay, Peru Mexico), North America (USA).

Qualif.: Part-time volunteer experience (helpful), awareness of human and social needs, high school graduate, college-educated or have 2 years work experience, maturity, flexibility, sense of humor, commitment to people.

Nonpro: Yes, with some college education and work experience.

Age: Minimum 21.

Duration: 1 year (US sites) or 2 years (international sites) renewable.

Lang.: Spanish for the programs in Latin America.

Benefits: Room and board, small stipend, medical insurance, deferred student loans, help with travel costs, supervision, workshops.

Costs: Fundraising of US$3,000-5,000 only for international programs.

Applic.: On-lne form. Applications are accepted on a rolling basis and site placements are in priority of application received.

Goodwill Community Center

PO Box 645
00902 Kikuyu Kenya
Tel.: ++254 (733) 877-804 or 063-2175 or (020) 272-3374
E-mail: goodwillkenya@yahoo.com

Desc.: Goodwill Community Centre is a rural based organisation situated at Kanjeru slum, Kikuyu west of Nairobi. The 3 programs are: childcare and support, HIV/Aids prevention and control, and socio-economic empowerment. Since 2001, free educational services to orphans and needy children from the slum and its environs have been offered. A fully fledged educational centre targeting orphans and the destitute is being established. Volunteers will have an opportunity to participate in the local culture and values; and interact with other poor communities in Kikuyu. While in the post, volunteers will learn from a mentor who will look after them during their stay.

Sector: Child welfare, community development, education.

Country: Africa (Kenya).

Qualif.: Skills in NGO and project planning and management, fundraising, and financial management and monitoring.

Nonpro.: Yes, with relevant skills.

Age: Minimum 18. No maximum age limit but must have physical ability to partake in occasional walking.

Duration: 3 months to 1 year. Placements can start throughout the year.

Lang.: English.

Benefits: No guaranteed food and accommodation.

Costs: US$15 per day to cover living expenses (food and accommodation). Optional single-time contribution of US$500.

Applic.: E-mail CV. References required by accepted volunteers.

Notes: Once accepted the applicant can request to be put in contact with former volunteers. Note that in the past only short time visitors from Kenya and abroad and not volunteers visited the project. Please see note on page 36.

Greenway International Workcamps

PO Box 21, Had Yai Airport, Had Yai, Songkhla 90115 Thailand
Tel.: ++66 (74) 473-506
Fax: ++66 (74) 473-508
E-mail: info@greenwaythailand.org
www.greenwaythailand.org

Desc.: All projects Greenway engages in are geared to alternative ways of thinking about environmental care, small-scale economical development, and sustainable growth. Greenway is an example of a local member organisation of CCIVS (see listing). The local member organisations are not branches of CCIVS, but the creators of the network of cooperation. The national organisations work mainly in their own countries and cooperate with each other by exchanging volunteers and meeting regularly so as to exchange experiences and new ideas, etc. In each workcamp, the national organisation cooperates with a local partner organisation.

Sector: Agriculture, construction, culture, education, environment, small-enterprise development.

Country: Asia (Thailand, China).

Qualif.: No particular skills required.

Nonpro: Yes.

Age: Minimum 18.

Duration: 14 days, and the participant stays for 1 or a few camps. Medium- to long-term positions are for those who prefer to stay 2 months or longer; sometimes a minimum period is requested for project reasons.

Lang.: English.

Benefits: Contact the organisation for details.

Costs: US$150 plus airfare.

Applic.: Send applications via a sending workcamp organisation in country of residence (see CCIVS for a complete list).

Notes: The organisation suggests places tom stay in Bangkok upon arrival before proceeding to the workcamp.

Habitat for Humanity International

Partner Service Center
121 Habitat Street, Americus, Georgia 31709 USA
Tel.: ++1 (229) 924-6935, ext. 2551 or 2552
(toll free in N. Am. 1-800-HABITAT ext. 2549)
E-mail: publicinfo@hfhi.org or VSD@habitat.org or gv@hfhi.org or .
www.habitat.org

Desc.: Habitat for Humanity International is a non-profit, ecumenical Christian housing ministry. Habitat for Humanity relies heavily on volunteers to carry out its mission around the world. Habitat "Global Village" short-term teams serve in international locations for 10 to 20 day periods.

Sector: Construction, housing.

Country: Over 80 countries in Africa, Asia, Caribbean, Europe, Latin America, Middle East, Oceania.

Qualif.: Some building skills are helpful, but team members work at the direction of local supervisors in a service-learning context

Nonpro: Yes.

Age: 18 for international programs. Students and school children can sometimes join 'home based' programs in their home country.

Duration: Habitat Global Village short-term trips last 10 to 20 days.

Lang.: Habitat Global Village trip leaders should speak the local language or budget for translators. No requirements for team members.

Benefits: Global Village short-term trip volunteers must bear all the costs of the trip.

Costs: Global Village Trips costs depend on destination and length of program. Fares below include international airfare, room and board, travel insurance, and a donation to the local affiliate. Many participants raise funds to pay their team fee by contacting local churches, civic groups, friends and family. Assistance is available on how to start a fundraising campaign. Costs per person are: Africa US$2,800—4,000; Asia and South America US$2,000—3,800; Central America and the Caribbean US$1,200—1,800; Europe US$1,800—2,800.

Applic.: To request more information, contact the Global Village department by mail, phone, or e-mail.

Notes: Travel, medical and evacuation insurance is required. Participants should be in good health. Work assignments normally require strenuous manual labour, sometimes at high altitudes. Habitat for Humanity Ghana is one example of a local chapter. It works in rural areas to build decent affordable housing for people in need in Ghana. Homeowners work to build their own home and the homes of others in the community. Repayment of the no profit, no interest loan in the form of building materials goes into a Revolving Fund for Humanity to build more houses. This revolving fund is maintained at the community to create a sustainable community based housing program. See www. habitatghana. org.

Heifer International

55 Heifer Rd
Perryville, Arkansas 72110 USA
Tel.: ++1 (501) 889-5124
Fax: ++1 (501) 889-1574
E-mail: ranchvol@heifer.org
www.heifer.org

Desc.: Heifer International provides livestock and training to small-scale farmers worldwide. Along with the gifts of livestock, Heifer helps communities develop sustainable agriculture while improving the environment and strengthening the community. Heifer International's education program increases understanding of issues related to hunger and poverty, and empowers and inspires people to take action to create a sustainable, socially just, economically viable, and environmentally sound world. Heifer International has three Learning Centers which offer a variety of experiences designed to fulfil that mission, while also serving as working examples of the type of sustainable agriculture supported around the world.

Sector: Agriculture, community development, education, environment.

Country: United States: at Learning Centers in California, Arkansas and Massachusetts.

Qualif.: Experience and education in relevant fields.

Nonpro.: No.

Age: Minimum Age 18

Duration: Enquire with the organisation.

Lang.: English.

Benefits: Housing and stipend

Costs: All expenses including travel, insurance, etc.

Applic.: Contact the organisation directly.

IBO – International Building Organization

St. Annastraat 172
6524 GT Nijmegen The Netherlands
Tel.: ++31 (24) 322-6074
Fax: ++31 (24) 322-6076
E-mail: info@bouworde.nl
www.bouworde.nl

Desc.: IBO aims to assist with the implementation of construction projects for people who need help, regardless of their race, nationality, or philosophy. Aid is provided by volunteers who do short-term manual work. The IBO wants to assist in creating conditions for real peace between people and nations by encouraging volunteers of different nationalities to work together and live with people in other countries. IBO's most important field of work is the improvement of the housing conditions of underprivileged people: homes for handicapped children, old people's homes, orphanages, and hostels for the homeless.

Sector: Construction, housing, human rights.

Country: Europe (Albania, Austria, Belgium, Bulgaria, Croatia, Czech Republic, Denmark, France, Germany, Hungary, Italy, Lithuania, Moldova, Netherlands, Poland, Portugal, Romania, Russia).

Qualif: No specific qualifications needed.

Nonpro: Yes.

Age: Minimum 18.

Duration: 3 weeks.

Lang.: English, German.

Benefits: Available accommodation or tents. Meals are usually prepared by the volunteers. IBO takes care of travel and insurance.

Costs: 40 hours per week without pay. Partial camp costs (about EUR100–300 depending on the country).

Applic.: Preferably via e-mail. Alternatively phone, write, or fax to request an application form.

ICYE – International Christian Youth Exchange

Große Hamburger Str. 30, D-10115
Berlin Germany
Tel.: ++49 (30) 2839-0550 or 2839-0551
Fax: ++49 (30) 28390552
E-mail : icye@icye.org
www.icye.org

Desc.: ICYE is a non-profit youth exchange organisation that offers opportunities to young people all over the world to spend a semester or a year living abroad with a family or host-project and being involved in voluntary service or attending school.

Sector: Agriculture, child welfare, community development, culture, education, environment, health, human rights, IT, refugee aid, small-enterprise development, women's issues.

Country: Africa (Ghana, Kenya, Morocco, Mozambique, Nigeria, Uganda), Asia (India, Japan, Nepal, South Korea, Taiwan, Thailand), Europe (Austria, Belgium, Denmark, Finland, France, Germany, Iceland, Italy, Lithuania, Norway, Sweden, Switzerland, Russian Federation, UK), Latin America (Bolivia, Brazil, Colombia, Costa Rica, Honduras, Mexico), Oceania (New Zealand).

Qualif.: N/A.

Nonpro: Yes.

Age: 16–25; 18–30 for some international projects.

Duration: 6 or 12 months; some 2–8 week projects available.

Lang.: English.

Benefits: In general no scholarship as the ICYE program is self-sustained. Possibility to join the EVS (see listing) program subsidised by the European Union.

Costs: Varies from country to country (consult website). Average 1-year fee is approximately US$5,000–6,000.

Applic.: After registration application forms are provided by respective ICYE National Committees (see website for addresses).

ICYE-UK – Inter-Cultural Youth Exchange

Latin American House, Kingsgate Place
London NW6 4TA UK
Tel.: ++44 (207) 681-0983
Fax: ++44 (207) 681-0983
E-mail: admin@icye.co.uk or development@icye.co.uk
www.icye.co.uk

Desc.: ICYE-UK aims to promote peace, cultural understanding, and youth empowerment through opportunities of international exchange and voluntary work overseas.

Sector: Agriculture, child welfare, community development, culture, education, environment, health, human rights, IT, refugee aid, small-enterprise development, women's issues, various.

Country: Africa (Ghana, Kenya, Morocco, Mozambique, Nigeria, Uganda), Asia (India, South Korea, Taiwan, Thailand, Japan), Europe (Future countries may include Morocco, Mozambique, Egypt, Turkey, Palestine), Latin America (Bolivia, Brazil, Colombia, Costa Rica, Honduras, Mexico), Oceania (New Zealand).

Qualif.: N/A.

Nonpro: Yes.

Age: 18–30.

Duration: 6–12 months.

Lang.: Language course offered in orientation month in host country.

Benefits: International travel costs, Visa, flights to and from host country, board and lodging, health insurance, host country orientation and language course, mid-year camp and final evaluation, support and supervision during the year, pocket money.

Costs: 12-month participation fee is GB£3,250 and the 6-months participation fee is GB£2,850. Fundraising support offered. European Voluntary Service placements are sponsored by the European Commission.

Notes: UK nationals only. For non-UK residents, please refer to ICYE International or EVS (see listing). Consult the ICYE website for contact details.

Interconnection

5215 Ballard Avenue NW, Suite 5
Seattle, Washington 98107 USA
Tel.: ++1 (206) 310-4547
Fax: ++1 (206) 297-0891
E-mail: info@interconnection.org
www.interconnection.org

Desc.: InterConnection provides professional, technology assistance to non-profit organisations (working in the areas of environmental preservation, human rights, and local economic development) in developing countries. The Virtual Volunteers work from home creating webpages for these organisations allowing them direct access to global markets (such as through on-line stores for displaying handmade crafts and materials) and international support (marketing assistance for community tourism projects and financial support). A WWW Volunteer is an independent volunteer, already travelling on his/her own trip who chooses to visit a non-profit to help them gather information for a website (text and photos). A Virtual Volunteer then uses it to create a website. Tech Corps Volunteers travel abroad and stay in local communities teaching people how to build and design their own websites. The Tech Corps Bulletin Board lists projects that need on-site technicians to provide computer and internet instruction.

Sector: IT.
Country: Worldwide.
Qualif.: Web design, technical expertise, computer skills, etc.
Nonpro: Yes, with relevant skills.
Age: N/A with necessary experience.
Duration: Up to 3 months for Tech Corps Volunteers.
Lang: Varies with each organisation.
Benefits: Tech Corps volunteers receive food and lodging.
Costs: All costs born by the volunteer (except Tech Corps benefits as stated above).
Applic.: On-line form.

International Executive Service Corps

901 15th St NW, Suite 350
Washington, DC 20005 USA
Tel.: ++1 (202) 326-0280
Fax: ++1 (202) 325-0289
E-mail: iesc@iesc.org
www.iesc.org

Desc.: Volunteer experts work in dozens of countries around the world transferring their knowledge and skills to assist entrepreneurs, small and medium-sized businesses, NGO's, trade associations, and business support organizations in the developing world and emerging democracies. Volunteers are committed to promoting free enterprise and democracy by assisting, instructing, and inspiring people, businesses and organizations around the world.

Sector: Agriculture, IT, skills training, small-enterprise development, various.

Country: Various countires in Africa, Asia, the Caribbean, Europe, Latin America and the Middle East.

Qualif.: At least 10 years experience in a professional field. Volunteers with experience in tourism, food processing and agribusiness, are in great demand. Computers skills are very important.

Nonpro: Yes.

Age: Variable.

Duration: 1week to several months.

Lang.: English. Foreign language not required but helpful.

Benefits: Airfare and specified travel related expenses, such as immunizations and Visas, are covered. Volunteers receive a per diem set by the federal government for meals and housing.

Costs: Contact organization for more information.

Applic.: On-line form through our website: www.iesc.org

International Medical Corps

International Medical Corps,
1919 Santa Monica Blvd., Suite 300,
Santa Monica, CA 90404, USA.
Tel.: ++1 (310) 826-7800
Fax: ++1 (310) 442-6622
www.imcworldgroup.org

Desc.: International Medical Corps is a global, humanitarian non-profit organization dedicated to saving lives and relieving suffering by providing health-care training and medical-relief programmes worldwide. IMC is a private, non-political, non-profit, non-sectarian organization with the organizational flexibility to respond rapidly to emergency situations. IMC's mission is to improve the quality of life through health interventions and related activities that build local capacity.

Sector: Child welfare, emergency, health, sanitation, women's issues,

Country: Africa (Angola, Burundi, Chad, DRC, Eritrea, Ethiopia, Kenya, Liberia, Sierra Leone, Somalia, Sudan, Tanzania, Uganda), Asia (Afghanistan, Azerbaijan, Indonesia, Pakistan), Europe (Georgia, Russia).

Qualif.:: Qualifications preferred: physicians, registered nurses, psychosocial advisors, emergency medicine personnel, public health, country program directors, finance officers, nurse practitioners, logistics and administrative specialists.

Nonpro.: No. Volunteers with professional qualifications (licensed with International or Emergency Medical experience) only.

Duration: Minimum 3 months; paid positions minimum 6-months.

Lang.: English, French, Arabic.

Benefits: Medical evacuation, health insurance, shared housing.

Costs: Inquire with organisation for details.

Applic.: Submit CV on-line. No telephone calls.

Notes: Minority group members, women, and disabled individuals are actively recruited and hired as part of the commitment to equal opportunity employment. Positions are open to qualified professionals of any nationality.

International Mountain Explorers Connection

Volunteer Nepal Himalaya
PO Box 3665, Boulder, Colorado 80307-3665 USA
Tel.: ++1 (303) 998-0101
Fax: ++1 (303) 998-1007
E-mail: info@hec.org
www.hec.org

Desc.: Volunteer Nepal Himalaya offers participants a unique opportunity to volunteer in a local Sherpa village in the Himalayas. Participants spend 10 days in Kathmandu, doing an orientation in Nepali language and culture. Volunteers then fly to Lukla, the gateway to the Khumbu region of Nepal, and teach English in a Sherpa school for 3 months (while living with a family). While not teaching, volunteers may stay in the village or explore the trails and villages of the Khumbu region.

Sector: Culture, education, environment.

Country: Asia (Nepal).

Qualif.: No professional qualifications needed.

Nonpro: Yes the program is open to anyone with sufficient motivation.

Age: Minimum 18.

Duration: 8–16 weeks.

Lang.: English. Local language instruction provided.

Benefits: Travel in host country, accommodation (home-stay with local family), food, tourist excursions, staff support.

Costs: US$1,000. Additional costs include airfare to Nepal, program books/tapes (US$50), membership (US$30), immunisations, flight to Phaplu (US$170 roundtrip), hotels, meals in Kathmandu and Phaplu during the orientation (about US$15 per day), language/teacher training in Kathmandu and Phaplu (US$100), 60-day entry Visa in Nepal obtained at airport (US$30), 2, 1-month Visa extensions (US$100), home-stay in village, including all meals (US$120 per month), miscellaneous (US$50 per month), medical and evacuation insurance (US$110).

Applic.: Written application followed by a telephone interview. Processing time is 1 month to 1 year, but typically 4–6 months.

International Partnership for Service Learning and Leadership

815 Second Avenue, Suite 315
New York, New York 10017-4594 USA
Tel.: ++1 (212) 986-0989
Fax: ++1 (212) 986-5039
E-mail: info@ipsl.org   www.ipsl.org

Desc.: The International Partnership for Service-Learning and Leadership was founded in 1982 to promote a new pedagogy for higher education based on the ideals of service-learning and to develop programs that put these ideals into practice. All projects are locally-established and based and serve the local community. Service agencies are schools, orphanages, recreation, health, or education centres, community development projects, museums, and cultural centres, etc. A typical day, in most programs, consists of some time spent with the host family, attending class, doing assignments, serving in the agency, and also having free time to participate in day to day activities. There is usually time for field trips in the local area or for participating in special events on the weekend.

Sector: Child welfare, community development, construction, education, emergency, environment, health, housing, human rights, small-enterprise development, women's issues, various.

Country: Asia (India, Philippines, Thailand), Caribbean (Jamaica), Europe (Czech Republic, England, France, Russia, Scotland), Latin America (Ecuador, Mexico), Middle East (Israel), North America (South Dakota, USA).

Qualif.: No specific skills required.

Nonpro: Yes, with high school education.

Age: Minimum 18.

Duration: 3–52 weeks, typically 15. Programs are 3 weeks (in India only), 8–10 weeks (summer), or 3–4 months (semester long). The majority of students serve for a semester and some serve for the summer. There are some undergraduates who serve 1 year. Students in the MA program serve 1 year. (Semester 1: Jamaica or Mexico; Semester 2: London, England).

Lang.: English, Spanish, or French, depending on country. Spanish and French require at least 2 years high school or 1 year college background. English requires fluency.

Benefits:The costs (below) include instruction, administration fees, service placement and supervision, orientation, and accommodation (group or home-stay), meals (except for the Israel and Scotland programs), in-country travel, tourist excursions, staff support. Academic credit is available. Scholarships are available. The first 1 or 2 weeks of the program may be devoted to orientation.

Costs: US$3,700—32,400. Program cost per semester is US$8,700—11,200. The costs for the summer programs range between US$3,700—11,000. Students are responsible for airfare, books, spending money, local travel, Visas, and health insurance. The India program cost US$11,000 for the semester and US$11,000 for the 3-week programs in January and August. Both these costs include airfare. Master's Program: the year-long Masters Degree program in International Service costs US$26,900 plus US$5,500 for room and board for both semesters and thesis period.

Applic.: Written application, letters of reference, health records, and transcripts.

Notes: A physical exam will be required.

International Relief Friendship Foundation
307, rue de Rollingergrund L-1241 Luxembourg
Tel.: ++352 (21) 744-973
Fax: ++352 (21) 220-066
E-mail: Luxembourg@irff-europe.org or irffeu@yahoo.com
www.irff-europe.org or www.irff.org

Desc.: The Foundation aims to relieve poverty, suffering, and disease through projects under its direction by providing financial and other humanitarian aid to the poor, aged, disabled, or otherwise unfortunate people of the world, and charitable associations or institutions that further the same purpose. They conduct research projects, hold lectures, publish appropriate materials, and convene conferences and conventions on a national and international scale that further this vision and world peace.

Sector: Agriculture, child welfare, community development, education, environment, health, hunger relief.

Country: Africa (Cameroon, Ivory Coast, Kenya, Uganda, Zambia), Asia (India, Philippines), Europe (Albania, Austria, Bosnia-Herz, Croatia, Czech Republic, Germany, Italy, France, Hungary, Luxembourg, Romania, Spain, Slovakia, Slovenia, Switzerland, UK and Bulgaria).

Qualif.: Desired for teams leaders and families volunteers.

Nonpro: Yes. Some experience in volunteering will help.

Age: For youth programs minimum age: 18. Under 18 years permission from the parent-responsible person will be required. Age 18—30 for youth volunteer camps. Families with children accepted for the "Family and Service" projects.

Duration: Youth camps 1–3 weeks, family 9 days. Long-term available.

Lang.: English.

Benefits: Room and board. Some scholarships for youths available.

Costs: Airfare, registration/application fee US$300—450, depending on the projects; local volunteers fee reduced to US$ 100-20.

Applic.: On-line form. Some project requires a cover letter and CV. See website for local chapters and recruitment information.

International Volunteer Program

678 13th Street Suite 100
Oakland, California 94612 USA
Tel.: ++1 (510) 433-0414 (Toll free: 1-866-614-3438)
Fax: ++1 (510) 433-0419
E-mail: cynthia@swiftusa.org
www.ivpsf.org or www.frenchfoundation.com)

Desc.: The International Volunteer program (IVP) is a non-profit organization that promotes volunteering in Europe, the United States and Latin America. Programs are designed to facilitate hands-on service opportunities, with the aim of fostering cultural understanding and philanthropy at a local and global level. Participants work full-time in non-profit organizations while equipping themselves for effective citizenship. IVP volunteers work on a variety of projects in the areas of social justice, arts and culture, and the environment.

Sector: Child welfare, community development, culture, environment, health, human rights, various.

Country: Europe (UK, France, Spain), Latin America (Costa Rica) North America (USA).

Qualif.: No particular qualifications required.

Nonpro: Yes.

Age: Minimum 18. No upper age limit.

Duration: 6–8 weeks; typically 8.

Lang.: English, French, Spanish.

Benefits: In-country transportation, accommodation and meals with host families. In-country and pre-departure training/ orientation. Comprehensive health/accident/civic liability and repatriation
insurance. Language and training (Costa Rica Program)

Costs: Varies with program. See website for details.

Applic.: IVP admits volunteers after an application process that includes a written application, letters of reference, CV, and a phone interview. IVP candidates must be flexible, open-minded and demonstrate a strong commitment to helping others.

International Youth Link Foundation

Global Operations Centre
5th Floor, 44-46 Wimbourne Road, Poole, Dorset BH15 2BY UK
Tel: ++44 (1202) 666-078;
Volunteers/Internship Hotlines ++44 (7960) 225-370/ 575-627
Fax: ++44 (1202) 666-078
E-mail: iylf@yahoo.com   www.youthlinknet.org

Desc: The mission statement is to improve the living conditions of unemployed youth to comply with UN declarations and conventions on the rights of the child. Utilising self-efforts for wealth creation, peace building, and combating crime, volunteers work for the advancement and development of youth. They are involved in education, conservation, office work, or community services. Educators teach either young children or secondary/high school students, or they offer Therapeutic Counselling for university/college students. University Lecturers may have an exchange placement to a different university for 1–2 months. Conservation volunteers are groups of up to 10 stationed in a national park, game reserve, or coastal region to work on endangered species protection and collect scientific data. IYLF office volunteers help run the regional office and support with fundraising activities for the selected country or region.

Sector: Child welfare, community development, education, environment.

Country: Africa (Ghana), Asia, South America.

Qualif.: Educators, psychologists. Groups are welcome for conservation volunteering.

Nonpro: Yes. Volunteers with no experience are often accepted.

Age: Minimum 18.

Duration: Range from 6 months, subject to renewal.

Lang.: English.

Benefits: If possible volunteers will receive lodging.

Costs: Travel, food, personal expenses, and possibly lodging.

Applic.: On-line form.

i-to-i World Vision UK
Woodside House, 261 Low Lane, Leeds LS18 5NY UK
Tel.: ++44 (870) 333 2332
Fax: +44 (113) 205 4618
E-mail: info@i-to-i.com
Website: www.i-to-i.com

Desc.: i-to-i is an award-winning volunteer travel and TEFL training organisation. i-to-i arranges work placements for over 3,000 volunteers a year and trains a further 4,000 people worldwide to Teach English as a Foreign Language on Weekend and Online TEFL Courses. i-to-i volunteers are of all ages, nationalities and backgrounds and support the work of a number of NGOs worldwide, including Save the Children, Habitat for Humanity and Plan International, as well as government schemes and independent development projects. i-to-i volunteer projects have been recognised by the Variety Club Children's Charity in the UK, and the WWF 'Nedbank Green Trust Awards' in South Africa (2003 Winner 'Best Emerging Conservation Project'). There are 6,000 i-to-i work placements available in total every year, in 25 countries. i-to-i's TEFL qualification is also recognised worldwide and has trained 12,000 people in teaching English since 1994. In 2004, i-to-i celebrates ten years of volunteer travel and TEFL training.

Sector: Agriculture, child welfare, community development, construction, culture, education, environment, health, housing, human rights, refugee aid, small-enterprise development, various.

Country: Africa (Ghana, Kenya, South Africa, Tanzania), Asia (Cambodia, China, India, Korea, Mongolia, Nepal, Sri Lanka, Thailand, Vietnam), Latin America (Bolivia, Brazil, Costa Rica, Dominican Republic, Ecuador, El Salvador, Guatemala, Honduras, Peru), Europe (Croatia, Ireland) Oceania (Australia).

Qualif.: No formal qualifications are required to join i-to-i volunteer placements or TEFL courses, just fluent English. Business/media placements require a CV/resume in advance. Professional (non-volunteer) teaching placements in South Korea require a degree.

Nonpro: Yes. See above.

Age: 18-80.

Duration: 1 week to 6 months. Projects are extendable indefinitely and can also be combined between locations.

Lang.: All volunteers need English. Those travelling to Latin America should also know Spanish (advanced Spanish for some projects), and Spanish training is provided in the first orientation week. i-to-i also offers Weekend Spanish Courses in the UK.

Benefits: Detailed information on project and country, fundraising advice and support, visa instructions and forms, vaccination and inoculation recommendations, CD-ROM with advice on health & safety & culture shock, contact details to pass along to those at home, pick-up from the airport on the designated arrival date, welcome orientation, regularly-inspected accommodation, meals provided or self-catering accommodation (in most cases), a well-researched placement, comprehensive insurance policy, access to an emergency support team 24/7, assistance of the global i-to-i staff, guidance and advice from experienced i-to-i travellers.

Costs: GB£495—1,895 depending on the destination and length of placement. South Korea Teaching placements come with a salary of GB£800-1,000 a month.

Applic.: Apply online at i-to-i.com or phone your nearest i-to-i office.

Notes: i-to-i has three main offices worldwide: in the UK (0870 333 2332, uk@i-to-i.com), the US (1-800-985-4864, usa@i-to-i.com or canada@i-to-i.com) and Ireland (058 40050, ireland@i-to-i.com).

IVDN – Interactive Voluntary Development Service

PO Box 5671
80401 Diani Beach, Mombasa Kenya.
Tel.: ++254 (721) 393-347
Fax: ++254 (40) 320-2106
E-mail : info@intvolnetorg.org
www.intvolnetorg.org

Desc.: Volunteers are able to work in rural and marginalised areas in orphanages, children's homes, community health centres, hospitals, and community based organisations projects. A variety of skills are also needed to help build the organisations. The volunteer positions provide a unique opportunity for visitors to participate in the local culture and better understand the values of the people of the region. Volunteers will learn from a mentor who will look after them during their stay.

Sector: Child welfare, community development, culture, education, health, skills training, various.

Country: Africa (Kenya).

Qualif.: No particular skills required but initiative and adaptability are important requisites.

Nonpro.: Yes.

Age: Minimum 18.

Duration: 2 weeks to 1 year.

Lang.: English.

Benefits: Accommodation and food.

Costs: EUR250 for 3 weeks to cover living expenses.

Applic.: E-mail CV.

Notes: Once accepted the applicant can request to be put in contact with former volunteers. Please see note on page 36.

IVS – International Voluntary Service

IVS UK South
Old Hall, East Bergholt, Colchester CO7 6TQ UK
Tel.: ++44 (1206) 298-215
Fax: ++44 (1206) 299-043
E-mail: ivs@ivsgbsouth.demon.co.uk
www.ivs-gb.org.uk

Desc.: The International Voluntary Service is the British branch of SCI (see listing), a peace movement that was founded in the aftermath of the first world war. IVS organises workcamps in Britain and sends volunteers to over 40 countries throughout the world. IVS is a voluntary NGO that aims to promote international understanding and peace. It provides volunteers for projects in the United States and Europe for communities needing volunteer help.

Sector: Child welfare, construction, education, environment, refugee aid.

Country: Africa (Morocco, Tunisia), Europe (all Western Europe, Baltic Republics, former Yugoslavia, Greenland, Russia, Armenia, Latvia, Lithuania, Ukraine), Middle East (Palestine, Turkey), North America (USA).

Qualif.: No particular qualifications needed.

Nonpro: Yes.

Age: Minimum 21, for some countries, most programs accept volunteers from 18.

Duration: 1–4 weeks; a few longer term posts available.

Lang.: English. For other languages, inquire with local IVS office.

Benefits: Accommodation, food, insurance.

Cost: Workcamp registration fee plus IVS membership (GB£40–125 depending on destination) and travel costs.

Applic.: See website for nearest office. No need to be a member.

Notes: Only 2 volunteers from the same country per project.
IVS UK South: ivs@ivsgbsouth.demon.co.uk
IVS UK North: ivsgbn@ivsgbn.demon.co.u
IVS Scotland: ivs@ivsgbscot.demon.co.uk
IVS Northern Ireland: colin@ivsni.co.uk

Jesuit Refugee Service

Borgo S. Spirito 4, 00193 Rome Italy
Tel.: ++39 (06) 6897-7386
Fax: ++39 (06) 6880 6418
E-mail: international@jrs.net
www.jrs.net

Desc.: The Jesuit Refugee Service is an international Catholic organisation, active in more than 60 countries. Its mission is to accompany, serve, and defend the rights of refugees and displaced people. The mission includes all those who have been displaced form their homes because of conflicts of war, tragedy, and violations of human rights. The services include educational programs for children, teenagers, and adults, pastoral guidance, small economic activities, advocacy, social services, and health counselling and assistance.

Sector: Education, emergency, human rights, refugee aid, skills training.

Country: Over 60 countries; on every continent.

Qualif.: Social workers, skills trainers, educators, medical doctors, administrators, and project coordinators are desired.

Nonpro: No. Skilled personnel only and preferably with experience in emergency and/or conflict situations.

Age: Generally not under 25; exceptions based upon experience.

Duration: 2-year standard contract.

Lang.: English, plus the official language of country of placement.

Benefits: Round-trip travel, food, accommodation, insurance, contribution towards personal expenses (varies with country of placement).

Costs: None.

Applic.: Send CV via post, fax, or e-mail to christine.anderson@jrs.net. Apply only to a specific placement posted on the website. An e-mail newsletter posts available positions.

Notes: Volunteers must share and respect the mission and vision that underlies the organisation's philosophy.

Joint Assistance Centre, Inc.
PO Box 6082
San Pablo, California 94806 USA
Tel.: ++1 (510) 464-1100
Fax: ++1 (510) 217-6671
E-mail: jacusa@juno.com
www.jacusa.org

Desc.: Joint Assistance Centre is a voluntary group based in the USA. It works with various non-governmental organizations in India, Nepal and Bangladesh.. Most programs involve working with villagers in cooperation with non-governmental and community based organisations devoted to their welfare.

Sector: Agriculture, child welfare, community development, construction, education, environment, health, sanitation, women's issues.

Country: Asia (India, Nepal and Bangadlesh).

Qualif.: No particular qualifications needed.

Nonpro: Yes, with high school education.

Age: Minimum 18.

Duration: Short-term projects are 1–4 weeks; long-term projects are from 3 months.

Lang.: English. Long-term volunteers should be prepared to learn some basic Hindi or Nepali languages, preferably before arriving or can take a quick refresher course on arrival.

Benefits: Accommodation (group or home-stay), food, staff support, airport pick-up.

Costs: Application registration fee of US$50, short-term work camp programs are US$300 for 1 month, additional costs per month are US$150. Long-term placements cost US$500 for 3 months and US$125 per additional month.

Applic.: On-line form, letters of reference, telephone interview. Processing time from 4-6 weeks (typically 3 weeks).

Notes: Individual medical insurance coverage should be obtained before departure. Processing time may be longer if physically handicapped.

Kibbutz Program Center – Takam-Artzi

Hashomer Hatzair
18 Frishman Street/cr.
Ben Yehuda, Tel-Aviv 61030 Israel
Tel.: ++972 (3) 527-8874 or 524-6156
Fax: ++972 (3) 523-9966
E-mail: kpc@volunteers.co.il   www.kibbutz.org

Desc.:   Although Israel can not be considered a developing country the kibbutz movement has been an example of the success of voluntering and communal life. After the Six-Day War in 1967, a wave of volunteers from all over the world began arriving in Israel. Their intentions were to show their goodwill towards the State of Israel and the Israeli People by becoming kibbutz volunteers. The notion of a kibbutz community carrying out the true principles of a socialistic society, having all work, property, and profit equally shared by its members, intrigued the volunteers. The volunteers work 8 hours a day, 6 days a week. The agricultural work branches in the kibbutz are very varied. The work includes fruit picking, working in greenhouses, with irrigation systems, in fisheries, in chicken and turkey houses and egg incubators, and with cows and diaries. The work in tourism includes helping out in guest houses, restaurants, nature sights, health spas, and tourist shops. The services include work in the kitchen, the dinning room, and in the laundry. Sometimes the volunteers work in the metal workshop, the children's zoo, the children's houses, or help in the kibbutz industry and in any other service related work branch in the kibbutz. The Kibbutz Program Center of the United Kibbutz Movement and the Kibbutz Haartzi is the office officially representing all the approximately 250 kibbutzes spread throughout the country of Israel. Since 1967, more than 100,000 kibbutz volunteers have arrived in Israel to participate in this experience.

Sector: Agriculture, various.

Country: Middle East (Israel).

Qualif.: None. Volunteers with specific professions or trades can be placed where their skills can be used.

Nonpro: Yes.

Age: 18-35.

Duration: 2-6 months.

Lang.: English, Hebrew.

Benefits: Accommodations (rooms with between 2-4 people in each room), food, laundry service, pocket money each month (approx. US$80), tourist expeditions. The volunteers are free to use the sports facilities of the kibbutz and the swimming pool. In most kibbutzes, a pub and even a disco is arranged for the volunteers and the younger population. Each month the volunteers are given 3 free days.

Costs: International travel, Visas ($17 for 3 months), insurance (US$55), registration fee (US$100, valid for 1 year; there is no extra charge for transferring between kibbutzes), a US$50-100 security deposit that is returned to the volunteers after 2 months in the kibbutz, minimum US$250 personal funds.

Applic.: Contact a kibbutz representative in country of residence (see website for contacts) or register directly through the Kibbutz Program Center via e-mail or fax including name, a short bio, age, passport number and nationality, date of birth, and date of arrival. Volunteers with specific requests must apply at least 6 weeks in advance stating their job, education, and experience. Volunteers must bring a valid passport, a medical certificate, a return ticket, and at least US$250 (not to be paid to the kibbutz, but the volunteer must prove they have some personal funds).

Note: Upon arrival (especially in the busy seasons) there is no guaranty of being placed on a kibbutz immediately. Volunteers may have to wait a few days in a hostel for a free place in a kibbutz.

MADRE – International Women's Human Rights Organization

121 West 27th Street, Room 301, New York, New York 10001 USA
Tel.: ++1 (212) 627-0444
Fax: ++1 (212) 675-3704
E-mail: volunteers@madre.org
www.madre.org

Desc.: Since 1983, MADRE has worked in partnership with community-based women's organisations in conflict areas worldwide to address women's issues through training, emergency shipments of food, medicine and other material aid, human rights, and international law. MADRE educates and mobilizes its members in the US to demand alternatives to unjust and destructive US policies. Based on the priorities of the women with whom it works, MADRE provides resources and training for sister organisations and develops programs to meet immediate needs in communities hurt by US policy and supports women's long-term struggles for social justice and human rights.

Sector: Child welfare, community development, education, health, human rights, hunger relief, small-enterprise development.

Country: Africa (Kenya), Latin America (Mexico, Guatemala, Nicaragua, Peru).

Qualif.: Credentials and experience in the relevant field of work.

Nonpro: Yes, with skills relevant to the project.

Age: N/A with necessary experience.

Duration: Enquire with organisation.

Lang.: Spanish (except for Kenya), English.

Benefits: Enquire with organisation.

Costs: Volunteers cover their own travel costs.

Applic.: Contact the organisation directly.

Notes: MADRE leads "Voyages with a Vision" delegations to some of the countries in which their programs are based. All travel with MADRE is done with experienced guides, and translation is provided. Contact MADRE for specific information on trips.

Makindu Children's Center

Makindu Children's Program
PO Box 335, Brownsville, Oregon 97327 USA
Tel./Fax: ++1 (541) 466-5521
E-mail: makindu@peak.org
www.makindu.org

Desc.: The Makindu Children's Center is a charitable, community-based organisation in Makindu town, eastern province of Kenya. It serves the basic needs (nutrition, affection, basic medical care and access to housing) of approximately 100 destitute orphans within the region. The children and their families served are amongst the most in need in this impoverished area—those with no other source of aid. Typically the orphans live with elderly grandparents or distant relatives, within 1–8 km walk to the Center. The program is a day resource facility, where the children come for food, washing and laundering facilities, and emotional support and crisis intervention. Their medical concerns are attended to and access to the local educational system is provided. Members of the community can come to the resource center and receive training in survival and vocational skills, guidance on various health (e.g., HIV/AIDS) and nutritional and agricultural concerns (solar cooking and vocational education). Other projects include a shamba (farm), which provides a good portion of the food as well as produce for sale, bee-keeping for the production and sale of honey, and multiple craft items such as hand-made baskets for marketing and income generation. In 2002-2003 the program has built a water system which allows potable water from a nearby spring to be delivered and distributed to the Center and a large portion of Makindu residents. Recently, the Makindu Children's Program has expanded its AIDS project, and began a voluntary counseling and testing center for HIV, where youth and adults can come and receive free counseling, testing, and referral services.

Sector: Agriculture, child welfare, community development, education, environment, health, human rights, sanitation, small-enterprise development, women's issues, various.

Country: Africa (Kenya).

Qualif.: Core Volunteers do not need any particular qualification. Special Project Volunteers include a Shamba Farm Manager, a Beekeeper, a Makindu Regional Water Project Facilitator, and a Marketing Developer (for crafts, honey, etc.). Well-qualified medical volunteers can sometimes be placed at the Makindu-town Medical Clinic.

Nonpro: Yes, with strong skills such as communication, patience, flexibility, compassion, sense of humour, openness to cultural diversity.

Age: Minimum 21.

Duration: Core Volunteers stay from 3–6 months; Special Volunteers' duration is negotiable.

Lang.: Kiswahili, English, and Kikamba

Benefits: None.

Costs: There is no fee for volunteering, but volunteers bear virtually all of their own costs, including immunizations, travel, a required Kenyan work permit and bond (US$275–450 depending on length of stay), room and board (about US$20 per week).

Applic.: After contacts via e-mail and telephone, volunteers are required to come to Brownsville, Oregon, or to Kenya, at their own expense, for a personal interview prior to final selection.

Notes: A health clearance and a criminal record check are required. Prior third world volunteer or work experience is highly desirable.

MedAir

Chemin du Croset 9, CH-1024
Ecublens Switzerland
Tel.: ++41 (21) 694-3535
Fax: ++41 (21) 694-3540
E-mail : info@medair.org
www.medair.org

Desc.: MEDAIR is an international humanitarian aid agency based in Switzerland (with national offices in France, the Netherlands, and the UK). It provides emergency relief in underprivileged developing countries affected by war or natural disaster where crisis situations threaten to further undermine their future development and stability.

Sector: Child welfare, construction, emergency, health, housing, hunger relief, sanitation.

Country: Africa (Congo, Mozambique, Sudan, Uganda), Asia (Afghanistan, India), Europe (Kosovo).

Qualif.: Manager, administrator, health professional, water technician, logistician, shelter coordinator.

Nonpro: Occasionally recruits work alongside experienced field staff to become trained as professional relief workers.

Age: 21–55.

Duration: 6 months minimum.

Lang.: English, some positions need French.

Benefits: Medical insurance, local food, lodging, transport, US$100 per month and other project related costs. After the first year the pay increases, starting from US$1,000 per month.

Costs: For the first assignment volunteers have to pay for return flights. Seminar (see notes) costs EUR 500 (approx. US$450, GB£300) plus EUR30 (US$28, GB£20) for registration.

Applic.: E-mail CV to the nearest office: Switzerland, UK, France, or Netherlands. See website for contacts.

Notes: Christians in good health, married or single without children. All candidates must attend a 10-day seminar in Switzerland (held 3 times per year) and have a personal interview.

Mission Discovery

PO Box 612
Goodlettsville, Tennessee 37070 USA
Tel.: ++1 (615) 851-0088 (toll free in N. Am. 1-800-767-8720)
Fax: ++1 (615) 859-4411
E-mail: projects@missiondiscovery.org
www.missiondiscovery.org

Desc.: Mission Discovery began in 1991 as an effort to combine the mission resources of churches around the United States to meet the physical and spiritual needs of the world's poor through short-term team mission projects. Since Mission Discovery's beginning over 20,000 students and adults have served in Mexico, Jamaica, Nassau, Honduras, Tennessee, Missouri and Homestead, Florida, building homes and churches and sharing the gospel with hundreds.

Sector: Child welfare, construction, housing, religious.

Country: Caribbean (Jamaica, Haiti, Bahamas), Latin America (Mexico, Honduras).

Qualif.: Nurses, doctors, Spanish translators, bus-drivers.

Nonpro: Yes.

Age: Youth and adult programs are available.

Duration: 1 week to 1 month.

Lang.: English, Spanish.

Benefits: Enquire with organisation.

Costs: US$175–500, depending on country and duration.

Applic.: US$55 registration fee due 30 days after sign-up. Late registration is an additional US$20.

Mission Doctors/Lay Mission Helpers Associations

3424 Wilshire Blvd., Los Angeles, California 90010 USA

Tel.: ++1 (213) 368-1875 (MDA)

++1 (213) 368-1870 (LMH)

Fax: ++1 (213) 368-1871

E-mail: missiondrs@earthlink.net or info@laymissionhelpers.org

www.missiondoctors.org or www.laymissionhelpers.org

Desc.: Mission Doctors Association is a lay Catholic organisation. The formation program the physicians take part in, includes theology, mission culture, and Catholic social doctrine. The diocesan Bishop and religious orders administer the hospitals served, therefore, the first requirement is that physicians are practicing Catholics. The Lay Mission-Helpers support the work of all other professionals - medical and non-medical.

Sector: Health.

Country: Africa (Cameroon, Ghana, Kenya, Zimbabwe), Oceania (Micronesia, Samoa), Latin America (Guatemala, Ecuador).

Qualif.: Medical doctors with completed residency. Also teachers, nurses, social workers, agronomists, or people with technical, agricultural or technical skills (Lay Mission Helpers).

Nonpro: Yes, with college degree or needed skills (Lay Mission Helpers).

Age: Minimum 21; maximum 65 (can be extended if self-insured).

Duration: Two programs for physicians - 3 years, or 1 – 3 months. LMH – only 3-year program.

Lang.: Training provided for long term.

Benefits: Long-term and short term: room and board provided by site. L-term lay missionaries: travel, living expenses, and stipend.

Costs: Personal expenses.

Applic.: On-line form. Discernment weekend in Los Angeles; 4-month training program in Los Angeles. Lay mission applicants also submit a Preliminary Form, a written application, and letters of recommendation; participate in a discernment weekend; pass an interview; take a psychological interview, tests, and a medical exam; and be approved by the Admissions Team.

Notes: Practicing Catholics and US citizens only.

Mondo Challenge

Galliford Building, Milton Malsor, Norhampton NN7 3AB UK
Tel.: ++44 (1604) 858-225
Fax: ++44 (1604) 859-323
E-mail: info@mondoChallenge.org
www.mondoChallenge.org

Desc.: MondoChallenge is a not for profit organisation which sends volunteers (students, professionals, early retired, etc.) to help with development programmes in Africa, Asia and South America. Our programmes are community based providing our volunteers with a unique insight into the local culture and giving them the ability to understand and learn from the values of the community they are working with.· The normal stay is from 2-4 months and start dates are flexible.

Sector: Child welfare, community development, education, health, small-enterprise development, women's issues.

Country: Africa (Tanzania, Kenya, The Gambia), Asia (India, Nepal, Sri Lanka), Latin America (Chile).

Qualif: For many programmes, no specific qualifications are needed. Business development and healthcare projects require specific skills which can be discussed. Enthusiasm, adaptability, initiative and cultural awareness are all important requisites.

Age: 19-65. The average age of volunteers is 27.

Duration: 3-6 months.

Lang.: English.

Benefits: Pre-Departure briefing, in-country management support, accommodation, organised events, post-placement debriefing, evaluation, alumni network.

Costs: GB£800 contribution for a 3-month placement.

Applic.: Written application, references, interview (also by phone).

Notes: Couples and families are welcome and receive a 10% discount (this also applies to friends travelling together). Approximately 50% of volunteers are non-UK based, with a large number of volunteers from North America, Europe and Australia.

158

MS – Mellemfolkeligt Samvirke

Danish Association for International Co-operation
Borgergade 14, 1300 Copenhagen Denmark
Tel.: ++(45) 7731-0000
Fax: ++(45) 7731-0101 or 7731-0111 or 7731-0121
E-mail: ms@ms-dan.dk
www.ms-dan.dk

Desc.: MS is a Danish members' organisation combining development assistance with both political and grass-root action. Their goal is to fight poverty by means of practical development assistance as well as political efforts, mostly by posting Danish development workers with local partners.

Sector: Agriculture, community development, environment, health, human rights, various.

Country: Africa (Kenya, Lesotho, Mozambique, Tanzania, South Africa, Swaziland, Uganda, Zambia, Zimbabwe), Asia (Nepal), Latin America (El Salvador, Nicaragua).

Qualif.: Farmers and/or agronomists, foresters, teachers, journalists, social workers, accountants, etc.

Nonpro: Long-term development workers require a relevant education and 1-2 years of working experience.

Age: Minimum 22 for long-term development workers.

Duration: Long-term (1-5 years); short-term(3-12 months).

Lang.: Danish, good knowledge of English. If applying for a job in Mozambique or Central America knowledge of Portuguese and/or Spanish is an advantage.

Benefits: Travel expenses, local transportation, and regular living expenses such as housing, etc. Volunteers receive a fee to ensure living conditions as in Denmark. Some projects provide expenses to travel, housing, and insurance coverage, and a stipend DKK3,500 (US$580/EUR 470/GB£320) per month.

Costs: Personal expenses.

Applic.: Contact the organisation to verify eligibility.

Notes: MS Travels runs study-work trips and workcamps: see www.mstravels.dk (only in Danish).

MSF – Médecins Sans Frontières

MSF International Office
Rue de la Tourelle 39, 1040 Brussels Belgium
Tel.: ++32 (2) 280-1881
Fax: ++32 (2) 280-0173
www.msf.org
(See e-mail contacts of national offices on www.msf.org)

Desc.: MSF provides emergency medical assistance to populations in danger in countries where health structures are insufficient or non-existent. MSF collaborates with authorities such as the Ministry of Health to rebuild health structures to acceptable levels. MSF works in rehabilitation of hospitals and dispensaries, vaccination programs, and water and sanitation projects. MSF also works in remote healthcare centres and slum areas and provides training of local personnel. More than 2,500 volunteers of 45 nationalities have volunteered for MSF projects. MSF was awarded the Nobel Price for Peace in 1999.

Sector: Emergency, health, refugee aid.

Country: 80 countries in 5 continents.

Qualif.: Health professionals (general practice doctors, nurses, surgeons, anaesthetists, and other specialists in such areas as tropical medicine, public health, and epidemiology, midwives, laboratory technicians, and paramedics). Non-medical volunteers look after the administration and logistics.

Nonpro: MSF recruits exclusively professionally qualified staff.

Age: N/A with necessary experience.

Duration: 6 months. Some 3-month missions in acute emergencies.

Benefits: MSF covers all costs associated with a volunteer's mission plus medical/emergency insurance. Return airfare, travel costs, living expenses while on mission, a small indemnity .

Costs: Volunteers are responsible for personal expenses

Applic.: On-line form. MSF national offices are responsible for recruitment and coordination of volunteers. A contact form is on the website.

Notes: Volunteers must live in or be able to travel to one of the countries where MSF has an office for interview and departure.

NetAid Online Volunteering

267 Fifth Avenue, 11th Floor
New York, New York 10016 USA
Tel.: ++1 (212) 537-0500
Fax: ++1 (212) 537-0501
E-mail: volunteers@netaid.org
www.netaid.org/ov

Desc.: Since early 2000, NetAid, through a service managed by the UN-Volunteers programme, has brought Online Volunteers and organizations in developing countries together through the largest database of online volunteering opportunities anywhere in the world. Through this service, Online Volunteers translate documents, research information, create brochures and web sites, write articles, offer professional advice, moderate online discussion groups, mentor young people, and engage in various other activities for organizations working in or for developing countries. Each Spring, NetAid and UN Volunteers programme select 10 "top Online Volunteers", each of whom are profiled on the NetAid web site.

Sector: Education, IT.

Country: Worldwide.

Qualif.: Excellent written English skills, experience communicating with others online, and some area of expertise that can benefit NGOs (legal expertise, teaching experience, web design, technical expertise, computer skills, etc.).

Nonpro: Yes, with relevant skills.

Age: N/A with necessary skills.

Duration: Variable.

Lang: English. Some assignments are also in Spanish and French.

Benefits: Volunteers contribute time and skills from home.

Costs: None.

Applic.: On-line form.

Oikos

Via Paolo Renzi 55, 00128 Rome Italy
Tel.: ++39 (06) 508-0280
Fax: ++39 (06) 507-3233
E-mail: oikos@oikos.org or volontariato@oikos.org
www.oikos.org or www.volontariato.org

Desc.: Oikos is an association engaged in the protection of the environment and the promotion of voluntary service. Since 1979 it has organised workcamps in many countries to work towards habitat protection, forest fire prevention, or the defence of the cultural and natural heritage. Since a few years Oikos has extended its scope of action towards humanitarian activities. Young volunteers are recruited from around the world. The projects are carried out in collaboration with the local authorities, the communities, and other non-governmental organisations.

Sector: Agriculture, education, environment, health, human rights.

Country: Africa (Kenya, Tanzania, Togo), Asia (Bangladesh, India, Korea, Nepal), Europe (Austria, Cyprus, France, Greece, Russia), Latin America (Brazil, Chile), Middle East (Palestine, Turkey).

Qualif.: No specific qualifications necessary.

Nonpro: Open to people of any social or economic status, race, religion, or ethnicity. Flexibility is necessary.

Age: Minimum 18.

Duration: 1–3 weeks.

Lang.: English.

Benefits: Food and accommodation included in the costs.

Costs: Association cost of EUR80. Travel. Workcamp fees vary with each project; it must be paid to the partner organisation in cash upon arrival

Applic.: There is an application form to fill out on the website.

Notes: The projects are carried out in collaboration with local NGOs and accommodate volunteers from around the world.

Operation Crossroads Africa, Inc.

34 Mount Morris Park
New York, New York 10027 USA
Tel.: ++1 (212) 289-1949
Fax: ++1 (212) 289-2526
E-mail: oca@igc.org
www.igc.org/oca

Desc.: This organization offers many opportunities for concerned persons with interest in areas such as ecology and environment, traditional medicine, archaeology, reforestation, agriculture/farming and teaching.

Sector: Agriculture, community development, culture, education, environment.

Country: Africa (Gambia, Ghana, Kenya, Uganda, Senegal, South Africa, Tanzania, Malawi)

Qualif.: Group leaders must be 25 years of age. Volunteers should have an interest in Africa and a desire to live and work in a local community in Africa.

Nonpro: Yes

Age: Minimum age for volunteers is 17.

Duration: 7 weeks (mid June to mid August).

Lang.: English. No language requirement

Benefits: See website for details.

Costs: US$3,500, which includes airfare.

Applic.: Available on-line for volunteers and group leaders.

Notes: Students who want to get academic credit can arrange an independent study program with their school.

Oxfam International

Suite 20, 266 Banbury Road
Oxford OX2 7DL UK
Tel.: ++44 (1865) 313-939 or 313-639
Fax: ++44 (1865) 313-770
E-mail: information@oxfaminternational.org
www.oxfam.org

Desc.: Oxfam International is a confederation of 12 non-governmental organisations working together in more than 80 countries to find lasting solutions to poverty, suffering, and injustice. Oxfam is a strategic financer of development projects; providing emergency relief in times of crisis and campaigning for social and economic justice.

Sector: Emergency, health, human rights, hunger relief, sanitation.

Country: Various countries in Africa, Asia, Europe, Latin America, Middle East, Oceania.

Qualif.: Inquire with the organisation directly.

Nonpro: Local non-professional volunteers are accepted.

Age: Minimum 18.

Duration: Negotiable.

Lang.: English and/or language of partner organisation.

Benefits: None.

Costs: Volunteers are responsible for their expenses.

Applic.: Consult website for local branches.

Notes: Oxfam works with volunteers in the countries where they are based. Local volunteers are accepted to work in a shop or office, joining campaigns, advocacy, and fundraising work. A few Oxfams place volunteers overseas; those that don't may be able to provide advise or further contacts. The websites of all the members of Oxfam International contain information about projects and partner activities, project funding criteria, emergency responses, policy research, campaigns, publications, expenditure, accountability, vacancies, and volunteering. Oxfam GB (www.oxfam.org.uk) does not send volunteers overseas, but welcomes volunters to work locally.

Peace Brigades International

89-93 Fonthill Road London N4 3HT
Telephone: +44 (20) 7561-9141
Fax: +44 (20) 7281-3181
E-mail: info@peacebrigades.org
www.peacebrigades.org

Desc.: Peace Brigades International is a non-governmental organisation that protects human rights. They send teams of volunteers into areas of repression and conflict where the volunteers accompany "at risk" human rights workers, their organisations, and others under threat . Those responsible for human rights abuses usually do not want the world to witness their actions. The presence of volunteers backed by an emergency response network thus helps deter violence. In this way, space is created for local people to work for social justice and human rights within their own communities. The presence of Peace Brigades International volunteers assists to ensure their safety and the continuation of this important work.

Sector: Human rights, peacekeeping.

Country: Asia (Indonesia), Latin America (Colombia, Mexico, Guatemala).

Qualif: No particular skills required, but with strong motivation for justice and peace issues. The success of their work relies on recruiting dedicated, bright individuals to volunteer on its missions.

Nonpro: Yes, with previous experience of working with human rights NGOs, or development, aid, or cooperative organisations, community work, etc.

Age: Minimum 25.

Duration: 1 year.

Lang.: Spanish fluency in Latin America. English and Bahasa Indonesian for Indonesia and East Timor (volunteers are required to learn Bahasa Indonesian before joining the team).

Benefits: Accommodation, travel to the country, food, local travel, health insurance and a small monthly stipend of about US$50—200 dollars, plus a repatriation contribution upon return.

Costs: Volunteers are encouraged to raise funds prior to travelling to the team because funds available to support volunteers depends upon the fundraising efforts of everyone involved.

Applic.: Request an application form and 3 reference forms.

Notes: Due to the nature of the work involved, PBI has decided that citizens from Colombia, Guatemala, Indonesia and Mexico cannot volunteer within their own country. An exception will be made with reference to persons contracted by the project to work administratively or domestically within Colombia. Potential volunteers first attend an orientation weekend training in their home country (where such trainings exist), and then participate in a 1-week intensive and project specific training. The latter are usually held 4 times a year for each project. The trainings cover practical aspects of team work, bringing up various potential situations when providing protective accompaniment and discussing how best to react. Other topics include safety procedures, nonviolence, consensus decision-making, dealing with stress and fear, conflict resolution, cultural sensitivity, country-specific information and political analysis. There may also be ongoing "homework" to be done by correspondence and completed before the intensive training. See website for nearest office.

Peace Corps

1111 20th Street NW
Washington, DC 20526 USA
Tel.: ++1 (800) 424-8580 (toll free in N. Am.)
E-mail: See Regional Contacts on website
www.peacecorps.gov

Desc.: Since 1961 over 170,00 Peace Corps volunteers have served in136 countries, working to bring clean water to communities, teach children, help start new small businesses, and stop the spread of AIDS. Volunteers receive intensive language and cross-cultural training in order to become part of the communities where they live. They speak the local language and adapt to the cultures and customs of the people with whom they work. Volunteers work with teachers and parents to improve the quality of, and access to, education for children. They work with communities to protect the local environment and to create economic opportunities. They work on basic projects to keep families healthy and to help them grow more food. Their larger purpose, however, is to work with people in developing countries to help them take charge of their own futures. At the same time, volunteers learn as much, if not more, from the people in their host countries. When they complete their service in the Peace Corps, volunteers work to strengthen America's understanding of different countries and cultures.

Sector: Agriculture, community development, education, environment, health, peacekeeping, sanitation, small-enterprise development.

Country: 135 nations in Africa, Asia, Caribbean, Europe, Latin America, Middle East, Oceania.

Qualif.: Certain education and work experience requirements. In most cases, applicants with a BA in any discipline, strong motivation and a commitment to Peace Corps service will be competitive.

Nonpro: Yes.

Age: Minimum 18.

Duration: 2 years plus 3 months of training in country of service.

Lang.: Intensive instruction in local language is provided.

Benefits: A stipend to cover basic necessities—food, housing expenses, and local transportation. The amount of the stipend varies from country to country, but will be an amount that provides a living at the same level as the people in the community served. The Peace Corps pays for transportation to and from country of service and provides complete medical and dental care. At the conclusion of volunteer service a re-adjustment allowance of US$225 for each month of service will be received.

Costs: Personal expenses above basic needs (covered by the monthly stipend).

Applic.: On-line form or contact the Peace Corps directly. An interview may then be scheduled. It is recommended to apply as early as 1 year in advance.

Notes: US citizens only. It is best to apply early. Student loan deferment can be obtained.

Peacework

209 Otey Street
Blacksburg, Virginia 24060-4745 USA
Tel.: ++1 (540) 953-1376
Fax: ++1 (540) 953-0300
E-mail: mail@peacework.org
www.peacework.org

Desc.: Peacework arranges international volunteer service projects for colleges, universities, and service organisations to provide the opportunity to learn about different cultures and customs and gain insight into the interrelationship of the needs and problems of people around the world. Volunteers help meet the critical needs of marginalised communities in developing areas by working with host organisations on existing self-development projects. The work is both challenging and rewarding. Peacework promotes peaceful cooperation, understanding, and service through volunteerism.

Sector: Child welfare, community development, education, health, religious, small-enterprise development.

Country: Asia (Vietnam, China) Latin America (Belize, Guatemala, Honduras, Dominican Republic), Europe (Russia) .

Qualif.: Enquire with organization.

Nonpro: Yes.

Age: Enquire with organisation.

Duration: Varies with project from a few weeks to months or longer.

Lang.: No language skills required.

Benefits: All required in-country expenses are included n the cost of the program.

Costs: Enquire with organization.

Applic.: Enquire with organization.

Notes: Volunteers with disabilities are accepted depending on project and also special projects with children or indigenous groups with similar or other disabilities can be arranged. European office: Vratizlavo 1200 00 Prague, Czech Republic; Tel.: ++ 42 (60) 3733-748, E-mail: europe@peacework.org.

Philanthropy Host Family Service

PO Box 7781
Santa Rosa, California 95407 USA
Tel.: ++1 (707) 569-8171
Fax: ++1 (707) 569-8171
E-mail: benkeh1@msn.com

Desc.: Philanthropy Host Families is a non-government, non-profit organisation. Members welcome men and women to form a partnership through which they will provide direct services to communities, the disadvantaged women and children, and people in need so as to help them to become self-sufficient. The idea of volunteers living together as families or living with host families in the communities enables volunteers to respect and learn about each others' culture and share experiences, faith and hope since volunteers come with diverse backgrounds and expectations.

Sector: Agriculture, child welfare, community development, culture, education, small-enterprise development, women's issues.

Country: Africa (Ghana).

Qualif.: No specific skills required. Doctors and nurses are desired.

Nonpro: Yes. Also, volunteers with general expertise and computer literacy are desired as well as in fields such as carpentry, painting, mechanics, teaching, etc.

Age: Minimum 18.

Duration: Minimum 1 month.

Lang.: English.

Benefits: Accommodation, food, project-related transportation.

Costs: US$600. Airfare not included.

Applic.: Request an information packet, which will be sent through the regular post, that will include an application form to be completed and returned along with US$200 deposit. The US$400 balance is to be paid upon arrival to Ghana in cash.

Project Trust

The Hebridean Centre
Isle of Coll, Argyll PA78 6TE UK
Tel.: ++44 (1879) 230444
Fax: ++44 (1879) 230357
E-mail: info@projecttrust.org.uk
www.projecttrust.org.uk

Desc.: The main philosophy behind Project Trust is to provide young people with an opportunity to understand a community overseas by immersing themselves in it by living and working there. All the projects are vetted for their suitability for volunteers, and none deprive local people of work.

Sector: Culture, education.

Country: Africa (Botswana, Egypt, Lesotho, Malawi, Namibia, South Africa, Uganda, Morocco), Asia (China, Japan, Jordan, South Korea, Malaysia, Pakistan, Sri Lanka, Thailand, Vietnam), Latin America (Peru, Chile, Cuba, Dominican Republic, Guyana, Honduras).

Qualif.: N/A.

Nonpro: Yes.

Age: 17.5–19.5 at the time of going overseas.

Duration: 9 months (from January) or 1 year (from August or September).

Lang.: English.

Benefits: Airfare, room and board, insurance, support, and training.

Costs: GB£ 3,850, which covers nearly all costs of a year overseas.

Applic.: Contact organisation directly or consult website.

Notes: British or EU passport holders only. Currently in full-time secondary education or taking a gap year upon finishing; university entry qualifications; able to leave from the UK in August/September of gap year and spend 1 year overseas; 1-week selection course at Project Trust headquarters on the Isle of Coll in Scotland and a summer training course in July. London Office: alex@projecttrust.org.uk or annie@projecttrust.org.uk

Quaker Peace Centre Workcamps Project

Quaker Peace Centre
3 Rye Road Mowbray, Cape Town 7700 South Africa
Tel.: ++27 (21) 685 -7800 / Fax: ++27   (21) 686 -8167
E-mail: Short term: workcamps@qpc.org.za
        Medium term:martin@qpc.org.za
www.quaker.org/capetown

Desc: The aim of the new workcamps project is to facilitate the development of a strong workcamp movement in South Africa. For this purpose, it will offer workcamps, train workcamp leaders, and support workcamp organisations. Workcamps offer volunteers an opportunity to work on a community related project, including construction and renovation of community facilities, conservation of the natural environment and cultural heritage, and organising holiday activities for disadvantaged groups. Where possible, volunteers live together for the duration of the workcamp, otherwise with host families.

Sector: Child welfare, community development, construction, culture,education, environment.

Country: Africa (South Africa).

Qualif.: N/A.

Nonpro: Yes.

Age: Short term: 18–35. Workcamp leaders may be over 35.

Duration: Short term (3 weeks), usually in summer. August to November
            Medium term: Maximum length of stay is 10 months from February to November.

Lang.:   English.

Benefits: Short term: accommodation, food.

Costs: Short term: a participation fee of EUR 200 from volunteers from OECD countries and countries where the GDP per capita is US$10,000 or higher. The Quaker Peace Centre will negotiate with any international workcamp for South African volunteers to be exempt from this fee.

Applic.: Short term: volunteers should apply in April as many of the workcamps are very popular, and places are filled quickly. South African volunteers apply directly through the Quaker Peace Centre. International volunteers apply through a workcamp organisation in their country of residence. Addresses of workcamp organisations in America, Europe, and Japan can be found at www.alliance-network.org. Medium term volunteers: 30 October for the following year (e.g. 30 October 2003 for 2004), 30 March for the period July to November

Notes: International workcamps are open to South Africans and volunteers from around the world. The Quaker Peace Centre aims to create a balance of volunteers in terms of gender, ethnicity, and nationality. Each workcamp will accept no more than 2 volunteers per country (other than from South Africa) in order to achieve a balanced diversity. The Quaker Peace Centre welcomes volunteers and interns to work at its premises in Cape Town. Volunteers from overseas should have skills that they want to share with members and staff. Interns from overseas universities should be studying towards a post-graduate degree and apply through a sending organisation of their university or college. Only applications from organisations placing volunteers will be considered and not those of individuals.

Raleigh International

Raleigh House
27 Parsons Green Lane, London SW6 4HZ UK
Tel.: ++44 (20) 7371-8585
Fax: ++44 (20) 7371-5116
E-mail: info@raleigh.org.uk
www.raleighinternational.org

Desc.: Raleigh International is a leading youth development charity that inspires people from all backgrounds and nationalities to discover their full potential by working together on challenging environmental and community projects around the world. The expeditions are part of a longer programme of training weekends and workshops prior to expedition that concentrate on global issues andon the volunteer personal development.

Sector: Community development, environment.

Country: Africa (Namibia, Ghana), Latin America (Costa Rica, Nicaragua, Chile), Asia (Malaysia).

Qualif.: Volunteers must be physically fit, able to swim 200 metres and speak basic English.

Nonpro: Yes.

Age: 17—25.

Duration: 10 weeks.

Lang.: English.

Benefits: Accommodation in tents. Living conditions during the expeditions are very basic. Volunteers have the option of independent travel after the expedition.

Costs: GB£2,995/3,500 without/with airfare from the UK (reviewed annually). Volunteers can raise funds for the expedition through sponsorship. With support from Raleigh head office, 800 young people succeed every year to take a place on an expedition.

Applic.: Application forms can be obtained from the website, by emailing or by calling the Expedition Recruitment & Support Team.

RCDP-Nepal – Rural Community Development Program

Himalayan Volunteers
Kathmandu Municipality, PO Box 8957, Ward-14 Kathmandu, Nepal
Tel.: ++977 (1) 278-305
Fax: ++977 (1) 282-994
E-mail: rcdpn@mail.com.np or rcdpn@wlink.com.np
www.rcdpnepal.com

Desc.: RCDP-Nepal has a permanent office and staffs in Kathmandu, Nepal, and 2 contact offices in USA and Japan that co-ordinate the international volunteer and youth exchange program for Europe, USA, and Asia-Pacific respectively. RCDP-Nepal maintains 1 field office in Chitwan, Nepal to promote local level cultural exchange between international volunteers and local people. The mainstay of the Himalayan Volunteers is voluntary service in urban and rural projects located in the different parts of Nepal through international workcamps, home-stay programs, internship, and language programs.

Sector: Child welfare, community development, education, environment, health, various.

Country: Asia (India, Nepal).

Qualif.: No experience necessary. Professionals welcome.

Nonpro: Yes.

Age: 18.

Duration: 1–3 weeks; long term 1–5 months.

Lang.: 2-week language program recommended for volunteers joining for more than 1 month.

Benefits: Accommodation (with a host family near their project), Nepali food (3 meals a day) that includes rice, lentil soup, vegetable curry, meats (occasionally), and pickles.

Costs: Communicate directly with the national coordinator about the volunteer contributions and Visas. An airport tax is paid upon departure from Nepal, ranging US$15–25.

Applic.: On-line form.

Notes: Many placements are in collaboration with local partners. Confirm the project, job, and host family prior to departure.

Recife Voluntário Brazil (Volunteer Centre of Recife)

Av. Visconde de Suassuna, 255 Boa Vista
Recife PE 50.050-540 Brazil
Tel./Fax: ++55 (81) 3221-6911
E-mail: recife@voluntario.org.br or cvrecife@uol.com.br
www.voluntario.org.br

Desc.: The Volunteer Centre of Recife is a non-profit organisation working to increase the volunteering culture in the Metropolitan Area of Recife, in Brazilian Northeast, providing many NGOs and community organisations with volunteers for their social, cultural, and environmental projects. Recife has a population of 1,300,000 inhabitants on its municipal area and 3,300,000 on its metropolitan area. It also has many social problems, like any other big city in Brazil, and it has a low volunteering culture among the majority of the members of its civil society.

Sector: Community development.

Country: Latin America (Brazil).

Qualif.: The Centre is in contact with many NGOs, therefore a wide variety of qualifications can be needed.

Nonpro: Some organisations can take volunteers at their first experience. Contact the Centre for further details.

Age: In general the minimum age is 18, some organisation may accept only older qualified volunteers.

Duration: Negotiable with individual NGOs.

Lang.: Portuguese, French, English.

Benefits: Negotiable with the chosen NGO. Room and board may be possible, not a stipend.

Costs: Travel, personal expenses. Room and board when not provided.

Applic.: Contact the Centre for further information and assistance for choosing the organisation.

Notes: The website is very useful for finding other volunteering contacts in Brazil.

Red Cross – International Federation of Red Cross and Red Crescent Societies

PO Box 372, CH-1211 Geneva 19   Switzerland
Tel.: ++41 (22) 730 4222
Fax: ++41 (22) 733 0395
E-mail: secretariat@ifrc.org
www.ifrc.org

Desc.:   The International Federation of Red Cross and Red Crescent Societies is the world's largest humanitarian organisation, providing assistance without discrimination as to nationality, race, religious beliefs, class or political opinions.   Founded in 1919, the International Federation comprises 178 member Red Cross and Red Crescent societies, a Secretariat in Geneva and more than 60 delegations strategically located to support activities around the world. There are more societies in formation. The Red Crescent is used in place of the Red Cross in many Islamic countries. The Federation's mission is to improve the lives of vulnerable people by mobilising the power of humanity. Vulnerable people are those who are at greatest risk from situations that threaten their survival, or their capacity to live with an acceptable level of social and economic security and human dignity. Often, these are victims of natural disasters, poverty brought about by socio-economic crises, refugees, and victims of health emergencies. The Federation carries out relief operations to assist victims of disasters, and combines this with development work to strengthen the capacities of its member National Societies. The Federation's work focuses on four core areas: promoting humanitarian values, disaster response, disaster preparedness, and health and community care.

Sector: Emergency, health, hunger relief.

Country: The Red Cross works in 178 countries in the 5 continents.

Qualif.:   Medical and paramedical personnel are the major qualifications needed. However some national branches may need also administrative or technical personnel. For example, lawyers, fundraisers, and public relations professionals are among those who help the national society as expert volunteers at local, regional or national level. Contact the appropriate national branch for details.

Nonpro: Generally no, but contact the national branches for details.

Age: Minimum 18.

Duration: Contact the national organisation for details.

Benefits: Local volunteers usually do not receive specific benefits. For international volunteers, contact the appropriate national branch.

Costs: Contact the national organisation for details.

Applic.: Contact the appropriate national branch.

Notes: National Societies recruit volunteers to carry out tasks that directly or indirectly help vulnerable people. Each National Society has different volunteer programs and requires different skills to make these programs effective. To become a volunteer with the Red Cross or Red Crescent, contact the nearest branch of the National Society for details on the programs offered and the current needs for volunteers. Go to: www.ifrc.org/address/directory.asp to find details on all the National Red Cross and Red Crescent Societies. It is possible that individual National Societies may run exchange programs for people wishing to volunteer to work in another country.

American Red Cross: www.redcross.org
Australian Red Cross: www.redcross.org.au
British Red Cross: www.redcross.org.uk
Canadian Red Cross: www.redcross.ca

RedR International – Registered Engineers for Disaster Relief

1 Great George Street, London SW1P 3AA UK
Tel.: ++44 (20) 7233-3116
Fax: ++44 (20) 7222-0564
E-mail: info@redr.org
www.redr.org

Desc.:	RedR/ International Health Exchange is an international NGO with offices in the UK, Australia, New Zealand, East Africa, Canada and India. We recruit qualified relief workers for a variety of international humanitarian agencies. We also provide specialist training to individuals and agencies.
Sector:	Agriculture, community development, construction, environment, health, housing, hunger relief, human rights, sanitation, various
Country:	Worldwide.
Qualif.:	Must have a minimum of 2 years professional experience in any of the above specified sectors.
Nonpro:	No.
Age:	The only criteria is that the person must be within the minimum and maximum legal working ages for the relevant country.
Duration:	Normally 1 or 2 years, however short-term contracts can be available for consultants.
Lang.:	English. French, Spanish, Portuguese, Russian desired.
Benefits:	Salary, terms, and conditions widely vary between agencies ranging from volunteer status to daily consultancy rates.
Costs:	Those who attend for interview with RedR/ International Health Exchange are expected to fund their own interview expenses. Joining the recruitment database is free. Registered members may contribute a GB£60 donation. They may also choose to subscribe to the organisation's magazines and publications.
Applic.:	Request via e-mail an application form. The application pack is also available from the website (www.redr.org) or for International Health Exchange members: www.ihe.org.uk

Religious Youth Service

155 White Plains Road
Tarrytown, New York 10591 USA
Tel.: ++1 (914) 631-1331 ext. 452
Fax: ++1 (914) 631-1308
E-mail: jygehring@aol.com
www.rys.net

Desc.: This interfaith service learning program networks with NGO's, individuals and government agencies training youth to become "global citizens of good character". Participants work in and with communities that have requested their help and through mutual effort provide substantial service. The Service tries to include a mixture of religions, cultures, races, and nationalities in making up each group.

Sector: Community development, construction, culture, education, environment, health, sanitation.

Country: Africa (Ghana, Kenya, Uganda, Zambia), Asia (India, Philippines, Thailand), Caribbean (Trinidad and Tobago), Europe (Albania), Latin America (Guatemala), Oceania (Australia, New Zealand, Papua New Guinea, Salomon Islands), North America (USA).

Qualif.: No particular qualifications are necessary.

Nonpro: No previous skills necessary. Specify skills on application.

Age: 18-30. Exceptions for those 16 and 17 or over 30 possible.

Duration: 1-4 weeks, depending upon project. Internships may be possible for longer periods of work.

Lang.: English, some projects are bilingual.

Benefits: Accommodation, food (on-site communal meals), local programs, local transportation, fundraising guidelines. Limited scholarship funds are available for exceptional candidates from developing nations with financial need.

Costs: Approximately US$400 for 2 weeks not including transportation to the host city and personal expenses.

Applic.: On-line form plus a letter of recommendation.

Notes: International contacts available on the website.

Right to Play
111 Gordon Baker Road, Suite 505
Toronto, Ontario M2H 3R1 Canada
Tel.: ++1 (416) 498-1922
Fax: ++1 (416) 498-1942
E-mail: info@righttoplay.com
www.righttoplay.com

Desc: Right to Play's objectives are supported by programs that enhance each child's right to play through sustainable sports development, community development, inclusion, and transfer of knowledge. Volunteer SportWorks Project Coordinators initiate and establish sport and play programs for refugees, returnees, IDPs (internally displaced people), former child combatants, urban populations, and orphans of HIV/AIDS victims. They seek out and train approximately 20–50 adults to be coaches for the children of the camps. Volunteers must produce daily program plans, a monthly progress report, and a final report about the mission within 6 weeks of return.

Sector: Child welfare, community development, refugee aid.

Country: Africa (Benin, Ethiopia, Ghana, Guinea, Ivory Coast, Mali, Mozambique, Tanzania, Uganda), Asia (Nepal, East Timor).

Qualif.: Experience playing, organising, or developing programs for recreation or sport, working with children, experience or interest in teaching or coaching sport.

Nonpro: No need to be a professional coach but should have a strong background and interest in coaching and management skills.

Age: N/A with necessary experience.

Duration: 6-12 months, plus a 4-day pre-departure training.

Lang.: English. Bilingualism in local language useful.

Benefits: Transportation, room, board, stipend, holidays, insurance, sporting equipment and educational material for the camps.

Costs: All costs are covered.

Applic.: On-line form. Send all material to recruitment@ righttoplay.com

Notes: No criminal record, good physical health, cultural/racial acceptance. Branches in Norway and Netherlands (see website).

Rokpa UK Overseas Projects

Kagyu Samye Ling, Eskdalemuir, Langholm DG13 0QL UK
Tel.: ++44 (131) 652-1316
Fax: ++44 (138) 727-3223
E-mail: diana108@btopenworld.com or charity@rokpauk.org
www.rokpauk.org

Desc.: Volunteers are able to work at Tibetan-medium schools in East Tibet in the Chinese provinces of Gansu, Qinghai and Sichuan. The organisation is active in funding over 100 orphanages, schools, clinics and environmental projects in these areas. Volunteer English teachers are needed in 4 projects currently. They will be largely self-financing, self-supporting and will have full TEFL qualifications and experience. Accommodation and subsistence is provided.

Sector: Education.

Country: Asia (Tibet-China).

Qualif.: Minimum TEFL and/or primary teaching qualification and experience.

Nonpro: Yes, with relevant skills and qualifications.

Age: Minimum 25, no maximum. Elderly volunteers may find altitude affects poor respiratory health.

Duration: Volunteer placements can start at various times of the year. Minimum of six months requested.

Lang.: English.

Benefits: Accommodation and food.

Costs: Volunteers are expected to pay for their own day-to-day expenses beyond accommodation and food. These are most likely to be taxis, e-mail, telephone calls and visa extensions.

Applic.: Send detailed CV with a brief message explaining interest. References are required and interviews are usually arranged.

Notes: Once accepted the applicant will be given the contact of former volunteers for additional information, and all pre-departure relevant information will be provided. Volunteers are required to sign an agreement complying with the protocols.

Rural Reconstruction Nepal

PO Box 8130, Lazimpat, Kathmandu, Nepal
Tel.: ++977 (1) 4-415-418 or 4-422-153
Fax: ++977 (1) 4-418-296 or 4-443-494
E-mail: rrn@rrn.org.np
www.rrn.org.np

Desc.: Rural Reconstruction Nepal is a non-profit, non-governmental development organisation established in 1989. Initially, it was established with an aim of helping the flood-affected people in east Chitwan. It started its activities with rehabilitation work. It then expanded its work on rural development and research in the various districts of Nepal. Currently, it has been working with people in the 18 districts of Nepal to encourage and strengthen them to take their own initiatives in improving their socio-economic life. It is headquartered in Kathmandu having its regional offices covering 5 development regions and district offices in the 18 working districts. Currently, it has over 500 staff and volunteers.

Sector: Agriculture, child welfare, community development, education, health, human rights, sanitation, small-enterprise development, women's issues, various.

Country: Asia (Nepal).

Qualif.: Agronomists, foresters, educators, medical and paramedical personnel and many more.

Nonpro.: No.

Age: Minimum 18, depending on experience.

Duration: Negotiable.

Lang.: English.

Benefits: Accomodation can be arranged.

Costs: Travel and living expences.

Applic.: Contact the head office.

Notes: RRN accepts international volunteers on a one to one basis.

RUSO – Rural Upgrade Support Organisation

PO Box CE 11066
Tema Ghana
Tel.: ++233 (24) 294-408 or ++233 (24) 760-826
E-mail: benxzola@africanus.net
www.interconnection.org/ruso/

Desc.: RUSO employs volunteer humanitarian action to empower local communities and contribute grass-roots solutions to rural challenges of providing healthcare, education, and social development. Volunteers may be involved in environmental awareness or health education campaigns, career and youth counselling, training local women in income generating activities, assisting communities to set up micro-finance networks to provide capital for a sustainable income generating programs, seeking appropriate interventions from relevant institutions to solve abuse problems, etc.

Country: Africa (Ghana).

Sector: Child welfare, community development, construction, education, environment, health, skills training, small-enterprise development, women's issues, various.

Qualif.: A strong and experienced staff is central to the program.

Nonpro.: Yes.

Age: No age restriction. The age range of volunteers is 19-75.

Duration: 1-3 months, depending on the technical and financial support.

Lang.: English.

Benefits: Room and board with a Ghanaian family (although a token fee is appreciated). Assistance in finding suitable accommodation and airport pick-up upon request.

Costs: Accommodation (if volunteers prefers a hostel or hotel), living expenses, and rural tour program. Registration fee is US$300. Personal funds should not be less than US$1,000 for 2 months.

Applic.: On-line form.

Notes: Volunteers must have an insurance policy and will register with their Embassy. See note on page 36.

Save the Children

International Save the Children Alliance
2nd Floor, Cambridge House
100 Cambridge Grove, London W6 OLE UK
Tel.: ++44 (20) 8748-2554
Fax: ++44 (20) 8237-8000
www.savethechildren.net

Desc.: Save the Children is the largest international and independent movement for the promotion and protection of children's rights. Since 1932, it has worked to make real and lasting change in the lives of children in need. Today it is a network of 32 member organisations coordinated by an international office—the International Save the Children Alliance. Save the Children brings immediate relief to children in emergency situations such as wars and natural disasters and develops projects to guarantee a long-term benefit for future generations.

Sector: Child welfare, education, emergency, health, human rights, women's issues.

Country: Nearly 120 countries, including Africa, Asia, Caribbean, Europe, Latin America, Middle East, and North America.

Qualif.: Job vacancies are posted on the website; they often include postings for lawyers, doctors, nurses, paediatricians, educators, social workers, psychologists, economists, etc.

Nonpro: Some national offices offer internships and most will accept willing volunteers who are able to support themselves.

Age: N/A with necessary experience and/or qualifications.

Duration: International professional positions always last a few months. Internships vary in length. Enquire with the branch of interest.

Lang: English and/or the local language.

Benefits: International professionals receive a comprehensive benefits package and have their travel expenses covered.

Costs: Interns and non-professional volunteers must cover their costs including airfare. Some benefits may be negotiable.

Applic.: The application must be addressed to the national office of interest. Consult website for contacts and positions available.

Save the Earth Network
PO Box CT 3635
Cantonments, Accra, Ghana
Tel.: ++233 (27) 774-3139
Fax: ++233 (21) 667-791
E-mail: eben_sten@hotmail.com or ebensten@yahoo.com

Desc.: Volunteer opportunities in Ghana are offered to work in areas that include renovation and construction of school buildings for poor rural communities; child education (English, math, and Christian religion) at schools for under-privileged communities; care and education for orphans and destitute and abandoned children in foster homes and orphanages; HIV/AIDS education; and re-forestation (environmental conservation), agro-forestry and rejuvenation of degraded farmlands through tree planting.

Sector: Community development, construction, education, environment, health.

Country: Africa (Ghana).

Qualif.: Special skills, professional qualifications or previous experience are not required of volunteers in most of the programs, however some of the volunteers may undergo a short (1 week) training in Ghana prior to volunteering.

Nonpro.: Yes.

Age: Minimum 18.

Duration: 2 weeks to 1 year, dependent upon project and interest of the volunteer. Start date is flexible.

Lang.: English.

Benefits: Accommodation and food.

Costs: US$475 for 4 weeks, US$775 for 8 weeks, US$1,075 for 12 weeks. Payment due upon arrival.

Applic.: Request registration form.

Notes: Once accepted the applicant can request to be put in contact with former volunteers. Please see note on page 36.

SCI – Service Civil International

International Secretariat
St-Jacobsmarkt 82, B-2000 Antwerpen, Belgium
Tel.: ++32 (3) 226-5727
Fax: ++32 (3) 232-0344
E-mail: info@sciint.org
www.sciint.org

Desc.: SCI is a voluntary NGO founded in 1920 that aims to promote international understanding and peace. It provides volunteers for projects worldwide for communities that cannot afford labour. Every year more than 20,000 volunteers of all nationalities work in over 100 camps. There are presently 33 international branches organised in national working groups, local groups, and one national committee. Depending on their size branches may employ paid staff to support its activities.

Sector.: Child welfare, construction, education, environment, refugee aid, various.

Country: Africa, Asia, Europe, North America, Oceania.

Qualif.: Ability to work as part of a team and live simply.

Nonpro: Yes, with workcamp experience.

Age: Minimum 18 for Europe; 16 for North America.

Duration: 2–3 weeks. Year round, mainly June to September. Volunteers with workcamp experience can join projects for 3–6 months.

Lang.: English. For other languages, inquire with local SCI office.

Benefits: Accommodation, food and insurance are provided.

Costs: Approx. US$60 in the United States, US$100 in Europe, US$250 in eastern Europe. Transportation costs.

Applic.: Standard application; no need to be a member. Contact the nearest national branch for information.

Notes: Only 2 volunteers from the same country per project.

SCI Germany: www.sci-d.de
SCI Italy: www.sci-italy.it
SCI USA: www.sci-ivs.org
IVS UK: see listing

SENEVOLU Association Sénégalaise des Volontaires Unis
Golfe Atlantique
PO Box 26 557 P.A./Dakar
Cité Nations Unies Nno °175, Dakar – Sénégal
Tel.: ++ (221) 55-67 -35 Fax: ++ (221) 892-44- 64
E-mail: senevolu@mypage.org
www.senevolu.mypage.org

Desc.: The Senegalese Association of United Volunteers was founded in 2002 in Dakar by Mr Magueye SY, a former SYTO (Student Youth and Travel Organisation) collaborator, to promote Community Tourism and Volunteer Work in Senegal so that Senegalese people also benefit from the proceeds of tourism in their country. Therefore, SENEVOLU cooperates with numerous Senegalese NGO's, schools, host families, artists, and musicians.

Sector: Community development, education, small-enterprise development, various.

Country: Africa (Senegal).

Qualif.: No specific qualifications necessary; each project requires different skills and appropriate placement will be determined.

Nonpro: Yes, with relevant skills to the project.

Age: Minimum 18 years.

Duration: Minimum 1 month, no maximum duration.

Lang.: French.

Benefits: Accommodation, food, 5-day orientation, and support assistance.

Costs: EUR525 per month. EUR90 for supplementary week; EUR250 for subsequent month or EUR375 for 2 subsequent months, EUR100 for each additional month.

Applic.: On-line form. E-mail, fax, or post application together with a CV and passport photo.

Notes: Once accepted, applicants may request to be put in contact with former volunteers. For a stay longer than 3 months a visa is required. Please see note on page 36.

Shekinah Care Centre

PO Box 11693, Dorpspruit
KwaZulu Natal, 3206 South Africa
Tel.: ++27 (33) 396-3333
Fax: ++27 (33) 396-1249
E-mail: snellr@iafrica.com or milo@mjvn.co.za
www.scf.co.za

Desc.: Shekinah Care Centre is a Christian Care Centre that provides residential counselling and rehabilitation programs for sufferers of substance addiction. The Centre was formed in 1976. It is based in New Hanover, 40 kilometres from Pietermaritzburg, South Africa. This quiet country setting is the ideal residential base for those who are battling to come to terms with their addiction. Shekinah Care Centre is highly respected in its chosen field of operation, both nationally and internationally. It is also unique in South Africa in that it has had the same Director since its formation.

Sector: Health.

Country: Africa (South Africa).

Qualif.: Nurses, social workers, counsellors. All volunteers need to be registered members of their respective professional bodies (e.g., a nurse has to be a registered nurse in own country).

Nonpro: No.

Duration: 6–12 months.

Lang.: English.

Benefits: Accommodation, food, allowance.

Costs: Volunteers need to pay for their own return airfare to South Africa. No other costs will accrue to the volunteer.

Applic.: Send a CV with references and proof of professional affiliation.

Sithabile Child and Youth Care Center

PO Box 21184, Dawn Park,
Boksburg, Gauteng 1474 South Africa
Tel.: ++27 (83) 340-5938 or ++27 (11) 969-5938
Fax: ++27 (11) 862-2342
E-mail: thabisile2012@hotmail.com
www.angelfire.com/ct2/sithabile

Desc.: The centre works to rehabilitate families in poverty and children in distress through education, care, and counselling and rescues children from adverse situations. They provide a home for children at risk from abuse and provide them with counselling, education, and skills and help them to realise their potential. Volunteers can be involved in teaching computer literacy and/or repair to youths or adults, working on a farm, on women and children issues, or fundraising.

Sector: Agriculture, child welfare, community development, education, health, skills training, women's issues, various.

Country: Africa (South Africa).

Qualif.: Doctors and nurses are needed, as well as computer specialists, agronomists, fundraisers, researchers, teachers, social workers, lawyers, and accountants.

Nonpro: Yes, with skills such as carpentry, arts, etc.

Age: Minimum 18.

Duration: 3 months.

Lang.: English.

Benefits: Food and accommodation for the duration of volunteer period.

Costs: Personal expenses. Monetary donations are welcomed.

Applic.: E-mail details of arrival, duration of volunteer period, CV, and cover letter stating areas of interest, an original Police Clearance Certificate. Volunteers must apply for and receive a Visa for South Africa, which permits a volunteer to work in South Africa for the stated period of time.

Notes: Volunteers must have completed high school or an equivalent. See note on page 36.

Skillshare International

126 New Walk
Leicester LE1 7JA UK
Tel.: ++44 (116) 254-1862
Fax: ++44 (116) 254-2614
E-mail: info@skillshare.org
www.skillshare.org

Desc.: Skillshare International works for sustainable development in partnership with the people and communities of Africa and Asia by sharing and developing skills, facilitating organisational effectiveness, and supporting organisational growth.

Sector: Agriculture, child welfare, community development, construction, education, environment, health, sanitation, skills training, small-enterprise development, various.

Country: Africa (Botswana, Lesotho, Mozambique, Namibia, Swaziland, South Africa, Tanzania, Uganda), Asia (India).

Qualif.: Diverse skills covering a wide variety of occupations.

Nonpro: No. A combination of a relevant professional qualification and relevant work experience (about 2 years) is required.

Age: Minimum 21.

Duration:2 years, though shorter placements are sometimes possible.

Lang.: English. Language training is provided in country.

Benefits: Local salary or allowance; pre and post placement grants; travel to and from the country of placement; medical insurance cover and payment of the NI contributions or equivalent. In addition, health trainers and development workers receive accommodation with basic furnishings.

Costs: Usually include utility bills and personal expenses.

Applic.: On-line form, completed and returned either by e-mail or post. Do not send a CV—only fully completed application forms will be accepted.

Notes: Most applicants will need to attend a selection day at the UK office in Leicester. Applicants from within Africa and Asia can alternatively attend selection at one of our Country Offices in the region.

SPW – Students Partnership Worldwide

17 Dean's Yard
London SW1P 3PB UK
Tel.: ++44 (20) 7222-0138
Fax: ++44 (20) 7233-0008
E-mail: spwuk@gn.apc.org
www.spw.org

Desc.: SPW is a youth led development charity which runs education and environment programmes in developing countries. Volunteers are recruited from the UK and abroad to partner volunteers of a similar age recruited in Africa and Asia. Volunteers live and work in mixed nationality groups in a rural community. Through a non-formal, peer-led approach, volunteers help others to gain knowledge and understanding of the health, social and environmental issues that affect their lives- and to take action. Comprehensive 4 weeks training in-country includes language learning, development theory, team building skills and cross-cultural awareness. SPW works with local NGOs to ensure the sustainability of programmes.

Sector: Community development, education, environment, health.

Country: Africa (South Africa, Tanzania, Uganda, Zambia), Asia (India, Nepal).

Qualif.: No particular skills needed.

Nonpro: Yes.

Age: 18–28. Students with A-level or equivalent qualifications.

Duration: 4–9 months, depending on program.

Lang.: English.

Benefits: The total cost of the program covers airfare, insurance, Visa, training, in-country living allowance and local support.

Costs: Varies from GBP £2,900—3,300 (approx. US $5,000—5,000) Personal expenses are in addition.

Applic.: On-line form or request via e-mail. Application procedures differ for international, UK, and Australian volunteers.

Notes: Candidates must attend a selection day. SPW Australia: spw@borderlands.org.au.SPW USA: spw@ worldpath.net

Student Action India

C/o Volunteering Services Unit, University College London
25 Gordon Street London WC1H OAY UK
Tel.: ++44 (7071) 225-866
Fax: ++44 (8701) 353-906
E-mail: info@studentactionindia.org.uk
www.studentactionindia.org.uk

Desc.: Student Action India is a development organisation which relies on the dedication of returned volunteers for its activities in the UK. The aim is to enhance education in the UK and India in particular through the promotion of cultural exchange between the 2 countries. During the 7 years that the organisation has been running, through the work of volunteers, it has grown and continues to develop.

Sector: Child welfare, community development, education, health, women's issues.

Country: Asia (India).

Qualif.: No specific skills required.

Nonpro: Yes. Training is provided in the UK. Basic computer skills and Internet familiarity will be an advantage for writing reports and keeping in contact with the UK. Some development knowledge or awareness may be expected for certain placements.

Age: Minimum 18.

Duration: Summer placements run from July to September and 5-month placements from September to February.

Lang.: English. Hindi and Tamil language training provided where necessary.

Benefits: Accommodation paid for as part of the cost of the placement

Costs: GB£550 for the summer placement cost and GB£1,000 for the 5-month placement fee. Volunteers must organise their own flights, insurance and Visas (total cost about GB£350–550). Travel and personal expenses not included.

Applic.: On-line application form.

Notes: Placements are not restricted to UK citizens but interviews and training are in the UK.

Teaching & Projects Abroad

Gerrard House, Rustington
West Sussex BN16 1AW UK
Tel.: ++44 (1903) 859-911
Fax:
E-mail: info@teaching-abroad.co.uk
www.teaching-abroad.co.uk

Desc.: With Teaching and Projects Abroad you can enjoy adventurous foreign travel with a chance to do a worthwhile job. There are hundreds of projects to choose from; including teaching conversational English (no TEFL required), care work in an orphanage or gaining experience of medicine, veterinary science, conservation, journalism or business. Placements are available throughout the year and last from one month upwards. Volunteers receive substantial UK and overseas support and are not isolated.

Sector: Child welfare, education, environment, health, small-enterprise development.

Country: Africa (Ghana, Togo, South Africa), Asia (China, India, Mongolia, Nepal, Sri Lanka, Thailand), Latin America (Bolivia, Chile, Mexico, Peru), Europe (Romania, Russia).

Qualif.: Voluntary positions and work experience placements. No experience or qualifications needed.

Age: Minimum 17.

Duration: 1 month – 1 year.

Lang.: English.

Benefits: Fees include accommodation, food and insurance as well as full-time support from overseas staff.

Costs: Costs range from GB£995 to GB£2,295 depending on the project.

Applic.: On-line form. See website.

Tearfund

100 Church Road, Teddington
Middlesex TW11 8QE UK
Tel.: ++44 (20) 8977-9144
Fax: ++44 (20) 8943-3594
E-mail: enquiry@tearfund.org
www.tearfund.org

Desc.: Tearfund is an evangelical Christian relief and development charity working in partnership with other evangelical Christian groups and churches around the world. Tearfund maintains the Disaster Response Team ready to react quickly to developing complex humanitarian emergencies. They also have the Transform program for young volunteers focused on practical tasks like building, painting, and decorating. Many work with children or give spiritual support to the vulnerable.

Sector: Agriculture, community development, education, emergency, environment, health, refugee aid, religious.

Country: Africa (Guinea Conakry, Ghana, Kenya, Malawi, Rwanda, Sierra Leone, South Africa, Uganda, Zambia), Asia (Armenia, India, Nepal, Pakistan, Tajikistan, Thailand), Latin America (Brazil, Dominican Republic, Nicaragua), Middle East (Lebanon).

Qualif.: Nutritionists, public health educators, logisticians, administrators, water/sanitation engineers, program managers etc., are always required to join Tearfund's Disaster Response Register. See website for other long-term openings, not linked to the Disaster Response Team.

Nonpro: Yes. No specific skills required for the Transform program.

Age: 18 for Transform programs overseas (16 for the UK).

Duration: 6 months to 4 years; 2–16 weeks for the Transform program.

Lang.: English.

Benefits: All long-term posts are salaried with contracts of employment.

Costs: GB£1,000– 2,500 depending on length and destination.

Applic.: On-line package. Qualified professional openings e-mail CV.

Notes: Applicants should be committed Christians and available for interview in the UK. European Union residents or citizens only.

Terre des Hommes

International Federation Terre des Hommes
31, ch. Frank-Thomas, 1208 Geneva Switzerland
Tel.: ++41 (22) 736-3372
Fax: ++41 (22) 736-1510
E-mail: info@terredeshommes.org
www.terredeshommes.org

Desc.: Terre des Hommes has a network of 10 organisations (in Belgium, Canada, Denmark, France, Germany, Italy, Luxembourg, Syria, and Switzerland) and works for children's rights and equitable development without racial, religious, cultural, or gender-based discrimination. The Terre des Hommes movement was founded in 1959 in Lausanne (Switzerland), and subsequently, groups were created in various countries. In 1966, they joined together to form the International Federation Terre des Hommes. Over the years, the activities of the Terre des Hommes movements evolved from an initial concept of assisting individual children towards a community based approach to address the causes of the problems that affect children, whilst respecting local cultures.

Country: Approximately 850 projects in 65 countries located in Africa, Asia, Europe, Latin America and the Middle-East.

Sector: Child welfare, culture, human rights, women's issues, various.

Qualif.: Agronomists, architects, engineers, administrator, surveyors, doctors, nurses, logistical coordinators.

Nonpro: No. Local branches select professionals exclusively.

Age: N/A with the necessary experience.

Duration: Up to 3 years for long-term positions, with exceptions.

Lang.: English French, Spanish, or Portuguese.

Benefit: Long-term personnel receive a salary and all expenses paid

Costs: Only personal expenses.

Applic: Send CV to the national branches offering the positions.

Notes: It is recommended to periodically consult the websites for new position openings.

Ugunja Community Resource Centre

PO Box 330, Ugunja, Kenya
Tel.: ++254 (33) 434-365
Fax: ++254 (33) 434-365
E-mail: ucrc@swiftkisumu.com or info@ucrckenya.org
www.users.bigpond.com/ucrc

Desc: The Ugunja Community Resource Centre's mission statement is to facilitate sustainable development by providing access to information and training and through communication and cooperation between various development actors (government, NGO's, and community groups).

Sector: Agriculture, child welfare, community development, construction, education, environment, health, human rights, hunger relief, IT, peacekeeping, small-enterprise development, women's issues, various.

Country: Africa (Kenya).

Qualif.: High school teachers especially in sciences; environmentalists working in the areas of ecotourism development, GIS, biodiversity, and sustainable agriculture; social workers.

Nonpro: Yes. Tutoring, fundraising, internships, thesis opportunities.

Age: Minimum 18.

Duration: From a few days to 2 years; no time limits.

Lang.: English and Kiswahili.

Benefits: The Centre cannot offer any monetary support.

Costs: A weekly donation of US$25 is suggested. Volunteers can live either with a local family or rent their own accommodation in Ugunja town (approx. US$100 per month). Airfares, local travel costs, Visa, and insurance not included.

Applic.: On-line form plus 2 references. Applications via fax are not accepted. Successful applicants will be notified within 2 months and be sent more detailed information. A small application fee will then be required to confirm placement.

Notes: Contact the organisation regarding Visas and vaccinations. See note on page 36.

UNA Exchange

Temple of Peace, Cathays Park
Cardiff, Wales CF10 3AP UK
Tel.: ++44 (29) 2022-3088
Fax: ++44 (29) 2022-2540
E-mail: info@unaexchange.org
www.unaexchange.org

Desc.: UNA Exchange evolved from UNA (United Nations Association) Wales and was established in 1973, to organise and promoting international youth work in local communities. International Volunteer Projects (IVP) provide services to local communities to carry out tasks that would not otherwise be possible. Projects are organised on a local basis by the community that have recognised and identified a specific need. Communities then contact an IVP organiser such as UNA Exchange or another partner organisation. The aims of the program are to promote cultural understanding between the local community and the volunteer, while at the same time providing the volunteers with a unique experience. The principle emphasis is often the breaking down of cultural barriers rather than the outcomes of the work itself. IVPs provide services to local communities to carry out tasks that would not otherwise be possible. IVPs provide opportunities for people of different nationalities, ages, abilities, social, cultural, and religious backgrounds to live, work, and cooperate together. MTVs (Medium-Term Volunteers) are volunteers with previous international volunteering experience, office skills and a good working knowledge of the relevant language.

Sector: Agriculture, community development, construction, culture, education, environment, various.

Country: Africa (Botswana, Burkina Faso, Ghana, Kenya, Lesotho, Malawi Morocco, Mozambique, Namibia, South Africa, Swaziland, Tanzania, Togo, Uganda, Zimbabwe), Asia (Bangladesh, Cambodia, Indonesia, India, Japan, Mongolia,

Nepal, South Korea, Thailand), Europe (almost all countries), Latin America (Ecuador, Guatemala, Honduras, Mexico). Cultural exchanges in Europe, Latin and North America, and Asia.

Qualif.: No particular skills required, but experience should include independent travel, living or working overseas, previous residential voluntary work or participation on IVPs, experience in community or voluntary work.

Nonpro: Yes, with previous relevant experience (see notes).

Age: Minimum 18, though projects in some countries take 14–17-year-olds.

Duration: 2–4 weeks; 1–12 months with EVS or MTV.

Lang.: English, with knowledge in local language of the project an asset.

Benefits: Food and accommodation for the duration of the project (unless it states otherwise). As a group, volunteers are usually self-catering and sufficient money will be provided to buy food and cook together. Accommodation will vary from project to project, ranging from the basic tent to comfortable hostels.

Costs: Placements cost £100—120 (approx. USD 135 — 180) paid nearer the time. Volunteers organise and pay for their own travel, insurance etc. Costs vary depending on country, placement, budget, duration, etc.

Applic.: Applicants must also have attended a compulsory UNA Exchange North / South Preparation weekend in Cardiff.

UNAREC – Union Nationale des Associations Régionales Etudes & Chantiers

33, rue Campagne.Première, 75014 Paris France
Tel.: ++33 (1) 4538-9626
Fax: ++33 (1) 4322-8836
E-mail: unarec@wanadoo.fr
www.unarec.org

Desc.: UNAREC organises international workcamps for adults, and teenagers; it also has a program working with people facing social or economical difficulties. In 1997 UNAREC became involved with EVS and since 1962 has been working with many partners all over the world. Volunteers participate in projects such as: restoring a village bread oven, cleaning riverbanks, organising festivals and cultural activities.

Sector: Community development, construction, culture, environment.

Country: Africa, Asia, Europe, Middle East, Latin and North America.

Qualif.: No specific qualifications needed .

Nonpro: Yes.

Age: Minimum 18; 14–17 for youth workcamps.

Duration: 2–3 weeks.

Lang.: French; English is often used on adult workcamps since there may be many nationalities.

Benefits: Food and accommodation.

Costs: EUR140–420. Plus all travel and administrative costs. In France: EUR115 for an adult workcamp - EUR430 for a Teenage. Abroad: EUR145 for adults, EUR345 for teens.

Applic.: Outside of France contact the partner organisation in country of citizenship (consult website). Volunteers from a country without a partner organisation can contact directly the UNAREC international office: D.I. UNAREC, 3 rue des Petits Gras - F-63000 Clermont-Ferrand, tel.: ++33 (4) 7331-9804; fax: ++33 (4) 7331-9809; e-mail: workcamps.unarec@ wanadoo.fr

UNICEF – United Nations International Children's Emergency Fund

UNICEF House
3 United Nations Plaza, New York, New York 10017 USA
Tel.: ++1 (212) 326-7000
Fax: ++1 (212) 887-7465 or 887-7454
www.unicef.org

Desc.: For more than 53 years UNICEF has been helping governments and communities by finding solutions to the problems plaguing poor children and their families. Programs work to protect children's and women's rights, crisis response, reopening schools and establishing safe spaces for children when armed conflict and war, flood, and other disruptions occur.

Sector: Child welfare, education, emergency, health, hunger relief, sanitation, women's issues, various.

Country: 161 countries in the 5 continents.

Qualif.: Qualifications or education relevant to the above sectors.

Nonpro: Yes, with Bachelor Degree and 2–5 years relevant experience.

Age: Minimum 21.

Duration: A few months to 1–2 years. UNV does not offer short-term overseas summer camps or internships for students.

Lang.: English fluency and 1 other UNICEF working language i.e., French or Spanish.

Benefits: Settling-in grant; Volunteer Living Allowance intended to cover basic needs including housing and utilities; international travel; insurance; annual leave; resettlement allowance.

Costs: Personal expenses.

Applic.: UNICEF does not recruit volunteers directly. International volunteer opportunities are offered through UNV – United Nations Volunteers (see listing). US citizens must send their CV to: United Nations Volunteers, c/o The Peace Corps (see listing).

Notes: UNICEF National Committees in industrialised countries provide information on national volunteer activities for their respective citizens. See website for national contacts and links.

UNICEF Internship Programme

Internship Co-ordinator, Recruitment Programmes Section
No. 3 United Nation Plaza, Room 2500
Office of Personnel Services, United Nations,
Tel.: ++1 (212) 326-7000   Fax: ++1 (212) 887-7465 or 7454
New York, New York 10017 USA
E-mail: internships@unicef.org   www.unicef.org

Desc.: UNICEF's Internship Programme is independent of the United Nations. Interns work in a UNICEF office on a project or several projects, such as limited research or studies and creating or improving databases or websites.

Sector: Human rights.

Country: Offices worldwide.

Qualif.: N/A.

Nonpro: Graduate or post-graduate students in a field related to international or social development, child survival or development, or management and enrolled during the proposed internship period. Undergraduates are not accepted. Excellent academic performance demonstrated by recent university or institution records. University or related institution support—minimum requirement is a letter from a professor. Additional consideration is given for past work experience.

Age: Minimum 23.

Duration: 6–16 weeks.

Lang.: English fluency and another UNICEF working language, i.e., French or Spanish.

Benefits: UNICEF does not provide financial support for interns.

Costs: Travel, lodging, and living expenses.

Applic.: On-line form plus letter from university certifying enrolment, course of study, and expected date of graduation; a copy of an up-to-date university transcript; 2 references (1 from a college professor); personal insurance information.

Notes: See list of addresses of UNICEF National Committees on website. For internships not in the New York office, applications should be sent directly to the head of the office concerned.

United Action for Children
Balong PO Box 177
Muyuka, SWP, Cameroon
Tel.: ++(237) 772-0418
E-mail: unitedactionforc@yahoo.com
www.interconnection.org/unitedaction

Desc.: United Action for Children works to create and develop a caring society for children, in particular by fighting against child neglect, labour and all other forms of child abuse. Disabled children are the most affected by child neglect or abandonment, particularly in rural areas with no adequate health facilities. The organisation provides counselling to both children and parents. It is also planning to build a multipurpose centre called "The Star Centre". The objective is to permit parents to assist in the upbringing of their children, by identifying parents of at-risk children and providing them with adequate training.

Sector: Child welfare, community development, education, health.

Country: Africa (Cameroon).

Qualif.: Nursery or primary schoolteacher, project administrator or program officer, paediatrician, orthopaedic surgeon, and general surgeon.

Nonpro: Yes, with tutoring, fundraising, computer training, or computer installation skills, depending upon position.

Age Minimum 18 for non-professional volunteers.

Duration: Negotiable.

Lang.: English.

Benefits: Help in finding room and board will be provided.

Costs: The volunteer will have to bear all the costs: international airfare plus living costs, which in Cameroon are very affordable.

Applic.: Contact the organisation for further details.

Notes: Please see note on page 36.

United Children's Fund, Inc.
PO Box 20341
Boulder, Colorado 80308-3341 USA
Tel./Fax: ++1 (888) 343-3199 (toll free in North America)
E-mail: unchildren@aol.com or united@unchildren.org
www.unchildren.org

Desc.: The United Children's Fund has been in Uganda since 1994 and iscommitted to helping the people of rural Uganda realize a decent standard of living, adequate healthcare, unlimited education opportunities for their children, and proper care for the aged and the terminally ill. This organisation works on the premise that it is the responsibility and duty of all people to ensure that every child in the world has the right to live and grow in a stable environment, in an atmosphere of happiness, love, understanding and security, with the basic human right of education, healthcare, adequate shelter, food, and clothing.

Sector: Agriculture, child welfare, construction, education, housing, sanitation, small-enterprise development, women's issues.

Country: Africa (Uganda).

Qualif.: N/A.

Nonpro: Yes. Experience is appreciated but not required.

Age: Special conditions apply to minors.

Duration: 1–2 months.

Lang.: English, however Luganda is the local and first language.

Benefits: Accommodation (dormitory), food, ground transportation in Uganda, administrative costs, local government fees, and all other incidental costs associated with the program.

Costs: 1 month is US$1,850; 2 months is US$2,950. Transportation costs to and from Uganda are not included. US$35 non-refundable deposit

Applic.: On-line form plus deposit.

Notes: In year 2001 the volunteers program was temporarily suspended, verify with the organisation. International volunteers are welcome.

UNV – United Nations Volunteers Programme

Postfach 260 111, D-53153 Bonn Germany
Tel.: ++49 (228) 815-2000
Fax: ++49 (228) 815-2001
E-mail: enquiry@unvolunteers.org or information@unvolunteers.org
www.unvolunteers.org

Desc.: Administered by the United Nations Development Programme (UNDP), the United Nations Volunteers (UNV) programme is the United Nations organization that supports sustainable human development globally through the promotion of volunteerism, including the mobilization of volunteers. Since starting its operations in 1971, the Bonn-based UNV programme has mobilized more than 30,000 UN Volunteers to serve the causes of peace and development. Every year, more than 5,000 UN Volunteers representing some 150 nationalities serve in more than 140 countries. Possessing a university education or advanced technical training as well as several years of work experience, they support the activities of UN agencies, governments and non-governmental organizations (NGOs) in such diverse areas as humanitarian relief, peace-building, human rights, electoral supervision, HIV/AIDS, education, Information and Communications Technology (ICT), gender mainstreaming, environmental management and urban development.

Sector: Agriculture, child welfare, community development, education, environment, health, housing, human rights, hunger relief, IT, peacekeeping, refugee aid, sanitation, skills training, small-enterprise development, women's issues, various.

Country: The UN Volunteers programme recruits globally. Assignments only take place in developing or transition countries.

Qualif.: Minimum, an undergraduate degree, several years of relevant work experience, and an interest in long-term volunteer opportunities in developing countries.

Nonpro: Yes. With academic or technical credentials (secondary school and/or vocational certificate); several years of relevant work experience, practical experience working with communities, and participation among different community groups.

Age: Minimum 25.

Duration: Varies from a few months to 1–2 years. No short-term overseas summer camps or internships are available for students.

Lang.: Good working knowledge of English, French or Spanish is essential. Additional language skills are an asset, in particular Arabic, Chinese, Portuguese, or Russian but are not necessary.

Benefits: UN Volunteers are professionals who do not receive a salary but in return for their services receive some or all of the following benefits: settling-in grant at the beginning of the assignment; Volunteer Living Allowance (VLA) intended to cover basic needs including housing and utilities. The VLA ranges from US$750—2,000 (monthly) depending on the country of assignment and the number of dependents; travel expenses on appointment and if applicable at the end of assignment; insurances, (Life, Health, and permanent disability); annual leave (30 days annually); a resettlement allowance upon satisfactory completion of the assignment.

Costs: Personal expenses.

Applic.: Send CV to the UNV Offshore Processing Centre by e-mail: enquiry@unvolunteers.org, or fax: ++357(22) 878 361. One can also send a hard copy to: PO Box 25711, 1311 NICOSIA, Cyprus; or apply on-line at www.unvolunteers.org/volunteers

Notes: Main partners recruiting UN Volunteers are: the United Nations, UNDP/Government, UNHCR, UNOPS, WFP, UNICEF, UNFPA, NGOs and others. In 2003, more than 75% of assignments were requested by UNDP/Government and the United Nations.

VIA
PO Box 20266
Stanford, California 94309 USA
Tel.: ++1 (650) 723-3228
Fax: ++1 (650) 725-1805
E-mail: info@viaprograms.org
www.viaprograms.org

Desc.: VIA volunteers teach English or work for local NGO's and in turn, English teachers have the opportunity to become immersed in the day-to-day life of an Asian society. VIA is a private, non-profit organisation dedicated to providing cross-cultural service learning opportunities to young Americans and Asians.

Sector: Education.

Country: Asia (China, Indonesia, Laos, Vietnam).

Qualif.: None, but volunteers must be college graduates or graduating seniors.

Nonpro: Undergraduate opportunities exist for the summer and for 1 year.

Age: Minimum 21.

Duration: 1–2 years; 6 weeks for summer programs for undergraduates.

Lang.: English.

Benefits: International travel, accommodation (independent), stipend (only for 1- or 2-year programs), basic health and emergency insurance, medical services, in-country staff support, round-trip international airfare, cross-cultural training, Visa expenses, and in-country field support, a monthly housing and living stipend. Limited need-based scholarships are available.

Costs: US$975 for 2 years; US$1,975 for 1 year; US$975-1,975 for summer programs, depending on country. Additional costs include: immunisations, outside language study, and additional insurance. See the application package on the website for further details.

Applic.: Successful applicants are required to participate in a weekend training session in the Santa Cruz mountains, and a week-long training in Palo Alto, CA prior to departure. Participants are expected to participate fully in these VIA training activities as well as take language and Teaching English as a Second Language courses through a community college or university. Applications and in-person interviews are held on specific dates (please see the timeline on the website for all important dates).

Notes: Undergraduate positions are open to all continuing college undergraduates. Graduate positions are open to all graduating seniors and college graduates who will be living in the San Francisco bay area in the spring. VIA offers scholarships to applicants who cannot afford the entire participation fee and encourages volunteers to apply for outside scholarships.

VIA Netherlands: vianl@xs4all.nl.

VIP - Volunteers for International Partnership

Federation EIL
PO Box 595, 63 Main Street
Putney, Vermont 05346 USA
Tel.: ++1 (802) 387-4210   Fax: ++1 (802) 387-5783
Email: info@partnershipvolunteers.org
www.partnershipvolunteers.org

Desc.: Through Volunteers for International Partnership (VIP), enthusiastic, committed individuals are matched with volunteer service opportunities in communities around the world. Experienced program directors in each country arrange for VIP's unique blend of language training, homestay and community-based host projects. Through one to three-month immersion experiences, volunteers learn about the county and the people in real, life-changing and mutually satisfying ways.

Sector: Agriculture, child welfare, community development, education, environment, health, women's issues, various.

Country: Africa (Ghana, Morocco, Nigeria, South Africa), Asia (India, Nepal, Thailand), Europe (Ireland), Latin America (Argentina, Brazil, Chile, Ecuador). See website for updates.

Qualif.: Host projects are selected according to participant's experience, skills and physical condition. Volunteers include students, recent graduates, professionals and retirees.

Nonpro.: Yes.

Age: Minimum18. No maximum unless dictated by circumstances.

Duration: 3 weeks to 3 months (longer programs may also be arranged)

Lang.: Depends on the country (language training is often included).

Benefits: Cultural orientation, language training, housing, most meals, in-country travel and one-to-one support.

Costs: Fees vary by country and length of program. Financial assistance may be available. A 20% application fee is required. International travel is not included.

Applic.: Through any VIP sending country offices (see website).

Notes: Sample projects in each VIP host country, an Inquiry Form (for the proper office) can be found at the VIP website.

Visions in Action

2710 Ontario Road NW
Washington DC 20009 USA
Tel.: ++1 (202) 625-7402
Fax: ++1 (202) 625-2353
E-mail: visions@visionsinaction.org
www.visionsinaction.org

Desc.: Visions in Action provides hands-on educational experiences while offering opportunities for participants to assist in efforts to make a difference in the lives of individuals in the developing world. Visions in Action programs are funded by program fees, private contributions, and in-kind donations.

Sector: Agriculture, child welfare, community development, education, environment, health, housing, human rights, hunger relief, IT, refugee aid, small-enterprise development, women's issues, various.

Country: Africa (South Africa, Tanzania, Uganda), Latin America (Mexico).

Qualif.: Individuals with equivalent experience, building, mechanical or trade skills, as well as college graduates are encouraged to apply. College undergraduates who do not have equivalent experience are not eligible.

Nonpro: Professional qualifications are only necessary for specific placements, but always appreciated on any project.

Age: Minimum 20.

Duration: 6–12 months. A 9-week summer program and minimum 3-month internships are also available.

Lang.: English, Spanish, depending on country.

Benefits: Accommodation (group, independent, or home-stays), stipend, medical and emergency insurance, tourist excursions, language instruction, staff support.

Costs: US$3,000—6,200, depending on country and duration.

Applic.: On-line and written applications, references, phone interview.

Notes: The program is open to international volunteers.

VITA – Volunteers In Technical Assistance

1600 Wilson Boulevard, Suite 1030
Arlington, Virginia 22209 USA
Tel.: ++1 (703) 276-1800
Fax: ++1 (703) 243-1865
E-mail: info@vita.org
www.vita.org

Desc.: For over 4 decades VITA has empowered the poor in developing countries by providing access to information and knowledge, strengthening local institutions, and introducing improved technologies. Its particular focus is on support to entrepreneurs in the private, public, and community sectors and on facilitating connectivity and technical information exchange between and among individuals and organisations.

Sector: Agriculture, community development, environment, IT, sanitation, skills training, small-enterprise development, various.

Country: Various countries in Africa and worldwide.

Qualif.: Experience in the above listed sectors. Necessary skills vary between programs.

Nonpro: VITA has only positions for expert volunteers.

Age: N/A with the necessary experience.

Duration: Minimum 3 weeks

Lang.: English, French, Spanish depending on programs.

Benefits: Airfare, lodging, food, local transportation, project-related costs.

Costs: Volunteers donate only their time and unique skills.

Applic.: E-mail expression of interest.

Notes: Vita operates primarily in Africa, but it collaborates with local organisations in need of expert volunteers all over the world.

VOICA – Canossian International Voluntary Service

Via Aurelia Antica, 180
00165 Rome Italy
Tel.: ++39 (06) 3937-5103
Fax: ++39 (06) 6385-885
E-mail: voica@fdcc.org
www.fdcc.org   or   www.geocities.com/voicaworld

Desc.: VOICA is a Canossian mission sending volunteers to live as active participants in the worldwide Catholic Church and in the global society to share their talents with the poor overseas. Volunteers join groups or centres for voluntary service.

Sector: Community development, education, health, religious.

Country: Africa (Angola, Egypt, Malawi, Sudan, Tanzania, Togo, Sao Tomé), Asia (East Timor, India, Philippines), Latin America (Argentina, Brazil, Paraguay) Europe (Albania, Italy, Poland).

Qualif.: Professional volunteers preferred, generic on condition.

Nonpro: Yes. Contact the organisation for details.

Age: Minimum 21 for long-term volunteers; 19–30 for short-term.

Duration: 1–2 years (for teachers) long term; 2 weeks/2 months/2 years for doctors and other healthcare specialists; 1–6 months for teachers of short-term intensive courses; 5-week summer program (July/Aug.) for some projects in Africa and S. America.

Benefits: Accommodation (group). Long-term volunteers also receive training (3–months in Rome) stipend, medical insurance, travel between Rome and the overseas mission site.

Cost: No cost for long-term; travel, room and board for short-term. All volunteers are encouraged to raise funds for the projects.

Applic.: No deadline for long-term service. Starting date varies depending on the country and ministry. International summer program deadline is late February/early March.

Notes: Catholics only, married couples only for long-term placements. Volunteers must be in good health and able to adapt to the poverty and simplicity of the mission and community life. Willingness to take part in community prayer and undertake a formation itinerary before, during, and after the experience.

VOLU – Voluntary Workcamps Association of Ghana

PO Box 1540, Accra, Ghana
Tel.: ++233 (21) 663-486
Fax.: ++233 (2) 665-960
E-mail: volu@gppo.africaonline.com.gh or voluntaryworkcamp@yahoo.com
www.volu.org

Desc.: VOLU runs workcamps in Ghana, either independently or in collaboration with other voluntary organisations or government ministries. Campers work to help poor communities to do work that they would otherwise be unable to do themselves and to further intercultural and interracial understanding by inviting people from abroad to workcamps in Ghana and by sponsoring Ghanaians to go to workcamps abroad. VOLU organises a variety of projects, including the construction of primary or secondary schools, roads, and hospitals, as well as reforestation, cocoa plantation, literacy projects, community development, oil palm production, and AIDS awareness campaigns. Volunteers work about 7 hours per day, Monday to Friday and occasionally Saturday.

Sector: Agriculture, child welfare, community development, construction, education, health, various.

Country: Africa (Ghana).

Qualif.: No particular qualifications needed.

Nonpro: Yes.

Age: Minimum 16.

Duration: 3–4 weeks; summer June–October; winter Decem–February.

Lang.: English.

Benefits: Food and accommodation, airport pick up, camp expenses.

Costs: A US$200 non-refundable fee for 1 workcamp (US$300 for multiple camps). All travel to Ghana and within Ghana.

Applic.: Print the on-line form to mail or fax (e-mail is often problematic).

Notes: Yellow fever immunisation required; Hepatitis A and B, typhoid/typhus, meningitis, rabies, and diphtheria recommended.

Volunteer Africa
PO Box 24
Bakwell DE45 1YP UK
E-mail: admin@volunteerafrica.org
www.volunteerafrica.org

Desc.: Volunteer Africa has been established to give people from around the world the opportunity to work on community initiated projects in developing countries. Health Action Promotion Association (HAPA) is the host organisation for the project in Tanzania, in the villages of the Singida Region. Once in the villages, groups of approximately 10 volunteers live in a camp using equipment provided by the organisation. Volunteers work with the villagers on projects such as building school classrooms or health dispensaries and get involved in village life.

Sector: Community development, culture.

Country: Africa (Tanzania).

Qualif.: N/A.

Nonpro: Yes.

Age: Minimum 18.

Duration: 4, 7 or 10 weeks (first week training and rest in the villages).

Lang.: English. Language training is provided in Tanzania.

Benefits: Accommodation (group camp), food.

Costs: 4 week programme GBP920/US$1,380/EUR1,290;
7 week programme GBP1,290/US$1,935/EUR1,800;
10 week programme GBP1,660/US$2,490/EUR 2,300.
Volunteers are responsible for airfare, insurance, spending money, all personal supplies (i.e., sleeping bag, boots, backpack), vaccinations, and anti-malarial tablets.

Applic.: On-line form.

Notes: Past volunteers have bee from the USA, Canada, UK, Australia, Hong Kong, Ireland, or New Zealand. Specific medical requirements apply.

Volunteers for Africa

PO Box 2044, GPO
Nairobi 00100 Kenya
Tel.: ++254 (733) 240-7558
Fax: ++254 (733) 407-5580
E-mail: vfa@avu.org
www.kagoka.8m.com

Desc.: Volunteers fro Africa assists local, community, and grassroots organisations to carry on with their duties and perform well in poverty eradication. Training is a vital concept in Volunteers for Africa work, which assists volunteers and consultants in securing jobs or volunteer positions with a number of organisations in East Africa.

Sector: Agriculture, child welfare, community development, education, environment, health, IT, religious, women's issues, various.

Country: Africa (Burundi, Botswana, Cameroon, Chad, Congo Kinshasa, Congo, Eritrea, Ethiopia, Ghana, Ivory Coast, Kenya, Lesotho, Liberia, Malawi, Mozambique, Namibia, Rwanda, Somalia, Sudan, Tanzania, Uganda, Zambia, Zanzibar, Zimbabwe), Asia (India, Nepal).

Qualif.: University education (BA, BS, MA, MS, or PhD) desired.

Nonpro: Yes.

Age: N/A. Families may apply but several months in advance.

Duration: 1 month to 2 years.

Lang.: English, French, Spanish, Portuguese, Kiswahili.

Benefits: Variable. Stipends may be available.

Costs: Accommodation travel, spending money, etc. Processing fee US$200 (only US$4 for Third-World applicants).

Applic.: Via e-mail (CV as an attachment). Apply at least 1 month in advance to date of expected travel.

Notes: There is no denominational restriction to applicants. Individuals may register as consultants for international consulting jobs. Once accepted, applicants may request to be put in contact with former volunteers. Please see note on page 36.

Volunteer Missionary Movement

5980 West Loomis Road
Greendale Wisconsin 53129 USA
Tel.: ++1 (414) 423-8660
Fax: ++1 (414) 423-8964
E-mail: info@vmmusa.org
www.vmmusa.org

Desc.: The Volunteer Missionary Movement is an international community of Christians, with its origins in the Catholic tradition. They send volunteer Christian lay missionaries, who are from the United States or Canada to service-oriented ministries in Central America, the United States, and Africa. They share their lives, resources and skills, and thus challenge oppressive and unjust structures and promote equality, respect, and dignity for all. They are committed to international justice.

Sector: Agriculture, construction, education, health, human rights, religious.

Country: Africa (Kenya, Nairobi, Uganda), Latin America (Belize, Costa Rica, Guatemala, El Salvador, Panama), North America (USA).

Qualif.: Work experience and skills. A college degree is preferred.

Nonpro: Yes, with 1–2 years work experience.

Age: Minimum 23.

Duration: 2 years.

Lang.: Language instruction provided.

Benefits: Enquire with organisation, some positions have a stipend.

Costs: Only personal expenses.

Applic: On-line form. Attend a 3-day introduction/discernment weekend, usually held near the US headquarters in Milwaukee, Wisconsin.

Notes: Citizens of the United States or Canada only.

Volunteer Nepal – Nabin School

Aang Serian Peace Village
Jhaukhel 4, Bhaktapur 977, Nepal
Tel.: ++ (977) 1661-3724
E-mail: anishn@eliabroad.com
www.geocities.com/photos_nabinschool
www.nabinschool.np.org

Desc.: Volunteer Nepal is committed to sustainable tourism: travel that leaves only a positive trace of constructive contact between cultures. They provide opportunities for people from other countries to meet and work together through volunteer and internship programs. Volunteer Nepal encourages alternative approaches to travel such as eco-tourism, adventure travel, and study programs. Volunteers from around the world will find opportunities to immerse themselves in another culture and make a difference in a world troubled by cultural insensitivity and narrow-minded leaders.

Sector: Child welfare, community development, construction, education, environment, health, IT, religious.

Country: Asia (Nepal).

Qualif.: Ability to teach English. Mechanics, IT and medical professionals, engineers, and experienced carpenters or electricians are desired.

Nonpro: Students or young people recently graduated from college with some experience in relevant field for internship.

Age: Minimum 18.

Duration: Minimum 2 weeks to maximum 1 year, depending on project. Volunteer placements can start at various times of the year and can be of flexible duration.

Lang.: English.

Benefits: Accommodation and food.

Costs: Application fee of US$395 and monthly fee of US$100.

Applic.: Send CV via e-mail; applicants will be asked for references.

Notes: Volunteer Nepal collaborates with 15 schools, 3 health posts, and 5 community based organisations in Kathmandu Valley.

Volunteers For Peace International

1034 Tiffany Road
Belmont, Vermont 05730 USA
Tel.: ++1 (802) 259-2759
Fax: ++1 (802) 259-2922
E-mail: vfp@vfp.org
www.vfp.org

Desc.: Volunteers For Peace is a non-profit membership organisation that has been coordinating international workcamps since 1982 and is a member of CCIVS (see listing) at UNESCO and works in cooperation with SCI (see listing), EVS (see listing), and YAP (see listing). The office staff, board and thousands of volunteers in the field help facilitate this program.

Sector: Agriculture, child welfare, construction, culture, education, environment, health, housing, human rights, refugee aid, various.

Country: Many countries in Africa, Asia, Europe, Latin America, Middle East, North America, Oceania.

Qualif.: No particular skills required.

Nonpro: Yes.

Age: Minimum 18. Teen camps for volunteers under age 18.

Duration: 95% of workcamps occur June through September. There are about 80 programs between October and May; 2–3 weeks per workcamp; 25% of the volunteers register for multiple workcamps in the same or different countries.

Lang.: English is generally the language of most workcamps.

Benefits: Food and accommodation. Workcamps vary greatly in living conditions. Limited funding is occasionally available for under-represented groups (generally African, Latin, or Native Americans) in domestic (USA) programs only. Volunteers are kindly asked not to request a scholarship for a program outside of the United States. The scholarship would only cover the registration fee but not any travel expenses.

Costs: Registration fee of US$200 per workcamp (US$225 for volunteers under age 18) plus mandatory VFP membership of US$20. The registration fee covers all expenses including meals and accommodation for 1 camp. Russian, African, Asian and Latin American programs may cost US$300–500. All transportation is arranged and paid for by the volunteer.

Applic.: Complete and send/fax the registration form to VFP. There will be a penalty of US$100, payable in advance, for changing workcamp selections after registering.

Notes: Citizens/residents of the United States and Canada may register through VFP. Placement of nationals of other countries may be possible, but if a partner organisation exists, the recruitment will be through the partner, not through VFP.

Programs for Teenagers: Programs for 15–17-year olds in France and 16–17-year olds in Germany. Fees range from US$225–600. Family camps accepting parents with children are offered this year by SCI (see listing) in Switzerland and Italy and MS (see listing) in Denmark.

VSO – Voluntary Service Overseas

317 Putney Bridge Road
Putney London SW15 2PN UK
Tel.: ++44 (20) 8780-7200
Fax: ++44 (20) 8780-7300
E-mail: enquiry@vso.org.uk
www.vso.org.uk

Desc.: VSO is an international development charity that works through volunteers. They enable people to share their skills and experience with local communities in the developing world. VSO passionately believes it can make a difference in tackling poverty by helping people to realise their potential. Since 1958, they have sent out more than 29,000 volunteers to work in Africa, Asia, the Pacific region and, more recently, Eastern Europe. While overseas, young people work together on a wide range of community-based projects including working with marginalized people, sports development, HIV/AIDS, peer education, disability awareness, and environmental education.

Sector: Community development, education, environment, health.

Country: Africa (Burkina Faso, Cambodia, Cameroon, Egypt, Ethiopia, Eritrea, Gambia, Ghana, Guinea Bissau, Kenya, Madagascar, Malawi, Mauritius, Mozambique, Namibia, Nigeria, Rwanda, South Africa, Swaziland, Tanzania, Togo, Uganda, Zambia, Zimbabwe), Asia (Bangladesh, Bhutan, India, Maldives, Nepal, Pakistan, Sri Lanka, China, East Timor, Indonesia, Laos, Mongolia, Philippines, Thailand, Vietnam), Europe (Albania, Bulgaria, Bosnia-Herzegovina, Kazakhstan, Kyrgyzstan, Latvia, Lithuania, Macedonia, Romania, Russia, Slovakia), Latin America (Belize, Cuba, Ecuador, Guatemala, Guyana, Honduras, Mexico, Nicaragua), Oceania (Kiribati, Papua New Guinea, Solomon Islands, Tonga, Tuvalu, Vanuatu).

Qualif.: Several placements for professionals and graduates.

Nonpro: Several Youth programs offered, including an Overseas Training program.

Age: 17–70. People aged 17–25 can apply for youth programs.

Duration: The vast majority of placements for the standard volunteer program are for 2 years. Youth program volunteers must commit to a 10-month program.

Lang.: English. Language and cultural awareness training offered on arrival in the country of destination.

Benefits: Professional and graduate programs include return airfares, medical cover, pre-departure training in the UK (including training in teaching skills), language and orientation training overseas, a series of grants, the support of a VSO program office in country, accommodation, local salary. Youth programs include travel, Visas, agreed medical costs, and training. While overseas, modest accommodation, food, and a basic living allowance will be provided.

Costs: In order to assess young volunteers commitment to the youth program, they are asked to attempt to raise GB£500 (EUR 800) prior to departure.

Applic.: On-line form or contact VSO directly. It takes between 4 months and 1 year from initial application to the project start date. There is an assessment day (like an interview) required.

Notes: EU volunteers only. Canadian and US volunteers apply with VSO Canada. Pilot programs are recruiting volunteers from Kenya and the Philippines. Offices in Canada (see VSO Canada listing) and the Netherlands (www.vso.nl).

Youth program: Volunteers must not normally have the opportunity to participate in overseas development work, be aged 18–25, live locally to the project in the UK, attend and be selected at a regional assessment day, and be able to obtain a UK passport.

VSO Canada

806-151 Slater Street
Ottawa, Ontario K1P 5H3 Canada
Tel.: ++1 (613) 234-1364 (toll free in N. Am. 888-876-2911)
Fax: ++1 (613) 234-1444
E-mail: inquiry@vsocan.org
www.vsocan.org

Desc.: VSO is an international development agency that works through volunteers – the largest independent organization of its kind in the world. VSO promotes volunteering to fight poverty and disadvantage. Since 1958, more than 30,000 women and men have shared their skills through VSO. Volunteers work with local colleagues in more than 30 developing countries to share skills, creativity and learning to achieve shared goals. VSO recruits volunteers through agencies in Canada, India, Kenya, the Netherlands, the Philippines and the UK.

Sector: Community development, education, health, small-enterprise, various.

Country: Africa (Cameroon, Eritrea, Ethiopia, Gambia, Ghana, Guinea-Bissau, Kenya, Malawi, Mozambique, Namibia, Nigeria, Rwanda, South Africa, Tanzania, Uganda, Zambia), Asia (Bangladesh, Cambodia, China, India, Indonesia, Kazakhstan, Maldives, Mongolia, Nepal, Pakistan, Philippines, Sri Lanka, Thailand), Latin America (Guyana), Oceania (Kiribati).

Qualif.: Placements available to professionals from more than 80 occupations.

Nonpro: Minimum 2 years post-qualification experience. B.Ed graduates without experience are accepted for some teaching positions at junior secondary schools. Science teaching placements are also available to volunteers with a B.Sc. in math, science, or engineering, and recent graduates of Information Technology (IT) programs.

Age: 21—70 (VSO is obliged to respect the mandatory retirement requirements of host countries).

Duration: Most placements in the Volunteer Sending Program are for two years. Placements through the NetCorps internship program (Canada) and the VSO Business Partnership are for 6 – 9 months.

Lang.: English, French (Rwanda and Cameroon). In most programs, training and support given to learn local languages.

Benefits: Pre-departure training which includes associated costs for travel, food and accommodation; costs of medical examination and required immunizations return airfare to the country of placement ; motorcycle training and equipment such as motorcycle helmet if required by placement ; pre-departure grant of up to CAD$1,000 (Volunteer Sending Program) or CAD$450 (NetCorps) for purchase of supplies and equipment; costs associated with processing Visa application; health insurance; in-service grant (mid-way through a 2-year placement) and end of service grant; support for language training; quarterly payments to a North American bank account (CAD$300 per quarter).

Costs: Volunteers are encouraged to raise CAD $2,000 through pre-departure fundraising.

Applic.: Online form or request form via post. At the application stage, qualifications, work experience, and personal circumstances will be reviewed. If an applicant's skills and experience match those required by VSO's overseas partners they will be invited to attend an assessment day in either Ottawa or Vancouver.

Notes: VSO Canada accepts applications from people who are living in Canada or the United States. Applicants who are living outside of North America should contact VSO UK. (see listing). VSO Canada also offers 6-month placements to IT graduates between the ages of 19-30 through the NetCorps Canada International internship program(see listing). Interns will be asked to contribute up to CAD$500 through fundraising

VSO – NetCorps Canada International

2330 Notre-Dame Street West, 3rd floor
Montreal, Quebec H3J 1N4 Canada
Tel.: ++1 (514) 931-9306 (or toll free in N. Am. 1-800-605-3526)
Fax: ++1 (514) 939-2617
E-mail: secretariat@netcorps-cyberjeunes.org
www.netcorps-cyberjeunes.org

Desc.:   NetCorps Canada International is a government-funded program bringing together a coalition of 9 Canadian development agencies—VSO Canada, WUSC, CUSO, Canada World Youth, Alternatives, Oxfam Quebec, Human Rights Internet, Canadian Crossroads International, Canadian Society for International Health to match young interns with genuine Information Technology skills to placements where they can make a solid contribution to development work. The program was piloted in 1997 with 14 interns funded by the Canadian International Development Agency (CIDA). This program is separate from VSO Canada's (see listing) mainstream volunteer-sending program. With funding channeled through Industry Canada, and managed by the NetCorps coalition and Secretariat, NetCorps is a Youth Employment Strategy program that offers exciting Information and Communications Technologies internships of approximately 6 months in developing countries. Every NetCorps assignment is different, as are the partners and locations. Tasks range from establishing Internet connections, preparing manuals and documentation, designing and providing skills development for creating websites, developing databases, networking workstations, and setting up and configuring hardware. Interns share their Information & Communication Technology skills, to pass on what they have learned through their own education and work experience. In practically all cases, interns are placed with an overseas host agency such as a government department, non-governmental organisation or institution such as a school or hospital.

Sector: Agriculture, education, health, IT.

Country: Africa, Asia, Europe, Latin America.

Qualif.: Post secondary education, IT, and skills training desired.

Nonpro: Yes, with appropriate skills.

Age: 19–30 at the start of the internship.

Lang.: Willing to learn the language (as needed) of the host country.

Duration: 6 months. Most NetCorps internships are for 6 months. There are occasionally placements of 4 months.

Costs: Interns will be asked to contribute up to CAD$500 or help raise CAD$1,500 through fundraising.

Benefits: A comprehensive financial package and practical assistance, travel (to assessment, PFC training, overseas/return less CAD$50) not including personal travel. Emergency return flight in special circumstances. A work permit and Visa. Expenses related to attendance at PFC training the NetCorps Secretariat Training, except for expenses of a personal nature. Before leaving, interns are eligible for an equipment grant of up to CAD$450. Vaccinations, monthly living allowance, accommodation (shared or private house or apartment). Upon the return home, an end of service grant will be available to assist interns while resettling in Canada and finding employment.

Applic.: On-line form. The results will be received within 5 days. Once selected, interns attend a Preparing for Change training weekend, normally held in Ottawa, and a week-long training session that has been developed by the NetCorps Secretariat.

Notes: Canadian citizens or landed immigrants only; un/underemployed prior to the internship; cleared by medical clearance process; selected according to VSO organisational procedures and specifications; and not having previously participated in a Youth Employment Strategy program.

Women's Aid Organisation

PO Box 493, Jalan Sultan, 46760 Petaling Jaya
Selangor Darul Ehsan, Malaysia
Tel.: ++60 (3) 7956-3488
Fax: ++60 (3) 7956-3237
E-mail: wao@po.jaring.my
www.wao.org.my

Desc.: This organisation's work concerns issues of violence against women. Volunteers organise activities for children and women (craft sessions, language classes, cookery lessons, computer skills, etc.), providing transport and accompanying women who need to make police reports, go the hospital, or run errands, as well as help out with administrative work.

Sector: Child welfare, women's issues.

Country: Asia (Malaysia).

Qualif.: Professional volunteers desired but not exclusively selected.

Nonpro: Yes, with awareness of the relevant issues, good report writing and fundraising skills, ability to do research and study, good computer literacy, able to conduct programs, teach skills to women, and create activities for children,

Age: Minimum 18, families with children are not encouraged.

Duration: 4 weeks to 9 months.

Lang.: English, spoken and written.

Benefits: None.

Costs: International airfare. Room and board (US$70–160 for a room per month and US$210–400 for an apartment per month). Utility bills (water and electricity) may amount to US$11–21 per month. Transportation costs vary (approx. US$80 per month). Living expenses (food, etc.) approximately US$130 per month. In Kuala Lumpur a comfortable budget is US$650–700 per month, a tight budget is US$315–400 per month.

Applic.: Request application form to complete and return via e-mail (preferred), regular mail, or fax plus cover letter and CV, which should include relevant experience, research, and studies.

Notes: A Visa is necessary and the responsibility of the volunteer.

WorldTeach

c/o Center for International Development, Harvard University
79 JFK Street, Cambridge, Massachusetts 02138 USA
Tel.: ++1 (617) 495-5527 (toll free in N. Am 1-800-483-2240)
Fax: ++1 (617) 495-1599
E-mail: info@worldteach.org
www.worldteach.org

Desc.: WorldTeach is an NGO based at the Centre for International Development at Harvard University, which provides opportunities for individuals to make a meaningful contribution to international education by living and working as volunteer teachers in developing countries. WorldTeach was founded by a group of Harvard students in 1986, in response to the great need for educational assistance in developing countries.

Sector: Education.

Country: Africa (Namibia), Asia (China), Europe (Poland), Latin America (Costa Rica, Ecuador, Chile, Honduras), Oceania (Marshall Islands).

Qualif.: Native-English speaker. All year-long and 6-month programs require a Bachelor's degree (BA/BS) or equivalent. The degree must be completed and diploma received prior to departure, but application accepted while still a college senior.

Nonpro: Yes.

Age: Minimum 18 for Summer Teaching Programs.

Duration: 1 year, 6 month, and summer positions. Time of year varies. depending on school calendars.

Lang.: No requirement. Local language preferred.

Benefits: Small stipend; room and board, usually with host family. Some programs totally or heavily subsidized; see website.

Costs: Year programs: fully funded through US$5,990; summer programs US$1,500 - US$3,990. The fee covers airfare, health insurance, materials and organisational support, intensive in-country orientation including teaching and language training. Full-time in-country field director for all programs.

Applic.: Application form on-line. Hard copy available from WorldTeach.

World Vision UK

599 Avebury Boulevard
Central Milton Keynes MK9 3PG UK
Tel.: ++44 (1908) 841-007
E-mail: studentchallenge@worldvision.org.uk
www.worldvision.org.uk

Desc.: World Vision is one of the world's leading aid agencies, currently working in nearly 100 countries and helping over 75 million people in their struggle against poverty, hunger, and injustice. World Vision is a Christian organisation and a member of several major agency groups including the Disasters and Emergency Committee (DEC), British Overseas NGO's for Development (BOND), and the Consortium for Street Children (CSC).

Sector: Agriculture, education, health, human rights, hunger relief, small-enterprise development.

Country: Africa (Ethiopia, Ghana, Kenya, Mozambique, Rwanda, Uganda, Zimbabwe), Asia (Bangladesh, Cambodia, India, Indonesia, Laos, Mongolia, Sri Lanka, Thailand, Vietnam), Europe (Romania), Latin America (Bolivia, Brazil, Chile, El Salvador, Honduras, Malawi, Mexico), Middle East.

Qualif.: Job openings for highly qualified professionals on the website.

Nonpro: Yes, students in the Student Challenge program.

Age: 19–29 years old and either still studying or just graduated.

Duration: 4– 6 weeks; each year in late June through to the end of July or the beginning of August.

Lang.: English, French, or Spanish, depending.

Benefits: Flight, accommodation, food, internal travel, and full insurance for the Student Challenge. Long-term qualified professionals receive a stipend according to their experience.

Costs: GB£900–1,400 depending on destination for the Student Challenge. Personal expenses for long-term professionals.

Applic.: On-line form. See website for country contacts.

WWISA – Willing Workers in South Africa
PO Box 2413
Plettenberg Bay 6600 South Africa
Tel.: ++27 (44) 534-8958 / 534-8148
Tel.: ++27 (44) 534-8958
E-mail: info@wwisa.co.za
www.wwisa.co.za

Desc.: WWISA is a community development organisation aimed at facilitating international volunteer involvement in sustainable projects in Garden Route and in the Eastern Cape area of South Africa. WWISA believes that by responding to the identified needs of under-privileged communities, transferring skills or enhancing existing skills in local peoples, and acquiring new expertise to launch and further new projects promotes the development of productive communities.

Sector: Community development, education, environment, skills training, various.

Country: Africa (South Africa).

Qualif.: Professionals and students seeking experience are needed to help set-up projects and transfer skills to local people.

Nonpro: Yes.

Age: Minimum 18.

Duration: Minimum 1 month. 2–3 months for skills training and practicum projects. 2–4 weeks for groups of 5 or more volunteers for community infrastructure projects.

Lang.: English.

Benefits: Accommodation, food, Visa, airport transfer and project-related transport, fieldtrips, 3–5-day orientation. Accommodation varies from project to project.

Costs: GB£400 for 1 month, GB£780 for 2 months, GB£1,140 for 3 months, GB£340 per additional month. A 20% reduction may be offered to volunteers with urgently needed skills.

Applic.: On-line form and written application with CV and a telephone interview. Documentation including credit details, insurance, passport photos, must be faxed or sent by registered post.

YAP – Youth Action for Peace

3, Avenue du Parc Royal
1020 Brussels, Belgium
Tel.: ++32 (2) 478-9410
Fax: ++32 (2) 478-9432
E-mail: yapis@xs4all.be or yapis@yap.org
www.yap.org

Desc.: YAP is an international youth movement, with branches mainly in Europe and associated group and partner organisations elsewhere worldwide. It struggles against the different forms of violence, exploitation, and injustice against networks of ideological religious, sexist, political, cultural, and economic oppression. YAP, thorough partner organisations, organises workcamps in about 50 countries in the world.

Sector: Community development, environment, human rights, peacekeeping.

Country: Europe (Albania, Algeria, Belgium, France, Germany, Hungary, Italy, Latvia, Portugal, Romania, Spain, Switzerland, United Kingdom), Latin America (Mexico, Peru), Middle East (Israel, Palestine). However YAP sends volunteers to more than 50 countries in the world.

Qualif.: No particular skills are required for YAP workcamps.

Nonpro: Yes.

Age: Minimum 18 (some projects for teenagers).

Duration: Short-term projects are 1–4 weeks; medium- to long-term projects are 3 months to 1 year.

Lang.: English, French, Spanish, Portuguese, German, depending on destination.

Benefits: Accommodation, food.

Costs: A small registration fee and travel costs.

Applic.: Contact organisation (most convenient local branch—consult website).

YCI – Youth Challenge International

20 Maud Street, Suite 305
Toronto, Ontario M5V 2M5 Canada
Tel.: ++1 (416) 504-3370 (ext. 300)
Fax: ++1 (416) 504-3376
E-mail: yci@web.net or generalinfo@yci.org
www.yci.org

Desc.: YCI is a Canadian-based community development organisation that sends international youths to Costa Rica and Guyana. Work projects include construction, health education and environmental research. Adult volunteers are needed to accompany groups of youths.

Sector: Community development, construction, education, environment, health.

Country: Africa (Guyana), Latin America (Costa Rica), Oceania (Australia).

Qualif.: Adequate physical fitness level and ability to swim 200 metres. Leaders require previous field experience working with groups of youths aged 18–25, working in remote areas or developing countries.

Nonpro: Yes.

Age: 18–35 dependent upon program.

Duration: 5–12 weeks. Upon review, volunteers can work for another placement period.

Lang.: English; Spanish may also be required in Latin America.

Benefits: Accommodations, food, insurance, and local travel.

Costs: CAD$2,735–3,885, dependent upon program, plus airfare, vaccinations, and personal equipment. Non-Canadians must purchase excess medical insurance and an additional international fee of CAD$135.

Applic.: On-line form to submit by e-mail or fax. Telephone the YCI office to verify application is received. Volunteer field staff can apply at any time.

Youth Development Centre

PO Box 1659 or YMCA Building, 1 Durban Road
Pietermaritzburg 3200 South Africa
Tel.: ++27 (33) 3452970
Fax: ++27 (33) 3451583
E-mail: ydc@youthkzn.co.za
www.youthkzn.co.za

Desc.: The Youth Development Centre provides overseas volunteers the opportunity to serve at-risk and disadvantaged youth and to give them a chance to experience South Africa in a community setting. It has since expanded and now has volunteers in Durban, Pietermaritzburg and LAbri, a wilderness training camp, as well as running the Tembelisha Self-Employment program. Volunteers may be working in shelters for homeless youth, running programs at the local YMCA, facilitating leadership camps with school groups, working with youth who are living on the streets, leading classes and groups on youth issues with students, running workshops on HIV/AIDS, or coordinating a variety of programs in schools.

Sector: Child welfare, education, environment, health, women's issues.

Country: Africa (South Africa).

Qualif.: No particular qualifications needed. Certain volunteer positions require marketing, IT, PR, or computer skills.

Nonpro: Yes.

Age: Minimum 18.

Duration: 6–12 months, with longer periods available.

Lang.: English, however Zulu as their first language.

Benefits: Accommodation, food, training, project-related transportation, recreational trips relevant to the programme.

Costs: Approx. US$380/month. Travel expenses to and from South Africa, spending money (US$100 per month), medical insurance. An Application fee of about US$30.

Applic.: On-line form. E-mail CV plus at least 2 letters of reference and a current photograph. Response will be given in 2 weeks.

Notes: Orientations are in January, April, July, and October.

Youth Group Foundation

H/N E128/2, Kojo Thompson Road, Adabraka
Tudu, Accra Ghana
Tel.: ++233 (21)228-877
Fax: ++233 (21) 228- 810
E-mail: ygf2001other@yahoo.co.uk or ameg@ghana.com

Desc.: The Foundation is dedicated to improving the quality of life of the poor, particularly in deprived communities. It provides free medical care to selected rural communities. It is also building an orphanage for orphans and abandoned children is running an anti-AIDS campaign by seeking awareness of the disease among the youth.

Sector: Child welfare, education, health, housing, hunger relief, women's issues.

Country: Africa (Ghana)

Qualif.: Various skills, medical personnel, office manager, secretarial help, planners(architectural), and teachers, also unskilled workers with initiative and fundraising skills are welcome.

Nonpro: Yes, with with initiative and fundraising skills

Age: Minimum18, but with skills or experience is often necessary.

Duration: Negotiable.

Lang.: English

Benefits: Accommodation , food can be arranged.

Costs: International travel and personal expenses.

Applic.: Contact the organisation via e-mail.

Notes: Please see note on page 36.

YPSA – Young Power in Social Action

House-02, Road-01, Block-B, Chandgaon R/Area
Chittagong-4212 Bangladesh
Tel.: ++88 (31) 653-088 or 656-291 Ext. 134
Fax: ++88 (31) 650-145 Mobile: ++88 (18) 321-432
E-mail: ypsa@spctnet.com or info@ypsa.org
www.ypsa.org

Desc.: YPSA is a voluntary social development organisation directed towards positive change in Bangladesh. This organisation is playing an active role in empowering the poor, especially women, through the active participation of organised groups of the grass-root level. This organisation is also working to activate and help young people and women become a skilled human resource and engaging them in development activities. YPSA acts as a catalyst in implementing sustainable development programs alongside the government as a supplementary force.

Sector: Child welfare, community development, education, emergency, environment, health, housing, hunger relief, sanitation, small-enterprise development, women's issues.

Country: Asia (Bangladesh).

Qualif.: "A" level education completed with skills in any sector.

Nonpro: Yes.

Age: Minimum 18.

Duration: 2– 6 months (negotiable).

Lang.: English.

Benefits: No.

Costs: A small cost is charged for food and accommodation for the host family (US$75 per month). Volunteers are responsible for airfare and personal expenses.

Applic.: An application form will be sent upon request.

Core Program Office: College Road, Sitakund 4310, Chittagong, Bangladesh.
Swiss Office: ypsa_swiss@ypsa.org

YWTO – Youth World Travel Organization

PO Box KS 5283
Adum, Kumasi
Ashanti 23351 Ghana
Tel.: ++(233) 2423-0943 or 2462-5218
www.ywto.tk

Desc.: YWTO was founded in 1999 to encourage international friendship and understanding as well as youth development promotion. This NGO aims to establish and provide vocational training to youth by way of reducing poverty among the youth in Africa.

Sector: Agriculture, child welfare, community development, culture, education, environment, health, skills training, small-enterprise development, women's issues, various.

Country: Africa (Ghana).

Qualif.: Volunteers may be placed where their skills are of most advantage.

Nonpro: Yes.

Age: Minimum 18.

Duration: YWTO Voluntary Service offers short term and long term voluntary projects in Ghana.

Lang.: English.

Benefits: Project fee covers 1 meal, accommodation, preparatory materials and manuals, administrative expenses, and an experienced team leader and materials for the project.

Costs: From US$100 per month plus personal expenses.

Applic.: On-line form.

Notes: Once accepted the applicant may request to be put in contact with former volunteers. Please see note on page 36.

Zajel Youth Exchange Program

Public Relations Department, An-Najah National University
Nablus, Palestine
Tel.: ++970 (9) 238-1113 or 238-1117 or (59) 201-300
Fax: ++970 (9) 238-7982
E-mail: youthexchange@najah.edu
www.najah.edu

Desc.: Zajel is the Arabic word for the carrier pigeon, used for many years as an important mean of communication. It represents the way this program sees its volunteers: people that will deliver a message of peace and solidarity across the world. Zajel is an international self-financing, non-profit, educational program mainly supported by partner organisations. The Zajel Youth Exchange Program assembles youth from diverse backgrounds to interact with Palestinians and learn about Palestinian society and political reality. The intention is to provide foreign youth and An-Najah National University students a venue to create a type of symbiotic relationship that will surpass what other exchange programs have offered. Zajel aims to create a learning environment for experience sharing, and partnership to achieve a breakthrough in understanding and interpersonal respect.

Sector: Culture, education, environment, various.

Country: Middle East (Palestine).

Qualif.: No particular qualifications necessary.

Nonpro.: Yes.

Age: Minimum 18.

Duration: 1–12 months, with longer periods available.

Lang.: English.

Benefits: Accommodation. Food and local transportation provided for the youth exchange volunteers.

Costs: US$150 for 3-week. Volunteers must pay for transportation food, and personal expenses but no fees are charged.

Applic.: Volunteers may apply at anytime of year.

Notes: Orientations are anytime of the year via the Internet.

APPENDICES

Analytical Table by geographical area and volunteer type

ORGANISATIONS	Africa	Asia	Caribbean	Europe	Latin America	North America	Middle East	Oceania	Nonpro	Short-term	Workcamps
Aang Serian Peace Village	✗								✗	✗	
Abha Light Foundation	✗									✗	
ACDI / VOCA	✗	✗		✗			✗				
Action Against Hunger UK	✗	✗		✗	✗						
Adarsh Community Development Trust		✗									
AFS – International	✗	✗		✗	✗				✗	✗	✗
AFSAI – Association for Training and Inter-Cultural Activities and Exchange	✗	✗		✗	✗		✗		✗	✗	✗
AFSC – American Friends Service Committee				✗	✗				✗	✗	
AJED Youth Association for Education and Development	✗								✗	✗	✗
AJUDE – Youth Association for the Dev. of Voluntary Service in Mozambique	✗								✗	✗	✗
AJVPE-TOGO Association des Jeunes Volontaires pour la Protection de l'Environment	✗								✗	✗	
AJWS – American Jewish World Service	✗	✗		✗	✗				✗	✗	
Alliance Abroad Group	✗				✗	✗			✗	✗	
Amaudo UK	✗								✗	✗	
Amazon-Africa Aid Organization	✗				✗				✗	✗	
AMIGOS – Amigos de las Américas					✗				✗	✗	
Amizade, Ltd.	✗	✗		✗	✗	✗			✗	✗	
Amnesty International	✗	✗	✗	✗	✗	✗	✗	✗	✗	✗	
AMURT Global Network	✗	✗		✗	✗	✗			✗	✗	
Apostolic Hospital Banga Bakundu, the	✗	✗									
ARC – American Refugee Committee	✗	✗		✗			✗				
Australian Volunteers International	✗	✗			✗		✗	✗	✗		
AVSO – Association of Voluntary Service Organisations	✗	✗		✗	✗	✗	✗	✗	✗	✗	✗
AYAD – Australian Youth Ambassadors for Development		✗						✗		✗	
Balkan Sunflowers				✗					✗	✗	✗
BERDSCO – Benevolent Community Education and Rural Development Society	✗						✗		✗	✗	
BESO	✗	✗					✗		✗		✗

Note: The organisations are in alphabetical order by name or acronym. Short-term volunteering is considered to be up to three months in duration. For nonpro explanation see page 29.

238

ORGANISATIONS	Africa	Asia	Caribbean	Europe	Latin America	North America	Middle East	Oceania	Nonpro	Short-term	Workcamps
BMS World Mission	×	×		×	×				×	×	
Brethren Volunteer Service	×	×		×	×	×			×		
Bridge Foundation, the	×								×		
BRIDGES	×	×			×				×	×	
Buea Youth Foundation	×								×	×	
BUNAC	×								×	×	×
BWCA – Bangladesh Work Camps Association		×							×	×	×
Canada World Youth (Jeunesse Canada Monde)	×	×		×	×	×			×		
Canadian Crossroads International	×	×						×	×		
CARE Corps Volunteer Program					×				×	×	
Casa de los Amigos	×				×				×	×	
Catholic Institute for International Relations	×		×		×		×				
Catholic Medical Mission Board	×		×		×				×		
CCIVS – Coordinating Committee for International Volunteers	×	×	×	×	×	×	×	×	×		
CECI – Canadian Centre for International Studies and Cooperation	×	×			×						
CESVI – Cooperation and Development	×	×		×	×		×				
CFHI – Child Family Health International	×	×			×				×	×	
Chantiers Jeunesse				×					×	×	×
Chol-Chol Foundation for Human Development, the					×				×	×	
Christian Peacemakers Corps						×	×		×	×	
CIEE – Council on International Educational Exchange	×			×		×			×	×	
Clearwater Project, the	×				×				×	×	
CNFA – Citizens Network for Foreign Affairs				×					×	×	
COMENGIP – Community Engineering Programme	×										
Concern America	×				×						
Concern Worldwide	×	×	×	×	×						
Concordia	×	×		×					×	×	×
COOPI – Cooperation International	×	×		×	×		×		×	×	×

ORGANISATIONS	Africa	Asia	Caribbean	Europe	Latin America	North America	Middle East	Oceania	Nonpro	Short-term	Workcamps
CORD – Christian Outreach Relief and Development	X	X		X							
Cotravaux				X							X
Council for Mayan Communication in Sololá					X				X	X	
Cross Cultural Solutions	X	X	X	X	X				X	X	
CUSO	X	X			X			X	X	X	
Dakshinayan		X									
Desteens Volunteering Services	X								X	X	
EMERGENCY	X	X					X		X	X	
EVS – European Voluntary Service	X			X	X				X	X	
Foundation for Sustainable Development	X				X				X	X	
Fundacioón Aldeas de Paz – Peace Villages Foundation					X				X	X	
Geekcorps, Inc.	X	X		X			X		X		
Global Citizens Network	X	X	X		X	X			X	X	
Global Corps	X	X		X	X	X	X				
Global Routes	X	X	X		X	X					
Global Service Corps	X	X							X		
Global Visions International	X	X		X	X				X	X	
Global Volunteer Network	X	X		X	X	X		X	X	X	
Global Volunteers	X	X	X	X	X	X		X	X	X	
Global Works, Inc.				X	X	X			X	X	
Good Shepherd Volunteers						X			X	X	
Goodwill Community Center	X								X		
Greenway International Workcamps				X					X	X	X
Habitat for Humanity International	X	X		X	X		X	X	X	X	
Heifer International						X			X		
IBO – International Building Organization				X					X	X	
ICYE – International Christian Youth Exchange	X	X		X	X		X	X	X	X	X
ICYE-UK – Inter-Cultural Youth Exchange	X	X		X	X		X	X	X		

ORGANISATIONS	Africa	Asia	Caribbean	Europe	Latin America	North America	Middle East	Oceania	Nonpro	Short-term	Workcamps
Interconnection	X	X	X	X	X	X	X	X	X	X	
International Executive Service Corps	X	X	X	X	X	X	X			X	
International Medical Corps	X	X		X							
International Mountain Explorers Connection		X			X				X	X	
International Partnership for Service Learning and Leadership	X	X	X	X	X	X	X		X	X	X
International Relief Friendship Foundation	X	X		X	X	X			X	X	
International Volunteer Program				X					X	X	
International Youth Link Foundation	X								X		
i-to-i	X	X	X	X	X			X	X	X	
IVDN-Interactive Voluntary Development Network	X								X	X	
IVS – International Volunteer Service	X			X		X	X		X	X	
Jesuit Refugee Service	X		X		X		X	X	X	X	
Joint Assistance Centre, Inc.		X									X
Kibbutz Program Center – Takam Artzi							X		X	X	
MADRE – International Women's Human Rights Organization					X				X	X	
Makindu Children's Center	X								X		
MedAir	X	X		X							
Mission Discovery			X		X	X		X	X	X	
Mission Doctors / Lay Mission Helpers Associations	X				X			X			
Mondo Challenge	X	X			X				X	X	
MS – Mellemfolkeligt Samvirke	X	X			X		X		X	X	
MSF – Médicins Sans Frontiers	X	X	X		X	X	X	X	X		
NetAid Online Volunteering	X	X	X	X	X		X	X	X	X	
Oikos	X				X				X	X	X
Operation Crossroads Africa, Inc.	X				X		X	X	X	X	
Oxfam International	X	X		X	X				X		
Peace Brigades International	X	X		X	X	X	X		X		
Peace Corps	X	X	X	X	X			X	X		
Peacework		X		X	X						X

ORGANISATIONS	Africa	Asia	Caribbean	Europe	Latin America	North America	Middle East	Oceania	Nonpro	Short-term	Workcamps
Philanthropy Host Family Service	×								×	×	
Project Trust	×	×							×		
Quaker Peace Centre Workcamps Project	×				×				×		×
Raleigh International	×	×							×	×	
RCDP-Nepal – Rural Community Development Program		×			×				×	×	
Recife Voluntário Brazil (Volunteer Centre of Recife)									×	×	
Red Cross – International Federation of Red Cross and Red Crescent Societies	×		×	×	×	×	×		×	×	
RedR International – Registered Engineers for Disaster Relief	×	×	×	×	×	×	×	×			
Religious Youth Service	×	×	×	×	×	×		×			
Right to Play	×	×							×		
Rokpa UK Overseas Projects		×							×		
Rural Reconstruction Nepal		×							×		
RUSO – Rural Upgrade Support Organisation	×										
Save the Children	×	×	×	×	×	×	×		×	×	
Save the Earth Network	×	×							×		
SCI – Service Civil International	×	×	×	×	×	×	×	×	×	×	×
SENEVOLU – Association Sénégalaise des Volontaires Unis	×									×	
Shekinah Care Centre	×								×		
Sithabile Child and Youth Care Center	×								×		
Skillshare International	×	×							×	×	
SPW – Students Partnership Worldwide	×	×									
Student Action India		×									
Teaching & Projects Abroad	×	×		×	×				×	×	
Tearfund	×	×			×		×		×	×	
Terre des Hommes	×	×		×	×		×		×		
Ugunja Community Resource Centre	×										
UNA Exchange	×	×		×	×				×	×	×
UNAREC – Union Nationale des Associations Régionales Etudes & Chantiers	×	×		×	×	×		×	×	×	×
UNICEF – United Nations International Children's Emergency Fund	×	×		×	×	×	×	×	×	×	×

ORGANISATIONS	Africa	Asia	Caribbean	Europe	Latin America	North America	Middle East	Oceania	Nonpro	Short-term	Workcamps
UNICEF Internship Programme	X	X	X	X	X	X	X	X		X	
United Action for Children	X								X	X	
United Children's Fund, Inc.	X								X	X	
UNV – United Nations Volunteers	X	X		X	X			X			
VIA	X	X									
VIP – Volunteers for International Partnership	X			X	X				X	X	
Visions in Action	X				X				X		X
VITA – Volunteers in Technical Assistance	X	X		X	X						
VOICA – Canossian International Voluntary Service	X	X							X	X	X
VOLU – Voluntary Workcamps Association of Ghana	X								X	X	X
Volunteer Africa	X	X							X	X	
Volunteer for Africa	X	X				X			X	X	
Volunteer Missionary Movement	X								X	X	
Volunteer Nepal	X	X							X	X	
Volunteers for Peace International	X	X		X	X	X	X		X	X	X
VSO – Voluntary Service Overseas	X	X		X	X			X	X	X	
VSO Canada	X	X		X	X			X	X		
VSO – NetCorps Canada International		X		X	X				X	X	
Women's Aid Organisation	X	X						X	X	X	
WorldTeach	X	X		X	X				X	X	
World Vision UK	X	X		X	X		X		X	X	
WWISA – Willing Workers in South Africa	X								X	X	
YAP – Youth Action for Peace				X	X		X	X	X	X	
YCI – Youth Challenge International	X				X			X	X	X	
Youth Development Centre	X	X							X		
Youth Group Foundation		X							X	X	
YPSA – Young Power in Social Action		X							X	X	
YWTO – Youth World Travel Organisation	X						X		X	X	
Zajel Youth Exchange Program							X		X	X	X

243

Analytical Table by sector

ORGANISATIONS	Agriculture	Child welfare	Community devel.	Construction	Culture	Education	Emergency	Environment	Health	Housing	Human rights	Hunger relief	IT	Peacekeeping	Refugee aid	Religious	Sanitation	Skill training	Small-enterp. devel.	Women's issues	Various
Aang Serian Peace Village	X		X	X		X		X											X		
Abha Light Foundation									X												
ACDI / VOCA	X		X			X		X											X		
Action Against Hunger UK	X								X			X					X			X	
Adarsh Community Development Trust		X	X		X	X		X	X								X				
AFS – International		X	X		X	X		X	X									X			X
AFSAI – Ass. for Training and Inter-Cultural Activities			X		X	X		X		X	X										X
AFSC – American Friends Service Committee			X		X	X		X											X		X
AJED Youth Ass. for Education and Development			X	X	X	X		X	X										X		
AJUDE – Youth Ass. for Voluntary Servi. in Mozambique		X	X	X	X	X	X	X	X												
AJVPE–TOGO Ass. pour la Protection de l'Environment	X		X		X	X	X	X			X										
AJWS – American Jewish World Service	X	X	X			X			X		X									X	
Alliance Abroad Group		X	X		X	X		X	X												
Amaudo UK	X	X							X												X
Amazon-Africa Aid Organization		X	X		X	X		X	X												
AMIGOS – Amigos de las Américas		X	X	X	X	X		X	X												
Amizade, Ltd.				X	X	X		X	X												
Amnesty International											X										
AMURT Global Network		X	X			X			X	X		X	X								
Apostolic Hospital Banga Bakundu, the						X		X	X										X		
ARC – American Refugee Committee	X	X	X			X	X	X	X						X		X				
Australian Volunteers International	X		X		X	X		X	X	X	X							X			
AVSO – Ass. of Voluntary Service Organisations		X	X		X	X		X		X	X										
AYAD – Australian Youth Ambassadors for Development	X		X		X	X		X	X								X				
Balkan Sunflowers	X	X	X		X	X		X			X			X							X
BERDSCO –Community Education and Rural Dev.	X	X	X		X	X		X	X										X		X
BESO	X	X	X		X	X		X								X			X	X	X
BMS World Mission	X	X	X		X	X		X	X							X		X	X		X
Brethren Volunteer Service	X	X	X		X	X		X	X		X				X	X				X	X

Note: The organisations are in alphabetical order by name or acronym. See the meaning of the sectors on pages 26–28.

ORGANISATIONS	Agriculture	Child welfare	Community devel.	Construction	Culture	Education	Emergency	Environment	Health	Housing	Human rights	Hunger relief	IT	Peacekeeping	Refugee aid	Religious	Sanitation	Skill training	Small-enterp. devel.	Women's issues	Various
Bridge Foundation, the						X	X		X				X								X
BRIDGES		X	X			X													X		
Buea Youth Foundation		X	X		X	X			X										X		
BUNAC	X	X	X	X	X	X		X	X				X						X		X
BWCA – Bangladesh Work Camps Association	X			X		X		X	X				X								
Canada World Youth (Jeunesse Canada Monde)	X	X	X			X		X	X				X								
Canadian Crossroads International	X	X	X			X		X	X												
CARE Corps Volunteer Program		X	X			X		X	X												
Casa de los Amigos		X	X					X													
Catholic Institute for International Relations	X		X			X		X	X		X		X						X	X	X
Catholic Medical Mission Board									X												
CCIVS – Coord. Committee for International Volunteers														X							
CECI – Canadian Centre for Int.Studies and Cooperation	X			X	X	X		X			X								X		
CESVI – Cooperation and Development			X	X	X	X	X		X		X		X		X		X	X			X
CFHI – Child Family Health International					X				X												
Chantiers Jeunesse			X	X	X			X													
Chol-Chol Foundation for Human Development, the	X		X	X	X	X		X	X	X	X		X	X				X	X		X
Christian Peacemakers Corps														X		X					
CIEE - Council on International Educational Exchange		X			X	X		X	X												
Clearwater Project, the					X	X		X	X								X				
CNFA – Citizens Network for Foreign Affairs	X	X				X		X	X	X	X								X	X	X
COMENGIP – Community Engineering Programme	X	X				X		X	X	X	X				X		X		X	X	X
Concern America	X		X			X	X		X		X						X		X		
Concern Worldwide						X	X	X			X						X				
Concordia		X	X	X	X	X	X	X													X
COOPI – Cooperation International	X		X	X		X	X	X				X			X		X	X	X	X	
CORD – Christian Outreach Relief and Development	X					X			X								X				

245

ORGANISATIONS	Agriculture	Child welfare	Community devel.	Construction	Culture	Education	Emergency	Environment	Health	Housing	Human rights	Hunger relief	IT	Peacekeeping	Refugee aid	Religious	Sanitation	Skill training	Small-enterp. devel.	Women's issues	Various
Cotravaux					X			X													X
Council for Mayan Communication in Sololà		X	X			X							X						X	X	X
Cross Cultural Solutions		X			X	X													X	X	
CUSO	X				X	X							X						X	X	X
Dakshinayan			X			X		X	X												
Desteens Volunteering Services			X			X		X	X	X	X		X						X		
EMERGENCY							X		X												
EVS – European Voluntary Service					X	X		X													X
Foundation for Sustainable Development			X						X	X											X
Fundacioón Aldeas de Paz – Peace Villages Foundation	X	X			X	X		X	X	X											
Geekcorps, Inc.	X												X						X	X	
Global Citizens Network			X	X		X		X													
Global Corps			X			X					X								X	X	
Global Routes				X		X		X													X
Global Service Corps	X								X												
Global Visions International			X			X		X	X												
Global Volunteer Network					X	X		X	X												
Global Volunteers			X		X	X		X	X								X				
Global Works, Inc.			X	X	X	X	X														
Good Shepherd Volunteers		X	X			X										X					
Goodwill Community Center		X	X			X															
Greenway International Workcamps	X		X					X											X		
Habitat for Humanity International				X						X											
Heifer International	X		X			X		X													
IBO – International Building Organization				X					X	X											
ICYE – International Christian Youth Exchange	X	X	X		X	X		X	X	X	X			X	X				X	X	X
ICYE-UK – Inter-Cultural Youth Exchange	X	X	X		X	X		X	X	X	X			X	X				X	X	X
Interconnection													X								
International Executive Service Corps	X												X					X	X		X

246

ORGANISATIONS	Agriculture	Child welfare	Community devel.	Construction	Culture	Education	Emergency	Environment	Health	Housing	Human rights	Hunger relief	IT	Peacekeeping	Refugee aid	Religious	Sanitation	Skill training	Small-enterp. devel.	Women's issues	Various
International Medical Corps	X	X					X		X								X			X	X
International Mountain Explorers Connection			X		X	X		X	X	X	X								X	X	X
Internat. Partnership for Service Learning and Leadership		X	X	X		X	X	X	X	X	X										
International Relief Friendship Foundation	X	X	X		X	X		X	X												X
International Volunteer Program		X	X		X		X	X	X	X	X										
International Youth Link Foundation		X	X	X	X	X		X	X	X											X
i-to-i	X	X	X		X	X		X	X		X									X	X
IVDN-Interactive Voluntary Development Network		X	X	X	X	X			X						X			X	X		X
IVS – International Volunteer Service		X				X	X	X							X			X		X	X
Jesuit Refugee Service		X				X									X			X		X	
Joint Assistance Centre, Inc.	X		X	X		X		X	X		X						X		X		X
Kibbutz Program Center – Takam Artzi	X								X												
MADRE – Internat. Women's Human Rights Organization		X	X			X		X	X	X	X	X					X		X	X	X
Makindu Children's Center	X	X	X			X	X	X	X	X	X						X				
MedAir		X		X					X	X		X				X					
Mission Discovery		X		X					X		X										
Mission Doctors / Lay Mission Helpers Associations			X			X			X												
Mondo Challenge		X	X			X		X	X		X				X				X	X	
MS – Mellemfolkeligt Samvirke	X	X						X	X		X								X		
MSF – Médicins Sans Frontiers							X		X												
NetAid Online Volunteering													X								
Oikos	X					X		X	X		X										X
Operation Crossroads Africa, Inc.	X	X	X		X	X		X	X		X						X		X	X	
Oxfam International											X	X		X							
Peace Brigades International											X			X							
Peace Corps	X	X	X			X		X	X								X		X		
Peacework	X	X	X			X			X							X			X		

247

ORGANISATIONS	Agriculture	Child welfare	Community devel.	Construction	Culture	Education	Emergency	Environment	Health	Housing	Human rights	Hunger relief	IT	Peacekeeping	Refugee aid	Religious	Sanitation	Skill training	Small-enterp. devel.	Women's issues	Various
Philanthropy Host Family Service	×	×	×		×	×													×	×	
Project Trust					×	×															
Quaker Peace Centre Workcamps Project		×	×	×	×	×															
Raleigh International			×	×	×			×													
RCDP-Nepal – Rural Community Development Program		×	×			×		×	×												×
Recife Voluntário Brazil (Volunteer Centre of Recife)								×	×			×									×
Red Cross – Int. Fed. Red Cross and Red Crescent Soc.							×		×						×						
RedR International – Reg. Engineers for Disaster Relief	×		×	×				×	×	×	×	×					×		×	×	×
Religious Youth Service			×	×				×	×	×							×		×	×	
Right to Play		×	×		×										×					×	
Rokpa UK Overseas Projects						×															
Rural Reconstruction Nepal	×	×	×	×	×	×		×	×	×	×						×	×	×		×
RUSO – Rural Upgrade Support Organisation		×	×	×		×		×	×									×	×		×
Save the Children		×			×	×		×	×												
Save the Earth Network			×	×		×	×	×	×		×										
SCI – Service Civil International		×		×	×	×		×							×				×		×
SENEVOLU – Ass. Sénégalaise des Volontaires Unis			×	×		×															
Shekinah Care Centre						×			×							×					×
Sithabile Child and Youth Care Center	×	×	×			×		×	×								×	×			
Skillshare International	×	×	×			×		×	×								×	×	×	×	×
SPW – Students Partnership Worldwide			×			×													×	×	×
Student Action India						×			×												
Teaching & Projects Abroad		×	×	×	×	×		×	×										×	×	
Tearfund						×	×	×	×			×	×						×		
Terre des Hommes	×			×						×					×						×
Ugunja Community Resource Centre	×	×	×	×	×	×		×	×	×	×				×		×		×	×	×
UNA Exchange	×	×	×	×	×	×		×			×									×	×

248

ORGANISATIONS	Agriculture	Child welfare	Community devel.	Construction	Culture	Education	Emergency	Environment	Health	Housing	Human rights	Hunger relief	IT	Peacekeeping	Refugee aid	Religious	Sanitation	Skill training	Small-enterp. devel.	Women's issues	Various
UNAREC – Union Nat. des Ass. Régionales Et. Chantier		X	X	X	X		X	X												X	X
UNICEF – UN International Children's Emergency Fund		X				X			X			X					X			X	X
UNICEF Internship Programme											X										
United Action for Children			X			X			X	X											
United Children's Fund, Inc.	X	X		X		X				X											X
UNV – United Nations Volunteers	X	X	X			X		X	X	X	X	X	X	X	X		X	X	X	X	X
VIA			X		X	X			X	X											
VIP – Volunteers for International Partnership	X	X	X			X		X	X		X	X	X							X	X
Visions in Action	X	X	X			X		X	X				X						X	X	X
VITA – Volunteers in Technical Assistance	X							X	X				X				X		X		
VOICA – Canossian International Voluntary Service			X			X			X							X					
VOLU – Voluntary Workcamps Association of Ghana	X	X	X	X		X		X	X												X
Volunteer Africa			X		X																
Volunteer for Africa	X	X	X			X		X	X	X			X			X	X	X		X	X
Volunteer Missionary Movement	X			X		X			X	X	X					X					
Volunteer Nepal		X	X	X		X		X	X				X			X					X
Volunteers for Peace International	X	X		X	X	X		X	X	X	X				X						X
VSO – Voluntary Service Overseas						X			X				X	X							
VSO Canada			X			X			X										X		
VSO – NetCorps Canada International	X												X								
Women's Aid Organisation		X																		X	
WorldTeach						X													X		
World Vision UK	X	X	X			X		X	X		X	X									
WWISA – Willing Workers in South Africa			X					X										X			X
YAP – Youth Action for Peace			X	X				X			X			X							
YCI – Youth Challenge International				X		X		X	X												
Youth Development Centre		X		X		X		X												X	

249

ORGANISATIONS	Agriculture	Child welfare	Community devel.	Construction	Culture	Education	Emergency	Environment	Health	Housing	Human rights	Hunger relief	IT	Peacekeeping	Refugee aid	Religious	Sanitation	Skill training	Small-enterp. devel.	Women's issues	Various
Youth Group Foundation		X				X			X	X		X								X	
YPSA – Young Power in Social Action	X	X	X			X	X	X	X	X		X					X		X	X	
YWTO – Youth World Travel Organisation		X	X		X	X		X	X									X	X	X	X
Zajel Youth Exchange Program					X	X		X													X

ORGANISATION ALPHABETICAL INDEX

From the same publisher

(available from your bookstore or from the website www.greenvol.com)

Green Volunteers The World Guide
to Voluntary Work in Nature Conservation
Over 200 projects worldwide for those who want to experience active conservation work as a volunteer. Projects are worldwide, year round, in a variety of habitats, from one week to one year or more. From dolphins to rhinos, from whales to primates, this guide is ideal for a meaningful vacation or for finding thesis or research opportunites.

Price £ 10.99 € 16.00 $ 14.95   Pages: 256

World Volunteers The World Guide
to Humanitarian and Development Volunteering
Nearly 200 projects and organisations worldwide for people who want to work in international humanitarian projects but don't know how to begin. Opportunities are from 2 weeks to 2 years or longer. An ideal resource for a working holiday or a leave of absence. A guide for students, retirees, doctors or accountants, nurses or agronomists, surveyors and teachers, plumbers or builders, electricians or computer operators... For everyone who wants to get involved in helping those who suffer worldwide.

Price: £ 10.99 € 16.00 $ 14.95   Pages: 256

Archaeo-Volunteers The World Guide
to Archaeological and Heritage Volunteering
Listing 200 projects and organisations in the 5 continents for those who want to spend a different working vacation helping Archaeologists. Placements are from 2 weeks to a few months. For enthusiastic amateurs, students and those wanting hands-on experience. Cultural and historical heritage maintenance and restoration and museum volunteering opportunities are also listed. The guide also tells how to find hundreds more excavations and workcamps on the Internet.

Price: £ 10.99 € 16.00 $ 14.95   Pages: 256